T5-ADP-883

AVERROES' PHYSICS

Averroes' Physics

A Turning Point in Medieval Natural Philosophy

RUTH GLASNER

OXFORD
UNIVERSITY PRESS

Great Clarendon Street, Oxford OX2 6DP

Oxford University Press is a department of the University of Oxford.
It furthers the University's objective of excellence in research, scholarship,
and education by publishing worldwide in

Oxford New York

Auckland Cape Town Dar es Salaam Hong Kong Karachi
Kuala Lumpur Madrid Melbourne Mexico City Nairobi
New Delhi Shanghai Taipei Toronto

With offices in

Argentina Austria Brazil Chile Czech Republic France Greece
Guatemala Hungary Italy Japan Poland Portugal Singapore
South Korea Switzerland Thailand Turkey Ukraine Vietnam

Oxford is a registered trade mark of Oxford University Press
in the UK and in certain other countries

Published in the United States
by Oxford University Press Inc., New York

First published 2009

British Library Cataloguing in Publication Data
Data available

Library of Congress Cataloging-in-Publication Data

Glasner, Ruth.
Averroes' physics : a turning point in medieval natural philosophy / Ruth Glasner. p. cm.
Includes bibliographical references and index.
ISBN 978–0–19–956773–7 (alk. paper)
1. Physics–Philosophy–History–To 1500. 2. Philosophy, Medieval. 3. Science, Medieval. 4. Averroës, 1126–1198. 5. Aristotle. Physics. I. Title.
QC7.G65 2009
530.01–dc22
2009001721

Typeset by Laserwords Private Limited, Chennai, India
Printed in Great Britain
on acid-free paper by the
MPG Books Group, Bodmin and King's Lynn

ISBN 978–0–19–956773–7

1 3 5 7 9 10 8 6 4 2

In memory of my parents
Leah and Tzvi Adar
יהי זכרם ברוך

Acknowledgements

For having read this book at one or another of the various stages of its long elaboration and for having made numerous valuable comments and suggestions I warmly thank Gad Freudenthal, Steven Harvey, and Richard Taylor. To Horst Schmieja I am very grateful for his generous help, for his answers to my many questions on the Latin manuscripts, and for his suggestions and corrections to Part A of the book. I extend my thanks also to Orna Harari and Tanely Kikkunen for their advice on Averroes' logic, to Hagar Kahana-Smilansky who examined my translations and transliterations from Arabic, and to Anat Peri for having checked my translations from the Latin.

I am indebted to the Dibner Institute for having supported my research during the academic year 1999–2000, when I started the endeavour of writing this book.

R. G.

Jerusalem
August 2008

Contents

Abbreviations and Notations x

Introduction: Science through Exegesis 1

A. THE COMPLEXITY OF AVERROES' WRITING

1. Description of the Corpus 10

1.1. The Short Commentary 10
1.2. The Middle Commentary 11
1.3. The Long Commentary 12
1.4. The *Questions in Physics* 17

2. The Order of Writing 19

3. The Changing Cultural Contexts 22

4. Versions and Revisions 28

4.1. The Short Commentary 28
4.2. The Middle Commentary 30
Appendix 1: The Anonymous Translation of Version A 30
4.3. The Long Commentary 32
Appendix 2: An Attempt at Tracing Back the History of the Two Redactions 36

5. The Late Stratum of the Long Commentary 41

5.1. The Formal Introduction 41
Appendix 3: The Revision of Book I 42
5.2. The Uses of Syllogism 43
Example A 48
Example B 50
5.3. The Turning to Alexander 52

B. AVERROES' NEW PHYSICS

6. The Turning Point of *Physics* VIII: The Breakdown of Determinism 62

6.1. The Challenge of Indeterminism 62
6.2. Conflicting Messages in Aristotle 69
6.3. The Story of the Middle Commentary 73
Appendix 4: Averroes' Argument with Philoponus 89
6.4. The Riddle of the Long Commentary 92

7. The Turning Point of *Physics* VI: The Breakdown of Motion 109

7.1. Introduction: The Various Concepts of Motion in Aristotle's *Physics* 110
7.2. Aristotle's Divisibility Argument: A Crack in the Interval Model of Motion (*Physics* VI.4) 114
7.3. *Physics* V Reinterpreted: From Homogeneity to Heterogeneity 117
7.4. *Physics* VI Reinterpreted: From a Continuous Interval to a Contiguous Chain 120
7.5. *Physics* III Reintepreted: From Dimensional Entity to Boundary Entity 127
7.6. When did the Turning Point Occur? 133
Appendix 5: The Revision of the Middle Commentary and the Role of Alexander 139

8. The Turning Point of *Physics* VII: The Breakdown of Physical Body 141

8.1. Can Physical Body be a True Homoeomer? 142
8.2. Aristotle's Moving-Agent Argument (*Physics* VII.1) 146
8.3. Alexander vs. Galen on the Meaning of Essentiality 147
8.4. Averroes' Notion of First-Moved Part 152
8.5. Averroes' 'Aristotelian Atomism' 155
8.6. The 'Divorce' between Mathematics and Physics 159

Abbreviations and Notations

PRIMARY sources are referred to by author and title or abbreviated title. Works by Aristotle and Averroes are referred to by title or abbreviated title only. Modern editions and translations are listed among the primary sources and are also referred to among the secondary sources under the name of the editor or translator. Primary sources are arranged in chronological order and the order of Aristotle's corpus; secondary sources are listed and referred to by author–date.

In the translations of Aristotle I preferred the new Clarendon Aristotle Series (Oxford University Press) and Wardy's new translation of Physics VII (Cambridge University Press). When new translations were not available I used the classical Oxford translations. In the translations of the Greek commentators I used the Ancient Commentators on Aristotle series (Cornell University Press) when available. For commentaries that are not yet translated I have used the standard CAG (Commentaria in Aristotelem Graeca) edition.

I refer to the books of the *Physics* (Aristotle and commentators) by Roman numerals and to the books of the *Metaphysics* by Greek capital letters because of the inconsistency in the numbering of the books in Averroes' commentaries.

Special signs used in quotations:

[ ]	Addition for the sake of clarification
< >	In quotations from the long commentary: words that appear only in the Hebrew version; in quotations from the middle commentary: words that appear only in Kalonimus' translation.
<< >>	In quotations from the long commentary: words that appear only in the Latin version; in quotations from the middle commentary: words that appear only in Zeraḥya's translation.

Introduction: Science through Exegesis

THE great twelfth-century Muslim philosopher Abu al-Walid Muhammad Ibn Rushd,[1] known in the Latin west as Averroes, has the reputation of having been Aristotle's most faithful interpreter, and has been referred to as 'the Commentator'. He was viewed as a bold thinker in teaching Aristotle's philosophy in Islamic society, but not so much as an original thinker within the Aristotelian tradition. He was usually regarded as a competent, didactic exegete rather than as an original creative thinker, and sometimes was even depicted as a 'slavish' follower of Aristotle. At least as far as his physics is concerned, this image is far from true. In this study I present Averroes' surprisingly original physics; in particular, his major role in the history of atomism.

Averroes wrote three sets of commentaries on Aristotle's treatises. On almost all of Aristotle's books he wrote a short commentary or epitome (*jawāmi*ᶜ) and a middle commentary or a paraphrase (*talkhīṣ*). On five books—*Posterior Analytics*, *Physics*, *De caelo*, *De anima*, and *Metaphysics*—he also composed a long or word-by word commentary (*sharḥ* or *tafsīr*). Wolfson remarked that Averroes' writings belong not only to the language in which they were written, Arabic, but also to the languages into which they were translated: Latin and Hebrew.[2] The Scholastics studied Aristotle through the Latin translations of 'the Philosopher' and of 'the Commentator'; Jewish scholars relied almost exclusively on the Hebrew translations of the latter. Averroes' commentaries influenced the course of the world's philosophy mainly through the Latin translations. What was their impact?

Since Duhem, historians of science have realized that the new science of the sixteenth and seventeenth centuries owes more to medieval Scholastic thought than earlier generations of scholars had

[1] I shall use the Latin names for Avicenna and Averroes because the use of these names is so common, and transliteration for all other Arabic names.

[2] Wolfson 1973*a*, 430–3.

acknowledged. Aristotelianism was still a major frame of reference for European thinkers until well into the seventeenth century. In her landmark studies of Scholastic science, Anneliese Maier has shown the significance of the Scholastic theories of *minima naturalia* and of motion as *forma fluens*—that included some 'mildly atomistic' elements—for early modern thought on matter and motion.[3] Her studies on these subjects have been followed by Latin scholars, notably Murdoch and Sylla,[4] and several recent studies focus on the role of Aristotelian concepts in the development of the new atomism.[5] The contribution of Muslim philosophy, however, has not yet been duly acknowledged. According to the commonly accepted narrative, for example, the theory of *minima naturalia* was developed by the Scholastic scholars from a few preliminary remarks in Aristotle. I will show that the theories of *minima naturalia* and of motion as *forma fluens* had been crafted by Averroes into a systematic, thoughtfully elaborated new physics. He developed these theories further than his predecessors had done, and further than many of his followers were to do later. I shall refer to his physical system as 'Aristotelian atomism'.

At first glance, this expression appears to be a contradiction in terms. Aristotle, as is well known, was an adamant opponent of atomism, so much so that Aristotelianism and atomism are commonly considered two irreconcilable physical systems. Yet, as Newman has shown, the merging of Aristotelian and other, apparently conflicting theories was not uncommon in the Middle Ages and the early modern era.[6] Medieval Aristotelianism was a flexible system that accommodated a wide range of interpretations. Edward Grant captures its spirit well when he writes: 'It was always a domain of both traditional and innovative concepts and interpretations and was, therefore, inevitably elastic and absorbent. Hence its most interesting feature was a capaciousness that knew few limits'.[7] Aristotle, as is well known, took up themes repeatedly,

[3] Maier 1949, 1958; Murdoch and Sylla 1978; Murdoch 2001. These theories will be explained in Part B.

[4] See Murdoch and Sylla 1978; Murdoch 1972, 1982*b*, 2001; Sylla 1991.

[5] Sennert and Gassendi, for example, who deeply influenced such a major figure as Boyle, were still deeply rooted in the Aristotelian conceptual framework. See e.g. Lüthy, Murdoch, and Newman 2001, chapters by Newman, Michael, Osler, Clericuzio, and De Chenes.

[6] Newman (2001) does not hesitate to coin the terms 'experimental Aristotelianism' and 'Aristotelian alchemy' when following the development of an interesting corpuscular theory that unites Aristotelian and alchemical elements.

[7] Grant 1987, 352.

often probing new approaches to problems already discussed elsewhere. Therefore the Aristotelian corpus reveals internal tensions and ambiguities and sometimes contains variant or even contradictory statements on given problems. These statements offered commentators alternative points of departure for their thinking. Over many generations, commentators elaborated different positions which were all accommodated within Aristotelianism, making its 'cumulative' basis increasingly heterogeneous. We shall see how inconsistencies in Aristotle made it easier for Averroes to develop his new ideas and for these new ideas to flourish in Christian schools.

Averroes was the most influential of the medieval Muslim philosophers in the Latin West. The fact that his major role in the development of medieval physical thinking has eluded historians of science may therefore seem surprising. The reason, I suggest, was the literary genre in which they were exposed—that of the commentary. No single text presented Averroes' new physics straightforwardly. The genre of the commentary dictates the order of presentation and this sometimes makes it difficult for the commentator to organize his ideas systematically and for the reader to distinguish the ideas developed in the commentary from those already present in the commented text.[8] The Scholastics as well as their modern students accessed Averroes' physics mainly through the Latin translation of the long commentary on Aristotle's *Physics*, a text which is often confusing and inconsistent and, by itself, cannot provide a full and coherent picture of Averroes' new physics.[9] This had to be retrieved through a comparative study of the extant versions of all three commentaries on the *Physics*.

The genre of the commentary affected not only the way in which Averroes presented his ideas but also the way in which he conceived and elaborated them. Taylor describes him as 'a sophisticated mind at work weaving from Aristotelian threads a coherent cloth of metaphysical teachings'.[10] This is true also of his physical teaching. In his own way, Averroes was an 'exegetical scientist' who gained new insights into nature through a dialogue with texts of Aristotle and earlier commentators. In Part B below I shall study his way of 'innovation by way of exegesis' through three case-studies. In all three he follows a pattern to which I

[8] See Gideon Freudenthal 2004, 133–4; 2003, 7–11.

[9] In a different context Wolfson remarked that the Latin translations are not sufficient for studying Averroes. See Wolfson 1973*b*, 396.

[10] Taylor 1998, 508.

shall refer as *the turning point pattern*, which he uses when he wants to present new theses to which he attaches great importance. Let us look at this pattern.

The three turning points in Averroes' physics studied in Part B grew out of polemical situations, where earlier commentators pointed out difficulties in Aristotle's arguments. Averroes charges the commentators with misunderstanding Aristotle's meaning. In book VI 'And Aristotle's intention on this assumption escaped all the commentators.'[11] In book VII 'Therefore many of those who have not understood this demonstration became angry with Aristotle. Thus Galen wrote his famous treatise and Ibn Bājja . . . followed a way different from Aristotle's and thought that it was Aristotle's [way].'[12] In book VIII 'This [false] understanding of Aristotle started with Philoponus, and [continued with] al-Fārābī and other scholars who lived after al-Fārābī and whose books have reached us.'[13]

Confused by the commentators, Averroes goes through a period of hesitation and intensive study. In book VI 'It so happened that people were much in doubt about this demonstration, so that *we were also confused about it for a long time*. And it was difficult for us to understand the depth of Aristotle's [thought] on this.'[14] In book VIII '*After an intensive inquiry and a long time* it seems to me . . .'[15]

It was the polemical context that led Averroes to 'an intensive inquiry', which opened the way to a new interpretation. In the exegetical context he presents his new interpretation as revealing the true meaning of Aristotle. 'And since I understood what all the commentators missed and what escaped them I believe that my opinion is more adequate than that of the commentators.'[16] 'After I started commenting on Aristotle's statement, it seems to me that his words work out naturally

[11] *LC Phys.* VI.32 Latin 266F11–12, Hebrew 62^b22–3. Similarly in the middle commentary: 'It is the case that many people had not understood this demonstration and found fault with Aristotle.' *MC Phys.* VI.1 84^a3–4.

[12] *MC Phys.* VII.2, 84^a3–8. Similarly in the long commentary: 'And it was this premise that escaped Galen and others who have not understood this [Aristotle's] demonstration.' *LC Phys.* VII.1 Latin 307H; Hebrew 107a19–20.

[13] *MC Phys.* VIII.2.2 94^a24 6.

[14] *MC Phys.* VI.1 83^b25–84^a1. Also: 'We, as well as others, thought *for a long time* about what Ibn Bājja argued and approved of what he said, considering it to be the most satisfactory way. But a certain objection occurred to me' *MC Phys.* VI.7 72^b14–17.

[15] *MC Phys.* VIII.2.2, version A, NY MS 67^a8.

[16] *MC Phys.* VI.7 Kalonimus translation 74^b7–11.

in all respects and should not be subject to any doubt or demand any apology.'[17]

Averroes concludes with praise for Aristotle: 'How superior is Aristotle's thought to that of all the others and how far are they all from his understanding, for many things that he understood immediately people understood from his accounts after an intensive investigation and a long time. . . . Therefore we say that if his [Aristotle's] accounts of these matters had not been written, discovering them would have been almost impossible or difficult to achieve, or would have taken a long time. . . . And because God has elevated and exalted him, the ancients called him "the divine".'[18] 'And this accounts for how far is Aristotle's thought from that of everyone [else] and how limited is everyone's understanding compared to his understanding. . . . And the [true] meaning of our study of his treatises is different from what was said earlier. This is the case with respect to many issues in his treatises.'[19] 'Blessed be he who distinguished this man with human perfection.'[20]

Averroes conceived of his task as resolving difficulties arising in Aristotle's text, answering questions about it, and bringing forth its true meaning. He did not present his new ideas as innovative but, on the contrary, made a great effort to present them as the correct interpretation of Aristotle's text. In the exegetical context, the novelty of his new physics is dimmed. The way in which he developed his ideas out of Aristotle's philosophy illustrates to what extent 'legitimate Aristotelianism' could be stretched. The innovative character of his physical system would have been more discernible had he himself conceived of it and presented it as such.

[17] *LC Phys.* VI.32, Hebrew 62^b^2–5. Also in the middle commentary: 'After having honestly studied this issue I saw that Aristotle's argument conforms to nature, and there is nothing about it that should cause doubt or perplexity for which one should apologize, as the commentators did.' *MC Phys.* VI.7 73^a^2–4.

[18] *MC Phys.* VI.7 Kalonimus' translation 74^b^11–17, 21–2; Zeraḥya's translation 90^b^13–19, 90^b^23–91^a^1.

[19] *LC Phys.* VI.32 Hebrew only 62^b^23–5.

[20] *MC Phys.* VIII.2.2 version A NY MS 67a26–7.

PART A

THE COMPLEXITY OF AVERROES' WRITING

This research started in 1998 when I discovered by chance that there are two different versions of the middle commentary on the first argument of *Physics* VIII.1. When I turned to the short commentary I learned that Puig Montada had already discovered two versions of the short commentary on the same passage. This led me to look at the two translations of the long commentary, the Latin and the Hebrew (the Arabic original is lost), and I found two different versions of this chapter as well as of many other chapters. The two translations obviously reflect two very significantly different versions of the text. Pursuing the study of the three commentaries, I learned that Averroes had revised all three of them, and more than once.

Determining the chronology of the different versions turned out to be particularly difficult. Interested in the subject of motion, I focused mainly on the second half of the *Physics* and located those chapters on which all three commentaries of Averroes had been significantly revised. Following this criterion, I also selected, in addition to chapter VIII.1, chapters VII.1 and VI.4. The great surprise was that Averroes' commentaries on these chapters were revealed to be fascinating from the point of view of the historian of science. In order to unearth Averroes' interesting ideas, it was necessary to study his work diachronically, and thus to understand the chronological order of the different versions. The study of the contents and of the order of writing of the three commentaries and their revisions proved to be inseparable.

This book is, thus, addressed to two audiences: historians of medieval and early modern science as well as historians of Arabic philosophy interested in Averroes' intellectual biography, the development of his ideas, his repeated writing and rewriting, and his exegetical techniques. Readers of the first group may wish to skip Part A and proceed directly to Part B.

1

Description of the Corpus

AVERROES wrote three commentaries on Aristotle's *Physics*: a short commentary or epitome (*jawāmi*ᶜ), a middle commentary or a paraphrase (*talkhīṣ*), and a long commentary (*sharḥ* or *tafsīr*). These are at the core of the present study. He also wrote a book of questions (*masā'il*). The three commentaries present three very different approaches to the same text and differ significantly in structure and style. In this chapter I shall provide important information about the three commentaries and focus on their different orientations.

1.1. THE SHORT COMMENTARY

Of the three commentaries on the *Physics*, only the short is extant in the original Arabic. The text was recently edited and translated into Spanish by Josep Puig.[1] The edition is based on the Cairo manuscript (Q), the Madrid manuscript (M), and a group of manuscripts that Puig designates the 'oriental' manuscripts (*arquetypo Š*).[2] Puig considers Q as representing an early version of the text,[3] M and Š later versions.[4] The short commentary is also extant in a Hebrew translation by Moshe Ibn Tibbon, dated around 1250. This highly literal translation is based on a text that differs in several places from the Arabic texts used by Puig and can thus be used as another source (H). The Hebrew translation is represented by many manuscripts and a printed edition (Riva di Trento, 1559).

The short is the least 'structured' of the three commentaries. It more or less covers the entire *Physics*, but some topics receive more attention

[1] Puig 1983; Puig 1987.

[2] Puig 1987, 75–81; see also Puig 1991.

[3] Puig 1987, 87, 89–92.

[4] M and Š are closer to each other, but Puig rules out the possibility of a common origin because they contain different versions of the argument of *Physics* VIII.1 251a8–b10. See Puig 1987, 81.

while others are almost neglected.[5] The division of the *Physics* into eight books is maintained,[6] but the eight books are not further subdivided.

1.2. THE MIDDLE COMMENTARY

The middle commentary is the least-known of Averroes' three commentaries on the *Physics*. The Arabic text has not survived although, as Harvey has shown, an outline (*taqsīm*) or table of contents has been preserved.[7] There are two complete Hebrew translations of the middle commentary, as well as a sixteenth-century Hebrew-to-Latin translation of the first three books by Jacob Mantino. The first Hebrew translation, by Zeraḥya ben Isḥāq ben She'alti'el from 1284, is extant today only in two manuscripts;[8] the second, by Kalonimus ben Kalonimus from 1316, was widely used and is extant today in more than forty manuscripts. The Hebrew text of the first two books was edited (on the basis of both translations), translated into English, and studied thoroughly by S. Harvey.[9]

The Arabic term *talkhīṣ* is sometimes translated into Latin as 'paraphrasis', but Harvey and Gutas have shown that this is not always a suitable term.[10] In the case of the *Physics* it is definitely not. The middle commentary on the *Physics* can by no means be described as paraphrase. First, Averroes included in some chapters new interpretations, discussions of selected topics, and arguments with other commentators. Second, he made a particular effort to organize the subjects under discussion in a systematic and structured form. The division into eight books follows Aristotle. Each book (*maqāla*,[11] *ma'amar, liber*) begins with a table of contents that lists the parts included in this book; each part (*jumla, kelal, summa*) has its own table of contents, which enumerates its division into chapters. Evidently these divisions are meant to clarify the book's structure and make it more transparent to the

[5] See Harvey forthcoming. Another example: Book IV of the short commentary on the *Physics* does not include the second part (on void).

[6] This is not the case with all the commentaries. For example, the short commentary on the *Metaphysics* is divided into only five books. On this subject see also Puig 2002.

[7] In the Arabic manuscript British Library MS Add. Or. 9061. See Harvey 1982. This text was edited and translated into English in Al-Masumi, 1956.

[8] A third was destroyed by the fire in the Turin library. Zeraḥya lived in Italy and his translation was almost unknown in Spain and Provence. See Freudenthal 1993, 68.

[9] Harvey 1977.

[10] Harvey 1977, 114–16; Gutas 1993, 38–42.

[11] Perhaps a better English translation of *maqāla* is treatise, but since it is so common to refer to the division of Aristotle's *Physics* into eight books I shall use this term.

reader. To this end Averroes also enumerates premises, demonstrations, arguments, meanings of words, and statements.[12] The structure of the middle commentary reflects its highly systematic character.[13]

1.3. THE LONG COMMENTARY

Of the long commentaries, only that on the *Metaphysics* survives complete in the Arabic original.[14] Only of the *Physics* and the *Metaphysics* do we have two independent translations: a thirteenth-century Latin translation and a fourteenth-century Hebrew one.[15] The Latin translation of the long commentary on the *Physics* is commonly assumed to be by Michael Scotus, and is dated from the first third of the thirteenth century.[16] It is available in many manuscripts and several Renaissance editions,[17] of which the most commonly used is the Juntas edition: *Aristotelis opera cum Averrois commentariis*, vol. IV (Venice, 1562), reprinted by Minerva (Frankfurt am Main, 1962). Schmieja is preparing a critical edition and book VII has already been published.[18] He has also found

[12] Averroes lists three premises on the definition of motion (III.2.1 23a), five (following Aristotle) on the nature of place (IV.1.6 36b), and two on velocity (VI.3 69a), four demonstrations that a sensible body cannot be infinite (III.3.4.2 28a17–30a24), five demonstrations that the void does not exist (IV.2.5 43a–46a), two that the indivisible cannot move essentially (VI.12 81b). He lists arguments (I.2.2.2 7a–b; I.3.2 8b15–26) and statements (IV.1.1–2); five parts (III.3.3 27a3–14), nine facets (IV.1.3 35b19–36a1), four effects (IV.2.3 41b12–16) etc. Sometimes he numbers alternatives where Aristotle does not; sometimes his enumeration differs from Aristotle's.

[13] Puig 2002, 335.

[14] Parts of the commentary on *De caelo* have been preserved in a single manuscript in the National Library Tunis, and have been published by Professor Endress. See *LC De cael.* Arabic.

[15] As far as is known, the long commentary on *De caelo* has never been translated into Hebrew and that on *De anima* was translated into Hebrew from the Latin in the sixteenth century (Stuart Crawford 1953, p. xii; Wolfson 1973, 445–54; Zonta 1994, 15). The commentary on *Posterior Analytics* was translated from Hebrew to Latin in the sixteenth century. On all editions and translations see Endress and Aertsen 1999, 341–81.

[16] The Latin translation of the long commentary on *De caelo* is known to be by Michael Scotus. de Vaux (1933, 219) dates it to shortly before 1230. The translation of the long commentary on the *Physics* is most probably by Micael Scotus too. See Hasse 2007.

[17] See Wingate 1931, 121.

[18] See Schmija 2006. See also www.zdv.uni-tuebingen.de/tustep/prot/prot852-aver.html. On the Averroes project being carried out in the Thomas-Institute see: www.thomasinst.uni-koeln.de/averroes.

that there was another translation, perhaps by Hermannus Alemannus, of which only parts have been preserved.[19]

The Hebrew translation was produced in Provence about a century later, probably in the 1320s. Steinschneider suggested that the translator was Kalonimus ben Kalonimus, Renan that it was Moshe ben Shlomo of Sālon, who translated the long commentary on the *Metaphysics*.[20] The Hebrew translation is extant in several manuscripts.[21] The *prooemium* was edited and translated into English by S. Harvey.[22]

The Latin translation is well known and has been thoroughly studied from the thirteenth century until the present;[23] the Hebrew translation is less known. Both translations are far from satisfactory and are marred by copying errors and lacunae.[24] The Latin is the less readable of the two, because the Latin translator abbreviated words and quotations and

19 Schmieja 1999.

20 For a summary and assessment of their arguments see Harvey 1983, 59–60.

21 Oxford Bodl. 1388, books I–IV.72; Munchen BS hebr. 91/4, books I–II; Cambridge, Mass. Houghton Heb. 40, books V–VIII; Paris BN héb 883, complete; Paris BN héb 884, books I–IV; Cambridge Add. 632, books III–IV (beginning and end missing); Cincinnati HUC 723, books I–II incomplete; Vienna ON hebr. 169, books III–IV. There are four more manuscripts that include the texts of the long commentary (without the comments) and are compared to a 'Christian version' and to the middle commentary: Milan Ambr. 79 (S 38 Sup.), book I; Ambr. 80 (Q 24 Sup.), book III incomplete; Moscow Guenzburg 396, first part of book II; Cambridge Add. 631, second part of book II. These are parts of a text that was identified by Zonta as a commentary by Yehuda Messer Leon. See Zonta 2001.

22 Harvery 1983.

23 Hebrew commentaries were written mainly on the short and middle commentaries. Except for S. Harvey, modern scholars have not examined this text.

24 I shall list the major lacunae in the two translations. In the Latin Juntas edition:

VII.37 Forty-four lines of the Hebrew text are missing between text VII.37 and comment 37. These lines include: comment on text 37 (Hebrew 133b27–134a23); text 37a (Hebrew 134a23–6), which corresponds to *Physics* 250a15–19, Arabic 792.13–793.5; comment 37a (Hebrew 134a26–b4), text 37b (Hebrew 134b4–8), which corresponds to *Physics* 250a19–25, Arabic 793.6–13. Then follows the comment that appears in Juntas edition as comment 37.

III.45. Two Hebrew texts—45a (117a10–12, corresponding to 229.8–12 of the Arabic text) and 45b (117a17–20, corresponding to the Arabic 229.12–230.1)—correspond to the Latin text. In the Juntas edition, the last few words of text 45a and the first sentence of comment 45a are missing. The Latin text 45 consists of text 45a, comment 45a, and text 45b, with about two missing lines.

In the Hebrew manuscripts:

I.63. The major part of the comment (Latin 37M1–38F14) is missing in the Hebrew. In MS Oxford 1388 the missing part is copied in the margin, with the remark that it was found 'at the end'.

often employed a concise style,[25] presumably in an attempt to save time, paper, or parchment.

Of Averroes' three commentaries on the *Physics*, only the long one includes Aristotle's text. It consists of text-comment units: a passage from Aristotle, followed by Averroes' comment. The texts are quoted from Isḥāq Ibn Ḥunayn's Greek–Arabic translation.[26] This translation is extant today in one single manuscript, Leiden Warner 583, and has been edited by Badawi.[27] It is obvious that the manuscript that Averroes used is not the one that has come down to us,[28] and thus the text of the long commentary can be used, preferably via the Hebrew translation,[29] as a second source, supplementing the Leiden manuscript, to determine the correct reading of this important text.

In the printed Latin editions the texts are numbered. This numbering, which is commonly used for reference, is late.[30] In most Hebrew manuscripts the texts are not numbered but introduced by 'Aristotle said' in bold letters; the comments by 'the comment' (*ha-perush*) also in bold letters.[31] While the structure of the middle commentary is dictated by the argument, that of the long commentary is dictated by the word-for-word commentary genre. The comments usually follow a common structure, though not all the components of the comment are always present:

V.16. The comment is missing in the Hebrew. Texts 16 and 17 form one text (Hebrew 17a20–28, corresponding to *Physics* 226a12–23, Arabic 564.4–568.3) and are followed by comment 17 (Hebrew 17a28–b23).

VI.87. The text is missing, so that comment 87 seems to be a part of comment 86; the text, however, can be reconstructed from the secondary quotations in the comment (Hebrew 101a1–11, 15–18, 25–7, 29–30).

IV.127. Missing parts in Hebrew. The text and comment are not differentiated.

[25] e.g. 'et si non recipit, non'. The 'non' stands for 'there would have been no void' (Text IV.58, Hebrew 167a16, Latin 151C2).

[26] Isḥāq Arabic translation, as Mansion remarks, is 'nettement différent' from William of Moerbeke's Latin version, produced from the original Greek. See Mansion 1934, 208.

[27] Badawi 1964–5.

[28] Sometimes Averroes' text follows an alternative reading that appears in the margin or above the line in Leiden manuscript. Averroes' text is more complete than the Leiden manuscript and often seems to offer a better reading The most notable example is ch. I.7. This chapter is missing in MS Leiden and Badawi added a new translation to his edition. Isḥaq's original translation can be retrieved from texts I.57 (last sentence) to I.70 of Averroes' long commentary.

[29] Medieval Arabic to Hebrew translations are usually word for word.

[30] See e.g. Bouyges 1952, p. lxxvii.

[31] Except MSS Cincinnati and Vienna. In MS Cincinnati, the word 'said' is sometimes added in the margin.

1. A sentence that links the present discussion to the previous one.[32]
2. A discussion of the Aristotelian text, sentence by sentence. This may include 'secondary' quotations from Aristotle's text, followed by explanations. In the Hebrew version, these excerpts are quoted in full; in the Latin, usually only the first few words are cited. In the Hebrew version, the secondary quotations are introduced by אחר אמר, אמרו, עוד אמר, (then he said, his saying, he also said) the explanations usually by ירצה (he means) sometimes by יסבול (can be subject to). In the Latin version, the quotations are usually introduced by *Deinde dixit* or *et dixit* (often abbreviated as D.d., & d., or similar variations); the explanation, usually by *igitur, etcetera, idest, id est,* or a similar phrase (often abbreviated as &c.i, &c.i.&, i.&, or similarly). Although the explanations are usually brief, they sometimes develop into long discussions or arguments.
3. 'Independent' discussions or arguments that do not depend directly on the text.
4. Occasionally a concluding sentence that links up to the next text.

The division into text-comment units defines the basic structure of the long commentary. However, when he began to write the long commentary Averroes tried to follow also the structure of the middle commentary, namely the division into parts (*summae*) and chapters. In most Hebrew manuscripts,[33] this division coincides with that of the middle commentary and the titles are identical to those of the middle commentary. As in the middle commentary, a table of contents appears at the head of each book and each part. The titles are brief and appear at the beginning of the corresponding parts and chapters. The Latin printed edition is divided into parts and chapters throughout, but this division is late.[34] Starting with the third chapter of the second part, the divisions in the Latin and Hebrew redactions no longer match. The Hebrew continues to follow the divisions of the middle commentary and in the second chapter of the third part

32 e.g. 'cum declarauit . . . incoepit declarate . . .'.

33 With two exceptions: MS Cincinnati, in which the division is missing; and Oxford 1388, in which it is different, as described below.

34 The division into parts and chapters does not appear in the manuscripts known to us, but some manuscripts have marginal notes that are similar to some of the chapter headings. I would like to thank Dr Schmieja for this information.

Table 1. Divisions of books I and II of Averroes' *Physics* Commentaries

Middle commentary[a]					
Book I					
Parts	1	2A	2B	3	
Chapters	1 2 3	1 2 3 4	1 2	1 2 3 4 5	
Book II					
Parts	1	2		3	
Chapters	1 2 3 4 5 6 7	1 2 3		1 2 3 4	
Long commentary					
Book I					
Parts	1	2		3	4
Chapters	1 2 3	1 2 3 4		1 2 3 4 5	1 2 3 4 5
Text numbers of beginnings of chapters:					
Juntas edition	1 2 4	6 8 13 23		32 35	41 50 57 71 82
Paris MS	1 2 4	6 8 12 32		57 [division discontinued]	
Oxford MS	1 2 4	6 8 12 23/32[b]		41 51 58[c] 82[d]	
Book II					
Parts	1	2		3	4
Chapters	1 2 3 4 5 6 7	1 2 3		1 2 3 4	1 2
Text Members:					
Junta edition	1 4 5[e] 6 7[f]	16[g] 21		27 39	75 87
Oxford MS	1 4 5 6 7 12[h]	16 18 21		27 39 68 87	[i]

[a] Following Harvey 1977.

[b] The title 'fourth chapter' appears twice. The second corresponds to the first chapter of part 3 in the Juntas edition.

[c] In the commentary the title 'fourth chapter' is missing, but in the outline of part 3 it appears.

[d] Apparently the third part in Oxford manuscript is equal to the fourth part in the Juntas edition.

[e] In the beginning of text 5 appears the title Caps 3 & 4.

[f] In the beginning of text 5 appears the title Caps 6 & 7.

[g] In the beginning of text 5 appears the title Caps 1 & 2.

[h] According to the outline in Oxford manuscript the first part is divided into 6 chapters.

[i] According to the ouline at the beginning of book II Oxford manuscript counts three parts. Parts three and four of the Juntas edition equal part three of Oxford manuscript.

is discontinued.[35] Only one Hebrew manuscript, Oxford 1388, is divided into parts and chapters throughout books I–IV, in a division similar but not identical to the division of the Latin Juntas edition.[36]

[35] There is also a cruder division. In book II, the title 'the treatise on accident and chance' appears before text 39. In book IV, 'the treatise on void' appears before text 50 and 'the treatise on time' before IV.87. Book VIII is subdivided into two parts at 184b.

[36] In book I part 3 and in book II part 3, for instance, Oxford manuscript has more chapters than the Juntas edition.

The copyist of this manuscript has apparently consulted a Latin manuscript.[37]

Table 1 compares the divisions of books I and II in the middle and long commentaries. In the latter I compare the common Hebrew version (Paris manuscript), the special Hebrew manuscript (Oxford 1388), and the Latin Juntas edition. There is fairly cogent evidence that the discontinued division that we find in the Hebrew redaction reproduces the original Arabic. Averroes discusses the division of the book in the *prooemium* to the long commentary:

As for the parts of this book, Aristotle made it into eight treatises. Each one of these treatises is divided into large sections and the large sections are divided into small sections. In some instances the small sections are divided into yet smaller sections. At times the first sections will not be divided, and at other times the division process will take place more than three times. . . . We will enumerate these divisions at the beginning of each treatise.[38]

This description exactly matches the structure of the middle commentary. It may be that when he began writing the long commentary Averroes intended to carry over the division into parts and chapters from the middle commentary but then gave up the idea. The editor of the printed Latin edition (perhaps relying on earlier Christian scholars) decided to continue the divisions where Averroes left off but, not being acquainted with the middle commentary, he applied a different breakdown from that found there. His division is undoubtedly inferior to that of the middle commentary.[39]

1.4. THE *QUESTIONS IN PHYSICS*

The *Questions in Physics* (ספר הדרושים הטבעיים) is a collection of nine short treatises, which is extant in several Hebrew manuscripts. The *Questions* has been translated into English on the basis of the extant manuscripts, with an introduction and detailed notes, by Helen Tunik Goldstein. Questions VI and VII also survive in one Arabic

37 MS Oxford also includes one sentence that is found in the Latin version and not in the Hebrew, as well as a Latin word above the line on fos. 110b, 122b.

38 Harvey 1983, 80.

39 The Juntas Latin edition of the long commentary on the Metaphysics also features a late division into parts and chapters. There is no division in the Arabic and Hebrew.

manuscript.[40] The seventh of the *Questions in Physics* is relevant to the study of *Physics* VIII.1; the first, the seventh, and the eighth, to the study of *Physics* VII.1.

[40] Escurial 632. According to Goldstein (1991, p. xiv) it is not the exemplar on which the Hebrew translation was based, and that 'the ancestor of the Hebrew version frequently had better readings.'

2

The Order of Writing

It is usually assumed that Averroes' commentaries in general, and those on the *Physics* in particular, were written in the 'natural' order: first the short, then the middle, and finally the long commentary. The colophon of the Madrid codex, which includes Averroes' short commentaries on Aristotle's four major physical treatises, is dated 1159. The middle commentary on the *Physics* was written in Seville,[1] and completed on March 21, 1170.[2] The long commentary on the *Physics* is commonly dated to 1186, but Harvey has shown that there is no decisive evidence to support this dating.[3] In his comparative study of the three commentaries on the *Physics,* Harvey concludes that the commentaries were written in the accepted order.[4] He adduces Averroes' own testimony in the colophon of the middle commentary: 'I already have among the multitude a commentary that I made in my youth and it is short.[5] Now I saw fit to make this commentary more complete'.[6] Harvey remarks that the commentary of his youth is no doubt the short one and that the colophon makes no reference to a long commentary or an intention to write one. The short commentary was, he concludes, written years before the middle one. Averroes himself provides additional testimony in the long commentary (comment I.57)—evidence hitherto

1 In Averroes' words 'away from scholarship and from my home'.

2 'And the completion of this commentary took place on Saturday, the first day of the month of Rajab, in the year 565 according to the Muslim calendar, in the city of Seville.' The Hamburg MS reads 565, the Paris MS 555, and Zeraḥya's translation 575. The true date must be 565, because that year the first day of Rajab was indeed a Saturday. I am grateful to Gad Freudenthal for this observation.

3 Harvey forthcoming n. 15; Puig 1997, 118–19; al-ᶜAlawi 1986, 55–7, 73–4.

4 Harvey forthcoming.

5 Zeraḥya's translation is even more awkward: 'I had from people's books a short commentary in my youth.'

6 *MC Phys*. VIII.6.5, Kalonimus' translation 115a5–17, Zeraḥya's translation 137b20–138a10. The last sentence is quoted in Harvey, forthcoming.

unknown because it appears only in the Hebrew version. The words between angle brackets are found only in the Hebrew:

The treatise on minerals is not available to us, nor is the treatise on plants, except for two books of it <which are attributed to Aristotle; but we do have the book of animals and have already completed its commentary according to the signification (*ke-fi ha-ᶜinyan*). We shall work further, if God wills in our life, on a word-by-word commentary as we shall try to do, God willing, on the rest of his books. We have not yet had the opportunity to carry out this intention except in the case of *De anima*, and this book that we start now [the *Physics*]. But we have already laid down commentaries on *all his books* according to the signification in the three disciplines—logic, natural science, and metaphysics>.[7]

'Commentary according to signification' (*Be'ur ke-fi ha-ᶜinyan*) and 'word by word commentary' (*be'ur mila be-mila)* are, apparently, translations of the Arabic terms *sharḥ ᶜalā l-maᶜāna* and *sharḥ ᶜalā l-lafẓ*,[8] and designate the middle and long commentaries respectively.[9]

From this passage we learn that Averroes intended to write a complete set of long commentaries.[10] Of the five that he accomplished, that on *De anima* was the first and that on the *Physics* the second.[11] The long commentaries were written after the middle ones with the possible exception of *De anima*. It is possible that the middle and long commentaries on *De anima* were written at about the same time. The former might have been the last middle commentary to be written (possibly in 1181),[12] while the latter was the first long commentary to

[7] *LC Phys*. I.57, Latin 34K9–11, Hebrew 35b11–16.

[8] See e.g. the middle commentary on the *Sophistical Refutations*, Jéhamy 1982, ii. 729.12–13.

[9] This agrees with Averroes' use of the term 'word by word' when referring to Alexander's commentary, and 'according to the signification' when referring to Themistius'. *LC Phys*., introduction, Hebrew 1a2; Harvey 1983, 65.3. *LC Meta.*, introduction to book Λ, Hebrew 139a11.

[10] In the epilogue to his middle commentary on the *Sophistical Refutations* Averroes likewise remarks that this commentary is based on what he could understand at this stage and announces his intention (if God wills) to write a more extended commentary (Jéhamy 1982, ii. 729.9–11). Also in the conclusions to books M and N of the middle commentary of the Metaphysics. See Puig 2002, 345.

[11] This rules out Alonso's and Al-ᶜAlawi's proposal to date the long commentary on *De anima* to 1190. See: Ivry 1995, 77 n. 10; Al-ᶜAlawi 1986, 108–9.

[12] It is dated 1181, but this date is not certain. See Ivry 1995, 77 n. 9; Puig 1998, 125; Puig 2002, 342.

be written.[13] In the case of the *Physics* the commentaries were written in the 'natural' order: short, middle, and long. I emphasize this because sometimes, as we shall see, the textual evidence is very confusing.

[13] This can explain the quotations or similar passages in these two texts that Ivry has noted. I have not found similar passages in the middle and long commentaries on the *Physics*.

3

The Changing Cultural Contexts

THE study of the three commentaries on the *Physics* calls attention to the rather complex and changing attitudes of Averroes to his predecessors, the earlier commentators.[1] The most notable trend in the way from the short commentary in the 1150s to the long commentary in the 1180s, as Druart has shown, is the shift of the centre of gravity from the commentators to Aristotle.[2] The increasing attention to Aristotle's text is accompanied by a change of attitude towards several of the commentators, notably a growing objection to Philoponus, al-Fārābī and Avicenna, who pursued some Neoplatonic ideas and a new fervent interest in Alexander, who wrote the most conscientious word-for-word commentary on the *Physics*.

When writing the short commentary Averroes certainly learned from the commentaries on the *Physics* of Ibn Bājja[3] and Themistius,[4] and only these can be considered as certain 'sources' at this stage. Averroes mentions Alexander once[5] and Avicenna four

[1] On this subject see Druart 1994. Druart examines several texts of Averroes with special attention to *De anima*, while my study is confined to the *Physics*.

[2] My study supports Druart's conclusion that in the short commentaries Averroes 'did not pay full attention to Aristotle's text', while the long commentary is 'an intense and thorough examination of Aristotle's text in all its minutae, and ample but critical use of all available commentaries.'

[3] Five times in the Arabic, (*SC Phys*. Arabic 55.16–17, Hebrew 16b1; Arabic 56.4, Hebrew 16b10; Arabic 99.13, Hebrew 30b11; Arabic 100.7, Hebrew 30b19; Arabic 116.13, Hebrew 36a11). Once only in the Hebrew (Hebrew 31a19) and once more in version B of book VIII (*SC Phys*. Arabic 134.11, Hebrew 40b15–16).

[4] Themistius is referred to six times, five of which are in Book VI (*SC Phys*. Arabic 99.8, Hebrew 30b6; Arabic 100.3, Hebrew 30b16; Arabic 103.2, Hebrew 31b26; Arabic 105.16, Hebrew 32b29; Arabic 106.2, Hebrew 33a4; Arabic 141.4, Hebrew 43b22). On the context of book VI see Ch. 7 below: 'the Peripatetics' are referred to twice (*SC Phys*. Arabic 21.10, Hebrew 5b27; Arabic 26.17, Hebrew 7b8). Theophrastus is mentioned by name once, but this reference is certainly second-hand. Gutas (1999, 128–9) has shown that Averroes learned about Theophrastus' views from Themistius.

[5] Alexander's well-known dictum 'that were there no soul there would be neither time nor motion' (*SC Phys*., Arabic 62.16, Hebrew 19a1–2). Averroes could have learned about it from Ibn Bājja or from other sources. See e.g. Lettinck 1994*a*, 381–2.

times,[6] but these references reflect general knowledge, and can by no means prove that he was acquainted with their commentaries on the *Physics*. Al-Ghazālī and the mutakallimūn are mentioned only in the late stratum of the short commentary,[7] and so is Philoponus.[8] Al-Fārābī is mentioned only once in the main body of the short commentary,[9] and three times in the late stratum.[10] Al-Fārābī's treatise *On Changeable Beings* which played an important role in the development of Averroes' interpretation of the *Physics* and to which he refers in version B of book VIII, is not yet known in the main body of the short commentary

The new actor on the stage in the middle commentary is Philoponus. He is mentioned by name only three times. Averroes refers to him by name when he argues with him,[11] but often consults him without mentioning his name, notably in matters of logic.[12] The role of Philoponus in Averroes' *Physics* was studied by Harvey, who concludes that Averroes 'valued Philoponus as a logician who often made the text easier to understand through apt illustrations and examples and by providing the syllogisms behind Aristotle's argumentation'.[13] The commentator most frequently mentioned in the middle commentary is still Ibn Bājja (thirteen times),[14] but his role is less important than it was in the short commentary. The interest in Avicenna is still negligible.[15] Al-Fārābī is

[6] Three times in the Arabic (*SC Phys.* Arabic 21.10, Hebrew 5b26; Arabic 26.11, Hebrew 7a32; Arabic 56.11, Hebrew 16b17), once more in the Hebrew version only (Hebrew 3b5) and once more in version B of book VIII (*SC Phys.* Arabic 134.11, Hebrew 40b15).

[7] The former in the introduction *(SC Phys.* Arabic 8.5, Hebrew 2a16); the latter in version B of book VIII (*SC Phys.* Arabic 134.4, Hebrew 40b6). The reference to 'our contemporaries' in the introduction (*SC Phys.* Arabic 8.7, Hebrew 2a18) is probably also to them.

[8] In version B of book VIII (*SC Phys.* Arabic 135.1, Hebrew 40b16).

[9] *SC Phys.* Arabic 55.16, Hebrew 16b1.

[10] Once in the introduction *(SC Phys.* Arabic 8.9, Hebrew 2a20) and once in version B of book VIII *(SC Phys.* Arabic 134.10, 135.3, Hebrew 40.14, 40.19). The former reference is a recommendation to study logic from al-Fārābī's books or from his own short commentary on logic. This reference can well be early. The second is polemical and is certainly late, as I shall show in Ch. 6 below.

[11] All three in book VIII: once in version B *MC Phys.* 94a25, once in the common part *MC Phys.* 100a26, and once in version A *MC Phys.* MS NY 66a21.

[12] To mention a few examples: *MC Phys.* I.2.4, 5a16–b13, following Philoponus *On phys.* 58–60; *MC Phys.* II.3.2, 18b17–25, following Philoponus *On phys.* 271.27–272.13; *MC Phys.* III.2.1 23a1–26, following Philoponus *On phys.* 341.10–342.9; *MC Phys.* III.2.2, 23b10–15, following Philoponus *On phys.* 342.17–28; *MC Phys.* IV.3.3, 48a13–19, following Philoponus *On phys.* 709–10.

[13] Harvey 2004*a*, 103.

[14] *MC Phys.* 40a1, 14, 22; 44b19–20; 45a17; 72b4, 9, 15, 17, 20; 74b7; 84a5; 85a9.

[15] He is mentioned once in book VI (*MC Phys.* 81b1–2).

mentioned once in Book IV and in both versions of book VIII.[16] Al-Ghazālī's *Maqāṣid* is mentioned in the colophon.[17] The mutakallimūn are mentioned four times.[18] Of the Greek scholars Galen is mentioned once,[19] 'the Peripatetics' and 'the commentators' are referred to several times;[20] and Alexander is mentioned by name seven times.[21]

In the short and middle commentaries, Averroes mentioned earlier commentators mainly in polemical contexts.[22] In the long commentary, by contrast, references to commentators are frequent and routine. The lists in my footnotes do not claim to be complete, but give only a general picture of what was available to Averroes and what interested him.

Alexander is the commentator most frequently mentioned in the long commentary.[23] Averroes consults him frequently, and not only

[16] *MC Phys*. 40a14, 94a26, NY MS 67a5.

[17] *MC Phys*. 115a10.

[18] *MC Phys*. 34a26–b1, 67b26–68a1 (Kalonimus writes 'the ancients of our nation'. but it should be 'the mutakallimūn of our nation' and so Zeraḥya translates), 68a7, 94a9–10.

[19] *MC Phys*. 84a4.

[20] Peripatetics: *MC Phys*. 5b6, 115a9 (colophon); commentators: 72b11, 73a4, 73b15, 74b10, 84a9. Theophrastus is mentioned three times (72a20, 74a14, 77a26) but these are certainly second-hand references. See n. 4 above.

[21] *MC Phys*. 72a23, 74a25 (twice), 74b2, 84a10, 85b25, 88a24.

[22] e.g. MC VII.4 88a24–5.

[23] **Introduction** Hebrew only, 1a3, 25, 1b20, 3 (the introduction is not a part of Scotus' translation). **Book I**: I.30, Hebrew only, 19b28, 20a14, 23; I.31, Hebrew only, 20b27; I.52, Latin only, 32E15, F1. **Book II**: II.9, Latin 51H10, Hebrew 54a11; II.30, Latin 60L1, Hebrew 64a18; II.35, Latin 62I11, Hebrew 66b4; II.37, Latin 63E2, Hebrew 67a11; II.77, Latin 77I9, Hebrew 83b27; II.88, Latin 82M9, Hebrew 90a12; II.90, Latin 84H7, Hebrew 92a17. **Book IV**: *Place*: IV.11, Hebrew only 140b19; IV.20, Latin 129E11, Hebrew 144b8, Latin 129F10 (Latin and the Hebrew MS Oxford 1388 fo. 122b); IV.30, Latin 133H1, Hebrew 148b30; Latin 133H7, Hebrew 149a3; IV.37, Latin 137M1, Hebrew 153a2; IV.43, Latin only 142K1, Latin 143A5, Hebrew 159a11; IV.45, Latin 144H16, Hebrew 160b22. *Void*: IV.50, Latin 147E10, Hebrew 163a27; IV.58, Latin 151E5, Hebrew 167b3; IV.64, Latin 154B15, Hebrew 170a30; IV.65, Latin 154K6, Hebrew 170b30; Latin 155C9, Hebrew 171b2; IV.70, Latin 157I14, Hebrew 174a17; Latin only, 157L6; IV.77, Hebrew only, 183a25. *Time*: IV.90, Hebrew only 191a30; IV.101, Latin 181G6, G13, Hebrew 197b10, 11; IV.102, Hebrew only 197b29; Latin 182A5, Hebrew 198a9; Latin only 182E5; IV.129, Latin 201B4, 6, Hebrew 215b11(Alexander's name is mentioned twice, but these are not references). **Book V**: V.10, Latin 215F11, Hebrew 13b20; Latin 215I6, Hebrew 14a2; Latin 215L10, Hebrew 14a12; Latin 215M6, Hebrew 14a15; Latin only 216A8; Hebrew only 14a20 (twice); V.20, Latin 222B10, Hebrew 19b15; Hebrew only 19b23; V.22, Hebrew only 20b30; V.38, Latin 231C2, Hebrew 28b18; V.50, Latin 238B4, Hebrew 35b30; V.59, Latin 243H4, Hebrew 41b11; Latin 243H6, Hebrew 41b12. **Book VI**: VI.1, Latin 246M2, Hebrew 45a6; VI.10, Latin 252A10, Hebrew 50a20; VI.15, Latin 255L7, Hebrew 53a20; VI.32, Latin 265L14, Hebrew 62a7; Latin 265M9, Hebrew 62a11; VI.34, Hebrew only 65a27; VI.37, Hebrew only 67a11; VI.46, Latin 275I5, Hebrew 72b15; VI.56 Latin 283C2, C9, Hebrew 80a20–21. **Book VII**: VII.20, Latin 323I13, Hebrew 123b23.

on disputed points. Sometimes he uses Alexander's commentary to establish Aristotle's correct text.[24] Usually he paraphrases Alexander, sometimes he quotes him verbatim.[25] A comparison of Averroes' and Simplicius' reports of Alexander's views would be an interesting subject for research.[26] Averroes also refers to Themistius[27] and Philoponus,[28] and sometimes more generally to 'the commentators'[29]

Book VIII: VIII.4, Latin only 341K11 (to Alexander's *On the principles*); VIII.42, Latin only 381I5; VIII.79, Latin 426K2, Hebrew 226a14; Latin 426L11, Hebrew 226a22.

24 The expressions 'libro Alex' נסחת אלסכנדר and העתקת אלסכנדר usually refer to Aristotle's text as quoted by Alexander: I.30, Hebrew only 20a14; I.31, Hebrew only 20b27; II.35, Latin 62I11, Hebrew 66b4; II.37, Latin 63E2, Hebrew 67a11; II.88, Latin 82M9, Hebrew 90a12; IV.50, Latin 147E10, Hebrew 163a27; IV.70, Latin 157I14, Hebrew 174a17; IV.77, Hebrew only 183a25; IV.90, Hebrew only 191a30; V.59, Latin 243H4, Hebrew 41b11; VI.10, Latin 252A10, Hebrew 50a20; VI.56, Latin 283C9, Hebrew 80a21. See also *LC Metaphysics* Λ, Arabic vol. IV 1537.12–14, Hebrew.153b15–16; Bouyges 1952, i. pp. cxxx–cxxxi.

25 Quotations usually open with 'dixit Alexander': II.9, Latin 51H10, Hebrew 54a11; I.30 Hebrew only 19b29–20a1; IV.58 Latin 151E5, Hebrew 167b3; IV.101 Latin 181G6, Hebrew 197b10.

26 Two examples: (1) Simplicius is clearer and more informative than Averroes: The question whether celestial motion can be faster or slower was raised by commentators on *Physics* VI.2. Both Simplicius (*On phys*. 941.22–942.24) and Averroes (*LC Phys*.VI.15, Latin 255L7–M7, Hebrew 53a20–27) ascribe two answers to Alexander and add that the second goes back to Eudemus. Simplicius' description of Alexander's two arguments is long and detailed (941.23–942.13, 942.13–24); Averroes' consists of two sentences, more or less corresponding to Simplicius 941.27 and 941.23–4. For more on this example, see Kukkonen 2002*c*. (2) Averroes is clearer and more informative than Simplicius: Averroes begins, 'and Alexander contends that this chapter is obscure and offers two interpretations' and then describes the two interpretations at length (IV.37, Latin 137L15–138E2, Hebrew 153a2–b1 [the last sentence is missing in the Latin]). His interpretation is more complete than Simplicius' (*On phys*. 576.30–577.6).

27 Themistius: **Book I:** I.25, Latin 17K7, Hebrew 16a30; I.61, Hebrew only 38b5. **Book II**: II.48, Latin 66G15, Hebrew 70b12; II.55, Latin 70A14, Hebrew 74b6; **Book III**: III.53, Latin 110A13, Hebrew 123a17. **Book IV**: IV.43, Latin 141F12, Hebrew 157b5; Latin 141H14–15, Hebrew 157b17; Latin 141I3, Hebrew 157b23; Latin 141L5, Hebrew 158a3; Latin 141L7, Hebrew 158a6; Latin only 141M2; IV.102, Latin 182C2, Hebrew 198a19; IV.106, Latin 185H5, Hebrew 201b5; IV.127, Hebrew only 214a15; IV.132, Latin only 203L10; **Book V**: V.10, Latin 215K9, Hebrew 14a8; Latin 215L10, Hebrew 14a12; Latin 216A8, Hebrew 14a20; V.28, Latin 226A3, Hebrew 23a31. **Book VI**: VI.32, Latin 266A1, Hebrew 62a14; Latin 266C2, Hebrew 62a29. **Book VII**: VII.9, Hebrew only 111b27. **Book VIII**: VIII.33, Latin 372B4, Hebrew 169b20; VIII.37, Latin only 377B13; VIII.76, Latin 421F4, Hebrew 221b11; VIII.82, Latin 431B11, Hebrew 229b30; VIII.42, Latin only 381I4.

28 Philoponus: **Book IV**: IV.43, Latin 141F9, Hebrew 157b3; Latin 142C1, Hebrew 158a22. **Book VI**: VI.61, Latin 288A2, Hebrew 85b24. **Book VIII**: VIII.4, Latin 341A12, Hebrew 138b14; VIII.15, Hebrew only 149b17; VIII.23, Latin 359K3, Hebrew 156b28; VIII.79, Latin 426K14, Hebrew 226a18.

29 Commentators: **Book II**: II.50, Latin 68A12, Hebrew 72a19. BookIII: III.53, Latin 110A13, Hebrew 123a17. **Book IV**: IV.43, Hebrew only 158b23; Latin 142K6,

or to the Peripatetics.[30] Other Greek scholars mentioned are Galen,[31] Archimedes,[32] and the Epicureans.[33] References that are clearly second-hand (e.g. to Eudemus or Theophrastus) are not listed here.

The Arabic scholars referred to are al-Fārābī,[34] Avicenna,[35] al-Ghazālī,[36] Ibn Bājja,[37] the mutakallimūn, and 'our contemporaries'.[38]

Hebrew 158b24; IV.71, Hebrew only 177a14, 16; IV.98, Latin 179G7–8, Hebrew 195b16; Hebrew only 195b16 (twice more); IV.129, Hebrew only 215a3. **Book V:** V.9, Latin 214K7–8, Hebrew 13a16. **Book VI:** VI.32, Latin 265L12, Hebrew 62a7; VI.46, Latin 275K3, Hebrew 72b21. **Book VII:** VII.1 Latin 306C2–3, Hebrew 105b13; VII.9, Hebrew only 111b27; VII.15, Hebrew only 118a27. **Book VIII:** VIII.23, Latin 359K3, Hebrew 156b28; VIII.42, Latin only 381I4 ('the commentators, Alexander and Themistius'); Latin only 382C2.

30 Peripatetics: **Book II:** II.22, Latin 57B6, Hebrew 60a11; II.48, Latin 66G11, Hebrew 70b10. **BookIV:** IV.71, Hebrew only 177a14; Hebrew 178b21. **BookVIII:** VIII.79, Latin 426K14, Hebrew 226a18.

31 Galen: **Book IV**: IV.97, Latin only 177M2 (twice); Latin only 177M8; IV.98, Latin 179E6, Hebrew 195b6; Latin 179E15, Hebrew 196b8. **Book VII:** VII.1, Latin 306C1, Hebrew 105b12; Latin 306G6, Hebrew 106a8; VII.2, Latin 307G16, Hebrew 107a19; VII.4, Latin 309B14, Hebrew 109a2; VII.10, Hebrew only 113b29; VII.15, Hebrew only 118b10. **Book VIII:** VIII.78, Latin only 424L14.

32 V.24, Hebrew only 21b14.

33 I.60, Latin 36I7 (Zenodic), Hebrew 38a8 (אפיקורוסים).

34 Al-Fārābī: **Book IV:** IV.43, Latin 142B14, 15 Hebrew 158a22; IV.101, Latin 181E7, Hebrew 197a29. **BookVIII:** VIII.1, Latin only 339B5–6; VIII.4, Latin only 341I10; VIII.9, Latin 345A6 Hebrew 142b20; VIII.23, Latin only 360E5; Latin 360F5, Hebrew 157b6; VIII.78, Latin only 424M1.

35 Avicenna: **Book I:** I.60, Hebrew only 37b15 (on this comment in the Latin and the reference to Avicenna, see Schmieja 1986, 180–2); I.83, Latin 47G10, Hebrew 49a20; Latin 47K5, Hebrew 49b11. **Book II:** II.3, Latin 49B14, Hebrew 51a5–6; II.22, Latin 56M, Hebrew 59b19; Latin 57B3, Hebrew 60a7; II.26, Latin 59C2, Hebrew 62b7; II.48, Latin 66G11, Hebrew 70b10; Latin 66G15, Hebrew 70b12; Latin 66H9, Hebrew 70b15; Latin 66M3, Hebrew 71a7. **Book IV:** IV.32, Latin 134F10, Hebrew 149b17; IV.45, Latin 144G7 Hebrew 160b15, Latin 144H9 Hebrew 160b21, Latin 144H13, Hebrew 160b22; IV.67, Latin 156B10 Hebrew 172a19. **Book VIII:** VIII.3, Latin 340E10–11, Hebrew 138a8; VIII.78, Latin only 424L2; Latin only 424L10; VIII.83, Latin 432D1, Hebrew 231a12–13; VIII.79, Latin 426L10, Hebrew 226a22.

36 al-Ghazālī: **Book I:** I.60, Latin 36I7, Hebrew 38a8. **Book VIII:** VIII.3, Latin 340E14, Hebrew 138a10; Latin 340F6, Hebrew 138a12.

37 Ibn Bājja: **Book IV:** IV.43, Latin 141M11, Hebrew 158a10; Latin 142B14, Hebrew 158a21; Latin 142C4, Hebrew 158a24; Latin142G4, Hebrew 158b14; Hebrew only 158b16; Latin 142K8, Hebrew 158b25; IV.71, many times; IV.74, Latin 154M8, Hebrew 181a28. **Book VI**: VI.32, Latin 266B7, Hebrew 62a25. The contexts are discussions of controversies. *Physics* IV.5: the question of the place of the outermost sphere (LC IV.43; MC IV.1.9). *Physics* IV.8: the question of motion in the void (LC IV 71, a brief note in IV.74; MC IV.2.5). *Physics* VI.4: the question of instantaneous motion (LC VI.32 and MC VI.7). *Physics* VII.1: the argument with Galen (MC VII.1–2).

38 Mutakallimūn and 'our contemporaries': **Book** I: I.30, Hebrew only 20a10; I.60, Latin 36D4 Hebrew 37b5; Latin 36E2, Hebrew 37b13; Latin 36F6, Hebrew 37b22; I.71, Latin 42C1, Hebrew 43b3. **Book II:** II.22, Latin 57B7, Hebrew 60a11. **Book IV**:

Several times Averroes refers to grammarians 'of our time' or 'of our language'[39] and to 'our friends'.[40]

The question of whether Averroes was acquainted with Alexander's views when he wrote the middle commentary is crucial for the understanding of the development of his physics and the chronology of his commentaries. I shall come back to this several times in Part B.

IV.6, Latin 124A5, Hebrew 138b29; IV.24, Hebrew only 145b25. **Book V:** V.13, Latin 218I11, Hebrew 16b18; V.38, Hebrew 29a3. **Book VIII:** VIII.4, Latin 341E3, Hebrew 139a2; Latin 341I1–2, Hebrew 139a28–9; Latin 344I1, Hebrew 142a5; VIII.15, Latin 349I10, Hebrew 146b22; Latin 349M15, Hebrew 147a8; Latin 350A10, Hebrew 147a11; Latin 350D4, Hebrew 147a22; Latin only 350E7, I11; Hebrew only 147b 9,12; VIII.20, Latin 355B10, Hebrew 152b4; VIII.47, Latin 388K10, Hebrew 188b18; VIII.53, Latin only 394K16–L1; VIII.74 Latin only 418I14; Latin 418K4–5, Hebrew 219a4; VIII.78, Latin only 424L1.

[39] Grammarians: **Book IV**: IV.23, Hebrew only 145b4–5; IV.115, Hebrew only 206a26–7; IV.119, Hebrew only 209b7.

[40] I.60, Latin 36E4, Hebrew 37b14; VIII.68, Latin 411B9–10, Hebrew 212a6.

4

Versions and Revisions

ALL three commentaries on the *Physics* were massively revised by Averroes himself. There is ample direct and indirect evidence of these revisions. The direct evidence includes passages that have come down to us in more than one version, the indirect evidence includes confused passages, with many differences, more than usual, among manuscripts and textual problems, which suggests that copyists encountered difficulties due to amendments in their source. Indirect evidence is not in itself sufficient but can be helpful when there are other grounds to suspect that a particular passage was revised.

4.1. THE SHORT COMMENTARY

Most of the text of the short commentary is clear, with relatively minor differences between the manuscripts, but there is direct and indirect evidence of revisions. The most noteworthy and instructive instance of direct evidence is the beginning of book VIII. Puig Montada found that different manuscripts preserve two different expositions of Aristotle's well-known and controversial argument that every motion must be preceded by another motion (*Physics* VIII.1, 251a8–b10).[1] He considers the Q-M version of this argument to be the early one, written before 1159, and the Š version to be a late revision, written after 1186.[2]

[1] Puig Montada studied the two versions of the short commentary in the introduction to his translation of the short commentary (1987). In his paper, 'Averroes y el problema de la eternidad del movimiento' (1999), he offers a comprehensive view of Averroes' interpretation of VIII.1. I shall rely frequently on his work.

[2] The differences between Q and M are listed in the apparatus of Puig 1983 and in Puig 1987, 87. He bases his late dating of version B on two references to the long commentary in books III and VIII (*SC Phys.* Arabic 43.8, 135.10; Hebrew 13a2–3, 40b27; Spanish 143, 237).

The Hebrew translation contributes additional information. Some of the manuscripts and the Riva di Trento edition include both versions: first version B,[3] and then version A. Version A is introduced by the sentence, 'another version is found in the margin (*gillayon*),[4] and this is . . .',[5] and concludes with the notation, 'up to this point is written in the margin (*gillayon*).'[6] Other Hebrew manuscripts contain yet a third version, which I shall refer to as A′. The word *gillayon* also appears in the margin in some of the A′ manuscripts.[7] Apparently version A itself is not a homogeneous text, and has been revised.[8] It seems that after writing the short commentary on VIII.1 Averroes modified it, possibly more than once, and eventually wrote the new version B. In other words, the same text has been both revised and rewritten. There are in the short commentary also quite a few noticeable instances of indirect evidence of revision: passages in which the text is obviously corrupt and the differences between the manuscripts are more frequent and significant than usual.[9]

The revision of the short commentary holds several surprises in store for the reader: in some of the revised passages we find ideas that apparently belong to the stage of the long commentary.[10] Puig dates version B of book VIII after 1186,[11] and I shall discuss this as well as other late passages in the short commentary in Part B and argue that

[3] *SC Phys.* Hebrew 39b–40b.

[4] The word *gillayon* in modern Hebrew means a sheet of paper. In medieval Hebrew it is usually used to denote the margin of the written folio.

[5] *SC Phys.* Hebrew 40b31.

[6] *SC Phys.* Hebrew 42a12.

[7] For example, in MS Vatican, the word *gillayon* appears in the margin where the passage begins (fo. 33a col. A, right margin) and the last sentence of the added passage reads, 'up to this point what has been written in the margin (*gillayon*)' (fo. 33b col. a13–14).

[8] On the differences between the Arabic manuscripts see the apparatus to pp. 129–35. For example in Q, which Puig considers to be early, the second part of the argument (*Physics* 251b29–252a4) is not included. The missing part has been completed twice: in M (134.12–135.16) and in the Hebrew translation (41b20–42a2) A comparison with the Hebrew yields: *SC Phys.* Arabic 133.19, 134.12–14, 135.17–19 missing in Hebrew; Hebrew 41b20–42a1, 42a5–6, 9–10 missing in Arabic.

[9] Interestingly the Hebrew commentators on the short commentary noted the many textual difficulties of this text. Yedaᶜaya ha-Penini testifies that he used 'several books' and paid close attention to textual differences. He mentions the problems of textual corruption and differences between versions in several chapters, e.g. V.1 Parma MS 91a5; V.2 ibid. 100a5; VI.4 ibid. 141b24–6; VII.1 ibid. 156a11–16, 156b16–20, 157a15–24; VII.4 ibid. 188a2–16.

[10] Puig (1987, 227) dates version B of book VIII after 1186.

[11] Puig 1987, 227.

sometimes, in the short commentary, we find Averroes' last word on issues that were of the utmost importance for him.[12]

4.2. THE MIDDLE COMMENTARY

In the middle commentary, as in the short one, there are two versions of the part on *Physics* VIII 251a8–b10, that is, chapters VIII.2.1–2. We have evidence that both versions of the middle commentary circulated *in Arabic* and were available in the thirteenth and fourteenth centuries, presumably in different manuscripts.[13] There is a clear correspondence between the versions of the middle commentary and those of the short one so I shall refer to the two versions of the middle also as versions A and B. The middle commentary, as noted above, is not extant in Arabic, but is preserved in two Hebrew translations. In Zeraḥya's translation we find version A, in Kalonimus' version B, and there is a second translation of version A added to some of Kalonimus' manuscripts. This translation is discussed in the Appendix below.

Aside from the two versions of chapters VIII.2.1–2, the middle commentary presents few textual difficulties. Fluctuations in style are scarce, and the text is relatively good and easy to understand. Nevertheless, there is some evidence, direct and indirect, of revision. The question to what extent the middle commentary was revised is crucial to an understanding of Averroes' intellectual biography, and I shall deal with it in detail in Part B.

APPENDIX 1: THE ANONYMOUS TRANSLATION OF VERSION A

Of the two versions of chapters VIII.2.1–2 of the middle commentary Zeraḥya translated version A and Kalonimus version B. In Spain and Provence only Kalonimus' translation was used and Zeraḥya's was practically unknown. Version A was 'rediscovered' by one of the readers or copyists of Kalonimus' translation and was translated again and added to some of the manuscripts. Of the manuscripts of Kalonimus' translation that include book VIII, the

[12] Notably on *Physics* VIII.1 and V.2. These passages are discussed in Chs. 6 and 8 below.

[13] For instance in the Hebrew encyclopedia *Midrash ha-Ḥokhma* we find version A and in *De*ᶜ *ot ha-Philosophim* version B.

majority (28 manuscripts) contain only version B, three contain version A,[14] and four contain both versions.[15] In these four manuscripts we find a few helpful comments:

In London MS 885 between chapters 1 and 2 of version B, the copyist left space for something to be added, and wrote in the margin: 'here appears the chapter of the Arabic book'. In this space chapter 1 of version A is copied in a different hand.[16]

In NY MS 2366 there are a few extra pages at the end, preceded by the note: 'In an Arabic manuscript that I have just received, there is a different version of the first and second chapters of the second summa of the eighth book of the Physics, the commentary of Averroes, and this is the translation: . . .'[17]

In NY MS 2358, the second summa opens with a full text of version A of the two chapters. At the end of the second chapter there appears the following note: 'Up to this point the version of the sage Narwinio (or Garwinio) of these two chapters . . .'[18]

In Oxford Bodl. MS 1381 the two chapters appear at the end of the commentary (fos. 95a–96b). The last sentence is: 'Up to this point the version of the sage Garwino of these two chapters'.[19]

The unusual terms used for 'succession' and 'contiguity' used in the second translation[20] confirm that it was not made by Kalonimus himself.[21] When was this translation done? All seven manuscripts which include the second translation of version A are from the fifteenth century. Let us look at the evidence of the super-commentaries.[22] The fourteenth-century Provençal commentators, Gersonides and an anonymous commentator who may have been a student of

14 Paris BNF héb. 943; Oxford Bodl. 1385; Vatican 209/8. In the Paris MS, version A of the two chapters appears twice, once in its place and once at the end (58b–60a, 74a–75a).

15 New York JTS 2358/2; New York JTS 2366; London BL 885; Oxford Bodl. 1381/2.

16 The first few lines are missing and the text actually begins in the middle of a sentence. It is possible that ch. 2 was also included but was lost. There are quite a few stylistic differences between this and the other manuscripts of this version, mainly towards the end of the chapter.

17 Fos.130a–140a in the microfilm. The first and last few lines are missing. These pages were added (not in the right order) before the last page which includes the colophon, and so they interrupt the text of the last chapter of book VIII.

18 Fo. 67a28–30. 19 Fo. 96b29.

20 The translator uses the terms המשכה and תכיפה for succession and contiguity respectively, following none of the early commentators. See Ch. 6, section 6.3.2, nn. 77–9 below.

21 Perhaps one of the copyists or readers of Kalonimus' translation who found version A in an Arabic manuscript asked someone else, possibly someone who knew Arabic better (but was not familiar with the rest of the book), to translate these two chapters.

22 Only a few of the fifteenth-century commentaries on the middle commentary on the *Physics* include books V–VIII. I examined all of them.

Gersonides,[23] used version B. Version A was used by three fifteenth-century Spanish commentators: Yisḥaq ben Shem Tov,[24] Shem Tov ben Yosef ben Shem Tov,[25] and a third commentator, probably from the same circle,[26] who was particularly interested in version A and commented on it in great detail.[27] It is possible that the second translation of version A originated in this circle but it is equally possible that it was done earlier.

4.3. THE LONG COMMENTARY

The long is the most heavily revised of the three commentaries on the *Physics* and possibly in the whole corpus of Averroes' commentaries. A comparison between the Latin and the Hebrew translations of the long commentary yields surprising results. The first notable difference that the reader encounters is the absence of the introduction (*prooemium*) in the original Latin translation.[28] In the body of the commentary the Latin and the Hebrew versions differ to various degrees. Many comments look like two translations of the same text, but others differ more significantly: some have modifications, others have short additions, some have long additions, while others are altogether different. In the texts (excerpts from Aristotle) there are only a few differences, due mainly to scribal errors.[29] This indicates that translators and copyists should not be blamed for more than a small fraction of the numerous differences in the comments. The many differences between the translations are due to changes made by Averroes himself. We can roughly distinguish two patterns of revision, which I shall call *editing* and *rewriting*.

[23] London BL MS 1012, fos. 158a–161a; Oxford Bodl. MS 2050/4 (Reggio collection 44).

[24] Cambridge MS 6.25/1 fos. 66b–74b. There is anoher copy Munich MS 45.

[25] Paris BNF MS héb 967/4 31a–32a.

[26] This commentator was erroneously identified by Steinschneider as Narboni. See Glasner, 2009.

[27] Paris BNF MS héb 967/1, fos. 86a–89a.

[28] See p. 42 below.

[29] Errors in texts are more common in the Hebrew. Sometimes a sentence appears twice—at the end of one text and at the beginning of the next: IV.73–4, V.4–5, V.19–20, VII.16–17. The last sentence of the Latin IV.27 appears in the Hebrew as the first sentence of IV.28. Sentences or parts of sentences are missing in Hebrew texts: III.66, Arabic 260.15–16, Latin 116K7–90; IV.101, Arabic 420.2–3, Latin 181B12–14; IV.128, Arabic 466.11, Latin 199D3–4; VIII.17, Arabic 819.3, Latin 353A5–7. There are also few errors in texts in the Latin. Sometimes a sentence appears twice—at the end of one text and at the beginning of the next: IV 97–8, VII.16–17. The last sentence of the Latin text is missing: VIII.52, Arabic 872.15–873.2, Hebrew 193a4–5. The last sentence of the Latin is incorrect: VII.35, 334F5–6.

By *editing* I refer to brief additions and modifications. These are common in both translations, but more numerous in the Hebrew. By way of example I will list those that appear at the ends of comments.[30] These are easy to locate and are very frequent, perhaps because the space between comments was a convenient place to add a few lines. The lists show that they are present in both translations but are more numerous in the Hebrew[31] than in the Latin.[32] Some of these additions are simple clarifications, some are editorial remarks[33] or references,[34] and some

[30] Minor differences between the Latin and Hebrew ends of comments (in some cases one sentence in one translation corresponds to several sentences in the other): **Book I:** I.41, Latin 27F6–9, Hebrew 27b18–19. **Book III:** III.19, Latin 94A13–B4, Hebrew 103b29–104a4. **Book IV:** IV.86, Latin 173F11–14, Hebrew 189b21–7. **Book V:** V.5, Latin 209 I4–17, Hebrew 8b21–2; V.33, Latin 227K14–L4, Hebrew 25a17–20. **Book VI:** VI.27, Latin 263E7–10; Hebrew 60a7–11; VI.40, Latin 272D13–15, Hebrew 69a27–30; VI.41, Latin 272K2–7, Hebrew 69b31–70a1. **Book VIII:** VIII.17, Latin 353I1–14, Hebrew 151a10–15; VIII.65, Latin 407C10–D3, Hebrew 208a13–17.

[31] Added sentences at the end of Hebrew comments or lacunae at the end of Latin comments: **Book I:** I.4, 5a28–30; I.5, 6a25; I.15, 11a17–18; I.21, 13b10–11; I.28, 18b6–7; I.35, 23b19–21; I.40, 26b17–18; I.47, 30a14–17; I.57, 35b11–16; I.61, 38b1–6; I.67, 41a7–9. **Book II:** II.1, 50a27–30; II.36, 66b30–67a1; II.42, 68b4–10; II.75, 82a10–14; II.91, 92b18–19. **Book III:** III.4, 95a22–6; III.21, 105a5–7; III.26, 107b3; III.36, 113a22–4; III.41, 115a18–19; III.42, 116a20–21; III.54, 123b7–8; III.55, 124a13–14; III.63, 130a7–9; III.72, 134a17. **Book IV:** IV.9, 140a15–17; IV.10, 140b4–5; IV.23, 145b4–5; IV.26, 147a27; IV.37, 153a30–b1; IV.43, 159a25; IV.50, 163b16; IV.53, 165b2–4; IV.57, 167a11; IV.71, 178b16–23; IV.77, 183a25–6; IV.88, 190b6; IV.95, 193a30–b4; IV.108, 202b21; IV.115, 206a24–8; IV.119, 209b6–9; IV.126, 214a4–6. **Book V:** V.11, 14b30; V.33, 25a17–20; V.36, 27b5; V.50, 36a7–9 (the Latin translator abbreviated the text); V.56, 40a10–11; V.59, 41b23. **Book VI:** VI.28, 60a27–8; VI.30, 61a11–13; VI.39, 68b27–31; VI.45, 72a16–18; VI.46, 73b22–3; VI.51, 77a29–30; VI.56,, 80a4–7; VI.68, 90a23–6; VI.74, 94a21–2. **Book VII:** VII.3, 108a11–16; VII.7, 110b13–14; VII.9, 112b9–12; VII.24, 126a26–7; VII.31130b21–3. **Book VIII:** VIII.8, 142a13–14; VIII.15, 149b10–17; VIII.28, 164a10–11; VIII.32, 169b5–6; VIII.44, 184a30–b6; VIII.54, 195b1–3; VIII.55, 197a11–16; VIII.62, 203b26–8.

[32] Added sentences at the end of Latin comments or lacunae at the end of Hebrew comments: **Book I:** I.11, 11K2–6; I.54, 33A2–6; I.83, 47K13–L2. **Book III:** III.3, 86L2–3; III.6, 88D15–E; III.60, 114G1–6. **Book IV:** IV.20, 129F10–14 (the missing sentence also appears in the Hebrew MS Oxford 1388); IV.28, 132L14–M5; IV.70, 157K13–L9. **Book V:** V.34, 228D5–7; V.52, 239D10–11. **Book VI:** VI.26, 263A15–B1; VI.33, 267M5–14; VI.36, 269K4–5 (in this comment there are many additions in the Hebrew, but an added final sentence in the Latin); VI.54, 281M8–13; VI.62, 289C14–D2. **Book VII:** VII.4, VII.10, VII.20, 323K4–9; VII.34, 334B12–14; VII.35, 335E1–6. **Book VIII:** VIII.53, 394K9–L1.

[33] Concerning the translation, errors in the texts, etc. see e.g. comment I.612, Hebrew 38b3–6; V.29, Hebrew 23b17–18.

[34] e.g., VII.3, Hebrew 108a6–7; V.24, Hebrew 21b14.

raise questions.[35] An interesting subset of the additions, which deserves special attention, consists of remarks on logical issues.[36]

By *rewriting* I refer to the replacing of paragraphs, sometimes of whole comments, by new ones, or to the addition of long passages to the comments.[37] In some cases it is apparent that the Hebrew is the revised version; in others, the Latin. Sometimes the Hebrew comment is the more elaborate, and sometimes the Latin. While short interpolations are more common in the Hebrew translation, long ones appear more frequently in the Latin translation.

This description, I believe, points out the difficulties in understanding the relation between the two versions of the long commentary. The writing of the long commentary on the *Physics* is very intricate and convoluted. The border between editing and rewriting is not always clear.[38] In addition, it is not always clear where the original writing ends and the editing begins. The fact that a sentence or a phrase appears in both translations does not always guarantee that it indeed belongs to the

[35] e.g., VIII.44, 184a30–b6. [36] p. 47 below.

[37] Rewritten or partly rewritten comments (the list is not complete):**Book I**: I.27, two Hebrew versions, the second agrees with the Latin (see p. 37 Appendix 2 below); I.30–31, the Hebrew is the revised version; I.52, significant additions in both translations; I. 60. **Book II**: II.66–7, two very brief comments in the Latin, a little more elaborate in the Hebrew; II.92, Hebrew 93a3–14 is more elaborate than Latin 85C13–D5. **Book III**: III.6, 7, 9, many differences, e.g., III.9, Latin 89D1–15 differs from Hebrew 97b16–21; III.12, many additions in the Hebrew (98b19–21, 25–7, 30–99a1, 99a3–6, 11–14, 17–20), significant difference between Latin 90G4–10 and Hebrew 99a21–30. **Book IV**: IV.27, IV.128, from Latin 199H6/Hebrew 214b10 the two translations diverge. The Hebrew includes one more sentence, the Latin is longer (until 200A4); IV.132, from Latin 203E4/Hebrew 217a14 the two translations diverge. The Hebrew includes only a few more lines, the Latin is long and important (until 203M14). **Book V**: V.10, significant differences, mainly between Latin 215L10 and 216A14, Hebrew 14a12–22; V.12, from Latin217E13/Hebrew15b2 the comments differ, with the Latin longer; V.15, Latin longer. **Book VI**: VI.23, from Latin 261K1/Hebrew 57b27 the comments differ, with the Hebrew longer; VI.33, 34, 37, 38, the two translations differ significantly. **Book VII**: VII.2, added passage at the end of the Latin comment (308A10–C14); VII.9, the order of the different parts of the comments is confused in the Latin and there are many differences; VII.13 Hebrew 116b29–117a2; Latin 317L6–M4 differ. **Book VIII**: VIII.1, 4, 5, added passages at the end of the Latin comments (339A5–F7, 341I9–L7, and 341M13–342B5); VIII.7, 12–14, rewritten; VIII.15, difference in the middle Latin 350D12–M1; Hebrew 147a25–b15; VIII.29, 38, 40–42, rewritten, in 40 the Hebrew is longer; VIII.49–50, rewritten, in 49 the Hebrew is longer; VIII.52, added passage at the end only in Latin 393C6–E8. VIII.66, the Hebrew is longer; VIII.78, rewritten.

[38] In some cases the rewriting looks more like 'extended editing', e.g., *LC Phys.* I.27, II.66–7. The first example is described in detail on p. 36 Appendix 2 below.

stage of the original writing.[39] Several comments in the long commentary went through both editing and rewriting.[40] Similarly, several passages in the short commentary were both edited and rewritten.[41]

Is the massive revision typical of the long commentaries or limited to that on the *Physics*? The only suitable candidate for comparison is the *Metaphysics*, because that is the only other long commentary for which we have two independent translations, from the thirteenth-century in Latin and from the fourteenth-century in Hebrew.[42] This is, however, fortunate because the Arabic original is extant and can be consulted. A comparison of the two translations to the Arabic original shows that the Hebrew is much closer to the Arabic than is the Latin,[43] but we cannot deduce much from this comparison because only one Arabic manuscript has survived. We can safely conclude, however, that not all the differences can be blamed on the Latin translator. Allowing for differences due to abbreviations in the Latin translation, to the different structures of the two languages, and to errors and copyists' mistakes—most of the differences undoubtedly go back to Averroes himself.

The commentary on the *Metaphysics* has no introduction, but several books have prologues and epilogues. All of these, except for the short prologue to book Z, are extant in the Arabic original and in the Hebrew translation, but missing in the Latin translation.[44] There are more differences between the texts (excerpts from Aristotle) in the case of the *Metaphysics*, presumably because Averroes used more than one translation of Aristotle.[45] The Hebrew translation, like the Arabic original, includes many remarks on the translations[46] and on lacunae.[47]

39 Several times the beginning of an added remark in the Hebrew translation appears also in the Latin and is then discontinued.

40 For example, in comment I.52 there are logical clarifications which are typical of the editing in the Hebrew translation; in the Latin translation, an important passage was added to the end of the comment.

41 e.g. *Physics* VIII.1.

42 In the case of *De anima* the Hebrew translation is from the Latin and in the case of the *Analytica Posteriora* the Latin translation is from the Hebrew. Of the long commentary on *De caelo* there is only a Latin translation. In all three cases the Arabic is no longer extant.

43 For what has been done so far on the Latin translation of the long commentary on the *Metaphysics*, see Endress and Aertsen 1999, 365.

44 See Glasner 2007.

45 See Bouyges 1952, i. pp. cxxvii–cxxxiii.

46 e.g. Γ.29, 47b27–8; E.1, 69a1–2; Z.48 96b39; I.21, 122b19, 20–21, 23; Θ.6, 127a27; Λ.26, 153b8, 153b15–16; Λ.34, 157b10. The emphasized words 'amar' and 'ha-perush' that introduce text 34 and comment 34 are missing in MS Paris.

47 e.g. B.4, 20b24; B.5, 6b12; B.8, 7b8, B.9, 7b39; B.17, 29a18; Γ.12, 37b25; Γ.29, 47a39; E.5, 70b15; E.8, 72a2; Z.23, 82b26, 32; Z.24, 83b19; Z.42, 93b40; Z.43, 94b7;

These remarks do not appear in the Latin translation, with a few exceptions.[48] In the comments editing is common, also in that on the *Metaphysics*, and also mainly in the Hebrew translation.[49] Rewriting is not found in the long commentary on the *Metaphysics*.

In conclusion, both long commentaries, on the *Physics* and on the *Metaphyscis*, were revised. The revision in both cases includes editing and addition of introductions. In the case of the *Physics* the instances of editing are more numerous and significant. Furthermore, the long commentary on the *Physics* was subject to an additional, more radical phase of rewriting. My impression, however, is that editing and rewriting are two distinct layers in Averroes' revision.

APPENDIX 2: AN ATTEMPT AT TRACING BACK THE HISTORY OF THE TWO REDACTIONS

There is no way to reconstruct the history of the two redactions of the long commentary on the *Physics*, as they have come down to us in the Latin and Hebrew translations, because no manuscripts of the Arabic text have survived, except in a few fragments.[50] My basic assumption is that the revision was done by Averroes himself. I am sure that the reader, if not yet convinced, will become convinced when reading Part B. Were there two Arabic manuscripts in Averroes' hand, carrying different texts from which the two textual traditions originated? It seems not. Nor does it seem to be the case that Averroes revised

Z.45, 96a24; Z.48, 96b32. On these remarks, see Bouyges 1952, i. pp. clix–clxi. In text B.4, after the remark (which appears in the Arabic and Hebrew), the rest of the text (Arabic 193.11–194.4) is missing in both the Hebrew and the Latin.

[48] e.g., B.8, 'in graeco album' (Latin 9E11); E.1, 'sed in omnibus libris a quibus coreximus istum librum, quem glosamus, invensimus sine non' (Latin 145C3–5); Z.54, 'et si non erit error scriptoris' (202D10–11).

[49] Minor additions at the end of Hebrew comments: A.15, 5a24–5; A.9, 8a20; A.14 9a40; A.16 10a28–9; A.17 10b11; A.23 11b38–19; A.24 12a6–10; B.1 18a37–8; B.3 20b11–12; B.9 23a22; B.10 24a12; Δ.15, 56b1–2; Δ.24, 62b39–40; E.7, 71b32; Z.1, 72b22, Z.17, 79b27–8; Z.23, 82b43; Z.25, 84a22; Z.28, 85b26; Z.28, 85b26; Z.37, 91b21; Z.44, 96a15–16; Z.46, 96b1; Z.50, 97b18; Z.51, 98a1; H.1, 103a12; H.8, 106b38; H.12, 109a17–18; I.13, 130b2; I.17, 132a39–40; Λ.1, 140b15–16; Λ.9, 144b23–4; Λ.17, 149a1–2; Λ.28, 155a16–18; Λ.29, 155b31–2; Λ.41, 163a33–4; Λ.71, 171b7–9. Minor additions at the end of Latin comments: Z.18, 167K4–6; I.4, 254D9; Λ.18, 305I6–7; Λ.48, 333C8–9.Minor differences at the end of comments: a.16; A.19; B.4; B.12; D13; Z.54; I.2. Bouyges (1952, i. p. lxxvii) also mentions 'petites omissions' in the Latin translation. Let me mention specifically one added logical remark (*LC Meta*. B.3 Arabic vol. II 192.4–5, Hebrew 20b11–12) and two linguistic remarks (*LC Meta*. D.32 66a41–42; Z.43, 95a12–14; Z.60, 101b36).

[50] See Puig, 2009.

the commentary while copying it. Rather, it seems that the two traditions stem from one single rather messy manuscript and were shaped by the decisions of copyists and, perhaps, of translators who encountered marginal insertions in the manuscript. We do not know whether copies of the long commentary were made in Averroes' lifetime under his supervision.[51] The Latin translation was made not long after Averroes' death. If Michael Scotus were indeed the translator, it is not impossible that he used Averroes' original manuscript,[52] and decided himself to leave the material in the margins. This might be one of the economizing techniques typical of the Latin translation. I shall adduce evidence to support my assumption about the formation of the two traditions.

The first occurrence of rewriting

The first 26 comments of book I show instances of only minor editing.[53] A different pattern surfaces in comment I.27: four of the Hebrew manuscripts contain the title 'Another comment on this chapter' in bold letters, followed by a different version of the comment.[54] In Latin, the comment is identical to the second Hebrew version. The first Hebrew version is more elaborate and seems to be the revised one.[55] Why is the second version explicitly introduced at this point and why are both versions included in the Hebrew redaction? A possible explanation is that the first time that one of the Arabic copyists or the Hebrew translator encountered two versions of the comment in his source

[51] Puig (1992, 258) concludes his paper on Averroes' circle with the remark that 'we cannot speak of any surviving school'.

[52] In an intriguing paper, Charles Burnett (1999) raises the possibility that Averroes' sons were invited to the court of Frederick II (as Aegedius Romanus testifies) and brought their father's manuscripts with them; and that the translations by Michael Scotus may have been sponsored by Frederick. Harvey remarked (in a conversation) that if Burnett's reconstruction is correct, Scotus may have worked from Averroes' original manuscript.

[53] Minor additions in Hebrew: comment I.4, Hebrew 5a28–30; I.5, 6a25; I.15, 11a17–18; I.21, 13b10–11; I.22, 13b25; I.23, 14a23, 25–9, 30, 14b2–3, 6; I.25, 15a30, 15b8–11,16–18. Minor additions in Latin: I.11, Latin 11K2–6. Opening lines of comment I.18, differ: Latin 14B5–8, Hebrew 12a18–19.

[54] Paris MS 884 fo. 17b7. This version appears also in Oxford MS 1388, Munich MS 91, and Milan MS 79. It is absent in Cincinnati MS 723. In Paris MS 883, a whole folio is missing at this point. The end of fo. 13b interrupts the first version of comment 27, while 14a begins in the middle of text 29.

[55] This is a typical example of rewriting that is really extended editing. The first Hebrew version is 31 lines long; the second (which agrees with the Latin), only 22 lines. The two versions share a common beginning of about six-and-a-half lines. This includes the introductory sentence, the first secondary quotation, and the first sentence of the explanation of this quotation. After that the secondary quotations are arranged differently. The text is *Physics* I.3 186b4–12. To facilitate the comparison I divided text I.27 into eight sentences. The Latin version includes secondary quotations of sentences 1, 3, 4, 5, 6, 8; the Hebrew version of sentences 1, 3–4, 5–6, and 7. In the Latin the explanations are very brief; in the Hebrew they are longer and somewhat more elaborate.

he included both and noted the fact. When he encountered the phenomenon again and again, he decided to select only one version. It is hard to blame him, considering the length of the commentary.

Original writing interrupted by added passages

In comments VIII.1 and VIII.5 passages that are added at the end (in the Latin translation) interrupt a link between the original comment and the next quotation from Aristotle.[56] Probably these passages were written in the margin and a copyist (or the Latin translator) placed them at the end of the corresponding comments.[57]

Parts of a comment copied in the wrong order

Text VII.9 includes the last two sentences of *Physics* VII.1 and the first two of VII.2.[58] The Hebrew version deals with the four sentences in sequence.[59] The Latin version is somewhat different,[60] and the order is confused.[61] The muddle may be due to copyist errors in the placement of marginal notes.

Copyist's indecision about what to omit

Where there are additions in the Hebrew, sometimes the first few words appear in both translations and then the Latin breaks off, sometimes in the middle of a

[56] See p. 101 n. 214. [57] These passages are studied in Part B.

[58] The text is: '[1] Thus, it is evident that there will be a stop sometime and that a sequence of things moved in turn by further things will not proceed without limit, but there will be some first moved thing. [2] We must not let the fact that this is demonstrated on the basis of a hypothesis make any difference: nothing absurd should have followed from postulating a possibility. [3] The first agent of motion, not in the sense of that for the sake of which, but rather the source of change, is together with what is moved. [4] By "together" I mean that there is nothing between them: this is common to all objects and agents of change' (*Physics* VII.1–2 version β 242b33–243a6, Wardy's translation with modifications). Sentence [1] is the conclusion of the argument of VII.1; [2] is a comment on the validity of the argument. Sentences [3]–[4], the beginning of VII.2, are 'out of context' and are not related to what comes next, so it is not surprising that Averroes quoted them with the end of VII.1. Isḥaq Ibn Ḥunayn's translation of sentences [3] and [4] is wrong. Instead of 'together' he had 'place'.

[59] *LC Phys.* VII.9, Hebrew [1]: 111b2–112a5; [2]: 112a5–11; [3]: 112a11–23; [4]: 112a23–b14.

[60] The Latin and Hebrew discussions of sentence [1] are altogether different. Sentences [2] and [3] are clearer and better presented in the Hebrew. Only in [4] are the two redactions the same, except for the last sentence, which is missing in the Latin (Hebrew 112b9–12).

[61] Latin: [1] The few first lines 311L2–13 coincide with the Hebrew. Then the discussion skips ahead to [2] 311L15–M11 and [3] 311M12–312 B5 before returning to [1] 312B10–D5; [4] again coincides with the Hebrew 312D5–F11.

sentence. See, for instance, the quotation from comment I.57.[62] Perhaps it was not always clear where the original text ended and the added sentence began. Another example: in comment VI.37,[63] the Latin version lists three entities that are equally divisible; the Hebrew version mentions 'three or four' and then refers to four. Apparently the copyist had in front of him both the original and the emended text.

Copyist's wrong decisions

In comment V.8, the Latin version counts three kinds of change, 'from subject to subject, from subject to non-subject, or the other way, and this is called generation and corruption.' The Hebrew counts two, taking generation and corruption as a single kind of change. The next sentence in both versions explains that generation and corruption are counted as one kind of change, like up and down movements and like changes from black to white and from white to black.[64] In the Latin this explanation is out of place. This example illustrates once again that the copyist could not always determine what belonged to the original and what to the amended text.

These examples suggest that Averroes' manuscript, from which all extant versions derive, was a kind of a working draft that included several strata or layers. The condition of the manuscript reflected the complex process of the writing of the commentary. The major question is how some additions found their way to the Hebrew redaction and others to the Latin. This question can be answered only by conjecture.

The editing, that is, the relatively minor additions and modifications that are preserved usually in the Hebrew translation, is easier to explain. Presumably when Averroes edited the commentary he wrote in the margins, in the space left at ends of comments, and perhaps also between the lines. A reasonable conjecture is that the Arabic copyist on whose copy the Latin translation was based, or possibly the Latin translator himself, left out marginal additions. This hypothesis explains why in the Latin text there are discontinued beginnings of sentences whose full text appears only in the Hebrew.

It is more difficult to understand the 'distribution' of the rewritten or added passages. For instance, in book I, alongside the standard editing preserved in

[62] p. 20 above. Sometimes beginnings of revised passages found their way to both translations. Perhaps it was not always clear where the marginal text starts.

[63] Comments VI.32–9 deal with *Physics* VI.4. These comments include both rewritten and edited parts.

[64] *LC Phys.* V.8, Latin 212G3–H2; Hebrew 11a1–5.

the Hebrew translation, there are a few instances of rewriting. In comments I.27, I.30, and I.31, the updated version is preserved in the Hebrew; in I.52, an added passage is attached to the end of the Latin comment. Apparently the added or rewritten passages written in the margin found their way to some manuscripts and not to others.

5

The Late Stratum of the Long Commentary

THE long commentary on the *Physics* was subject to massive revisions. From these revisions we can learn much about the late phase in Averroes' thought. A close examination of the late stratum—the edited and rewritten comments—reveals some recurring patterns: Averroes therein adopts standards for the writing of commentaries that had been established by the Greek commentators, most notably the formal introduction and the logical analysis of Aristotle's arguments.

5.1. THE FORMAL INTRODUCTION

The tradition of composing introductions to commentaries developed in antiquity, culminated in the school of Alexandria in the fifth and sixth centuries, and spread to the Arab and later to the Latin world.[1] It was adopted by al-Fārābī and other Arabic writers.[2] The introduction was a formal component of the commentary and followed a set pattern. In its most advanced form, the introduction included eight points,[3] but there are variations in the number, order, and exact phrasing of the points discussed. The eight points expounded by al-Fārābī, in his *Kitāb al alfāẓ*, are: (1) the intention or aim of the book, (2) its utility, (3) its parts or division, (4) its subject matter, (5) its rank or place (with regard to other

[1] See Westernick 1990, 341–2; Hadot 1990, 21–47; Klein-Braslavy 2005, 258 n. 2. I would like to thank Prof. Sara Klein-Braslavi for giving me a preprint of her paper, which helped me greatly.

[2] Harvey 1983, 72 n. 4; Klein-Braslavi, 2005, 258–9 and n. 9; Zimmermann 1981, pp. xci–xciv.

[3] The eight points in introductions to specific books should not be confused with the ten points found in more general introduction to the whole Aristotelian corpus, e.g. in Ammonius' and Simplicius' commentaries on the *Categories*. Cf. Simplicius, *Commentaire sur les catégories*, 9–17.

books), (6) the method used, (7) the title, and (8) the author.[4] In his extant commentary on *De interpretatione,* al-Fārābī covers seven of the eight points.[5] Averroes could have learned this tradition from al-Fārābī.

Averroes gradually adopted this stylistic element—the formal Alexandrian introduction. We find one-point introductions in many short commentaries, two points in the introduction to the short commentary on *De Generatione et Corruptione*, four in the middle commentary on the *Topics*, six and seven in the long commentary on the *Posterior Analytics* and in the short commentary on the *Metaphysics*.[6] The most complete example is the eight-point introduction to the long commentary on the *Physics*. The introduction to the long commentary on the *Physics* conforms most fully to this tradition of all those in Averroes' known corpus. It includes eight points: (1) the intention or aim of the book, (2) its utility, (3) its rank (compared to other sciences), (4) its division, (5) its relation (as a natural science to the theoretical sciences), (6) its method, (7) the meaning of the name, (8) the author.[7]

Many of the introductions to Averroes' commentaries were revised or were added late.[8] I shall argue that the introduction to the long commentary on the *Physics* is a late addition. The first reason to 'suspect' this introduction is that it appears only in the Hebrew translation.[9] It is not found in the thirteenth-century Latin translation.[10] In Appendix 3 I provide textual evidence that at least book I of the commentary had been written before the introduction and was modified after the introduction had been completed.

APPENDIX 3: THE REVISION OF BOOK I

The first five comments of the long commentary deal with the introductory first chapter of the *Physics*. Averroes concludes in comment I.5: (i) 'This is the

[4] S. Harvey 1997, 91–113, on 91 n. 1; 1983, 72–3 n. 4; 2004*b*, 21 n. 17.

[5] Al-Fārābī, *De int.* 1–9. Point (4) is not explicitly mentioned and is probably included in (1) and the order is somewhat different. From the passages of the commentary on the *Categories*, discovered by Zonta, we learn that al-Fārābī dealt with all eight points. See Zonta 1998; Harvey 2004*b*, 22 n. 19.

[6] See Glasner 2007.

[7] Harvey 1983, text 65–70, translation 71–84.

[8] Glasner 2007.

[9] This is true also of the short introduction to book V of the Physics as well as to the several introductions to the books of the Metaphysics. See Glasner 2007.

[10] It was translated into Latin by Theodorus Antiochenus (Wolfson 1973, 437). This translation appears in several Latin manuscripts in book VIII (Schmieja 1986, 185; Harvey 1983, 58). In the Juntas edition it is printed at the start, alongside a sixteenth-century translation by Jacob Mantino.

introduction of the book and it includes its intention, its rank, and the method of demonstration.'[11] Had he already written his own introduction, this concluding sentence would have been redundant: why should Averroes list these three points after having dealt in detail with all eight points in the introduction? The answer is found in the emendation of this sentence in the Hebrew version: (ii) 'and these three are the basis of the eight principles'.[12] Sentence (i) seems to belong to the original version while sentence (ii) to the late edition, preserved in the Hebrew translation. The last sentence of comment I.4—again only in the Hebrew translation—was also added after the writing of the introduction: 'We have already mentioned in the introduction all the reasons for giving priority to the general over the particular; the one he mentions here is the most important and most obvious among them and this is why he was brief about it here.'[13] The reference is obviously to Averroes' introduction, in which he lists three such reasons.[14] This sentence, too, was probably added after the external introduction had been written. It seems that book I was written before the introduction and was modified after the eight-point introduction had been written.

5.2. THE USES OF SYLLOGISM

The influence of late Greek logic on Averroes has been well noted. Butterworth remarks that Averroes does not hesitate to criticize the way in which Aristotle handles certain logical subjects, and turns to Theophrastus, Themistius, and Alexander, whose presentations of these topics he considers to be more orderly and comprehensible than those of Aristotle.[15] Of the Greek and Arabic commentaries on the *Physics* known to us, Averroes' long commentary is the most logically oriented.

Like all medieval intellectuals Averroes was already well versed in Aristotelian and Stoic logic when he was young.[16] In the debates with the

[11] *LC Phys.* I.5, Latin 8H2–5.

[12] *LC Phys.* I.5, Hebrew 6a24 5 .פינות הראשים השמונה.

[13] *LC Phys.* I.4, Hebrew 5a28–30.

[14] *LC Phys.* introduction, Hebrew 2a14–17.

[15] *MC Top.* Butterworth's introduction, 26.

[16] He composed an epitome on logic as well as middle commentaries on all the books of the Organon. Late in his life he composed a long commentary on the *Posterior Analytics*. In the introduction to his short commentary on the *Physics* he advises the reader to learn logic from al-Fārābī. In his epitome on logic he apparently relies on al-Fārābī's short commentary. In the part on the *Prior Analytics* he also mentions Alexander, Theophrastus, Themistius, Galen, and 'the grammarians'. In his middle commentaries on the *Prior Analytics* and the *Topics* he refers several times to Alexander, Themistius and al-Fārābī (Jéhamy 1982, iii. 848–9). On the question of whether Averroes' acquaintance with Alexander's commentary on the *Prior Analytics* was direct or through Themistius

theologians and with al-Ghazālī logical argumentation was employed,[17] and it is likely that the 'argumentative mood' of the polemical books[18] affected Averroes' late writing. At this period, as Kukkonen has shown, Averroes studied the border line between logic and metaphysics, trying to achieve a certain merging of the two disciplines.[19] The trend to apply logic to natural science and to offer a more formal presentation of Aristotle's arguments is accelerated in Averroes' late years. It is, of course, likely that in the long commentary, which was addressed to a select audience, Averroes could afford to be more 'professional'. Still the study of the commentaries shows that the increasing formalization reflects an inner development of Averroes' philosophy.

In a series of studies of Averroes' three commentaries on *De caelo*, Hugonnard-Roche shows that a trend toward logical formalization appears in the middle commentary and becomes more systematic in the long.[20] We do not know whether the long commentary on *De caelo* was edited because it has come down to us in only one version—the Latin translation.[21] In the case of the *Physics* we have more data and can distinguish three main stages in the formalization process: the middle commentary, the long commentary, and the late stratum of the long commentary.[22] Interestingly, a substantial part of the logically stated arguments appears only in the Hebrew translation,[23] and we can thus deduce that it belongs to the editing phase of the long commentary. The editing stage, I suggest, marks a somewhat more advanced stage in his employment of logic.

and the possibility that he was acquainted with other of Alexander's writings on logic, see Flannery 1995, 56 and nn. 9 and 10, 93–4. On Averroes' use of Stoic logic, see Van den Bergh 1954, ii. 178–9, 319 nn. 3, 6, 7.

[17] See Kogan 1985, 6–8, 21, 22.

[18] Notably the *Faṣl al maqāl* and the *Tahāfut al-Tahāfut* written about 1180.

[19] In a series of papers, Kukkonen explores some aspects of the connections between logic, notably the notion of modality, and metaphysics, with special attention to Averroes–Al-Ghazālī controversy. See Kukkonen 2000*a*, 2000*b*, 2001.

[20] Hugonnard-Roche, 1977, 1984, 1985, 2004. Notably 1977, 115–16.

[21] See *LC De caelo*, Latin, Endress' and Arnzen's new edition based on an old edition by Carmody.

[22] As to the short commentary, see Puig 1987, 94.

[23] Examples: *LC Phys*. Hebrew I.10, 8b15–16, 22–23; IV.95, 193a29–b4; IV.102, 197b20–30; V.8, 12a11–19 (the argument appears in the Latin (213I1–9) but is different; VI.45, 72a16–18; VI.68, 90a15–17; VII.7, 110b13–14; VII.9, 112a5–11 (the argument appears in the Latin (311L15–M11) but is different); VIII.15, 149b10–17; VIII.62, 203b26–8. I found one logical passage that appears only in the Latin, in comment VII.2. This, however, seems to be an added passage rather than an instance of the logical editing typical of the Hebrew translation.

The arguments of natural science are not easily set forth by means of syllogisms. Barnes has argued that, in his writings on the natural sciences, Aristotle does not follow the demonstrative method that he himself prescribed in the *Posterior Analytics*.[24] Most of the arguments in his works on natural science are dialectical rather than demonstrative and he does not use syllogisms in the strict sense defined in the *Prior Analytics*. Consequently, remarks Barnes, 'the ancient commentators were given to inventing syllogisms where they could not discover them.'[25] Hugonnard-Roche notes that in his long commentary on *De caelo* Averroes takes Aristotle's argument apart in order to reconstruct it as a demonstration. In this reconstruction he does not use the language of the Aristotelian syllogism but rather that of Stoic syllogism.[26] This also applies to the commentaries on the *Physics*. Several arguments in the middle commentary are presented in the form of syllogisms.[27] Already at this stage Averroes uses the Stoic style more often than the Aristotelian.[28] In some of the syllogisms he follows Philoponus;[29] others are probably his own work.[30] This trend becomes more prominent in the long commentary, where Averroes presents several of Aristotle's major arguments as syllogisms or a series of them.

[24] The case is strongly presented in Barnes 1969. Barnes' updated statement appears in 1994, pp. xviii–xx.

[25] Barnes 1981, 20.

[26] Hugonnard-Roche 1985, 245–6. For a short summary of the differences between Aristotelian and Stoic logic see Mates 1961, 2–3.

[27] *MC Phys*. I.2.4, 5a17–19, 19–21, 21–b7; I.3.1, 8a8–15; II.3.2, 18b17–25; IV.1.2, 35b16–19; IV.1.8, 37a24–6; IV.3.3, 48a13–19; VI.1, 67b16–26; VI.7, 72b23–73a2.

[28] He uses Stoic style in *MC Phys*. I.2, 7a20–23; I.3.1 8a8–15; II.3.2 18b17–25; VI.1 67b16–26; Aristotleian style in III.3.4 28a10–12, 15–17.

[29] *MC Phys*. I.2.4, on *Physics* I.3. Averroes lists four errors in Melissus' argument (5a17–19, 5a19–21, 5a21–b7, 5b7–13), using logical arguments and language in the first three. He seems to follow the four problems pointed out by Philoponus (*In phys*. 59.15–24, 59.25–60.18, 60.19–61.10, 61.11–21). *MC Phys*. II.3.2, 18b17–25 on *Physics* II.5 196b19–21. Averroes offers a syllogism of the third figure following Philoponus *On Phys*. 271.27–272.13. *MC Phys*. IV.3.3, 48a13–19 on *Physics* IV.10 218b5–9. Averroes remarks that the syllogism used by those who argued that time is the sphere is invalid. Compare Philoponus *On Phys*. 713.9–12.

[30] *MC Phys*. I.3.1, 8a8–15 on *Physics* I.5 188a30: Averroes presents Aristotle's argument as a syllogism of the second figure. Philoponus does not mention the syllogism. *MC Phys*. IV.1.8, 37a24–6 on *Physics* IV.4 211b5: Averroes remarks that the definition of place is implied not only by a categorical demonstration but also by a hypothetical disjunctive syllogism. I have not found it in Philoponus, Simplicius, or Ibn Bājja. *MC Phys*. VI.1, 67b16–26, on *Physics* VI.1 231b15–18: Averroes depicts Aristotle's argument as a hypothetical syllogism. *MC Phys*. VI.7, 72b23–73a2: Averroes doubts the logical validity of Aristotle's argument.

Examples A and B below illustrate the development of the formalization of arguments from the middle to the long commentary and from the early stratum to the late stratum of the latter. In both examples Averroes uses the technique of adding premises, found in other contexts as well.[31] This technique involves the attribution to Aristotle of arguments or parts of arguments that are not in his text and hence need justification. In example A Averroes remarks that Aristotle was silent (*tacuit*, שתק) about the two premises. Such remarks are common in the long commentary and more frequent in the late stratum (i.e. appear only in the Hebrew translation).[32] The following remark illustrates the 'formal mood' that is typical of the editorial revisions to the long commentary:

How puzzling (נפלא) is this man's [Aristotle's] brevity and how difficult (זר).[33] Had lengthiness not deterred us, we would have further pursued this aspect of the investigation [namely formal logical analysis] in all his [Aristotle's] books. But this analysis of what can be inferred from his words and from the inspection of his books is accessible to one who is knowledgeable in what is said in the *Prior* and *Posterior Analytics* concerning this issue.[34]

Naturally, the attempt to present some of Aristotle's arguments as syllogisms led the commentators to endorse a broad notion of this term. In the *Posterior Analytics*, Aristotle presents a strict conception of demonstrative science that proceeds from necessary premises to necessary conclusions.[35] In the *Prior Analytics* he divides syllogisms into categorical (or ostensive) and hypothetical, a special case of the latter being the argument *per impossibile*.[36] In the Hellenistic period, the notion of the hypothetical syllogism became commonplace,[37] even though its theoretical status was still a matter of debate.[38]

[31] e.g. Hugonnard-Roche 1985, 243–4.

[32] *LC Phys.* I.35, Latin 23I7, Hebrew 23b16; III.48, Latin 106C4–5, Hebrew 118a26; III.49, Hebrew only 120a23; III.52, Hebrew only 122a29; IV.9, Latin 125B1–2, Hebrew 140a10; IV.50, Hebrew only 163b16; IV.65, Latin 154I1, Hebrew 170b23; IV.102, Hebrew only 197b23, 26; V.17, Latin 220C9, Hebrew 17b17; VII.10, Latin 314D9, Hebrew 113a19; VII.20, Latin 323I11, Hebrew 123b21, VIII.2, Latin 339L4, Hebrew 137a28; VIII.29, Hebrew only 164b16; VIII.51, Latin 392A13, Hebrew 192b19.

[33] *LC Phys.* I.35, Latin 23I5–13, Hebrew 23b15–18.

[34] *LC Phys.* I.35, Hebrew 23b18–21.

[35] *An. post.* I.2, 71b20–25.

[36] *An. pr.* I.23, 40b22–6; see also *An. pr.* II.20. On the order of writing of the Analysics see Smith 1982.

[37] Alexander *C An. Pr.* 11.18–21; English: Barnes et al. 1991, 56 n. 25.

[38] Brunschwig, 1980, 127–8; Kneale and Kneale 1962, 128–38. Concerning hypothetical syllogisms, Aristotle admits that 'they have not been proved by deduction but assented to by agreement' (*An. pr.* I. 44 50a18). Similarly Alexander writes that

The use of hypothetical syllogisms occupies Averroes in the long commentary on the *Physics*,[39] most notably in the edited part, that is, in those passages that appear only in the Hebrew edition.[40] For example, in comments VI.1–3 Averroes makes seven remarks on logic,[41] four of which concern the use of the hypothetical syllogism. Three of these four appear only in the Hebrew.[42] Sometimes he specifies whether a syllogism used is categorical or hypothetical; and, in the former case which figure is used, and in the latter, whether the syllogism is conjunctive or disjunctive.[43] He speaks of definitions based on a hypothetical disjunctive syllogism in the middle commentary,[44] as well as in the Hebrew translation of the long commentary.[45] The

'hypothetical propositions, in and of themselves, do not produce syllogisms' (*C An. Pr.* 17. 9; English: Barnes et al. 1991, 64).

[39] See Hugonnard Roche 2004, 116–17.

[40] In the edited part: *LC Phys.* II.3, Hebrew 51b2–4; III.41, 115a18–19; III.42, 115b2–3; III.48, 118a28; III.49, 120a25–9; III.52, 122a28–9; IV.9, 139b22–3, 25, 25–6, 28, 140a1, 2, 8; V.9, 12b3, 13; VI.68, 90a23–7; VIII.29, 164b2–3, 6–7, 14–30. In the main body of the commentary: *LC Phys.* VI.3, Latin 248F12–G6, Hebrew 46b16–19; VI.9, Latin 251G6–15, Hebrew 49b21–4. In the second example he refers to 'this hypothetical syllogism' in the Hebrew, to 'this syllogism' in the Latin. The term 'hypothetical syllogism' appears a few lines later (Latin 251G14, Hebrew 49b23).

[41] *LC Phys.* VI.1, Hebrew only 45a8; Latin 247A6, Hebrew 45a16; Latin 247B10, Hebrew 45a25–6; VI.2, Hebrew only 45b7–8; 45b12–13 Latin 247K11, Hebrew 46a14–15; VI.3, Latin 248F12–G6, Hebrew 46b16–19.

[42] *LC Phys.* VI.1, 45a8; VI.2, 45b7–8; 45b12–13. The remaining remark, which appears in both translations, is *LC Phys.* VI.3, Latin 248F12–G6, Hebrew 46b16–19.

[43] On these terms see Alexander *C An. Pr.*, introduction to the Englesh translation Barnes et al. 1991, 23. This division is late and was introduced by the Stoics (Kneale and Kneale 1962, 148). Averroes was aware of it when he wrote the middle commentary on the *Prior Analytics* (see Harvey 1997, 100).

[44] *MC Phys.* IV.1.8, 37a24–6 on *Physics* IV.4 211b5: The definition of place is implied not only by a categorical demonstration but also by a hypothetical disjunctive syllogism. I have not found this remark in Simplicius, Ibn Bājja, or Philoponus. A hypothetical syllogism is used once more in ch. VI.1 of the middle commentary on the *Physics* (*MC Phys.* VI.1, 67b20, on *Physics* VI.1), but there are reasons to suspect that this is a late revision.

[45] *Physics* III.2, 201b16–18. The text is Aristotle's statement that the definition of motion is substantiated 'by what others say about motion, and from the fact that it is not easy to define it any other way.' Comment III.12 includes many additions that appear only in the Hebrew version (*LC Phys.* III.12, Hebrew 98b19–21, 25–7, 30–99a1, 99a3–6, 11–14, 17–20, 23–30). In the Latin and Hebrew versions Averroes counts three rationales (הישרות) for the definition of motion; he adds a fourth one in the Hebrew: 'a syllogism that is similar to a hypothetical syllogism.' The added passage is *LC Phys.* III.12, Hebrew 99a23–30; the quoted sentence is 99a24.

Hebrew translation distinguishes between the premises (הקדמות) of a hypothetical syllogism and the hypothesis to be refuted (הנחה),[46] whereas the Latin translation refers to all equally as *propositiones*.[47] Several of the logical remarks that appear only in the Hebrew translation of the long commentary deal with the type of syllogism involved.[48] Remarks in which Averroes specifies whether an argument under consideration is dialectical or sophistical are more common in the Hebrew version.[49]

Example A[50]

In *Physics* I.4 Aristotle offers four arguments that the first principles cannot be infinite.[51] The first argument reads: 'If the principles were unlimited both in number and in form, there could be no knowledge of the things they make up. For we think we have knowledge of something composite when we know the variety and number of its components.'[52] In the middle commentary, Averroes presents this argument as 'general and logical' and formalizes it as follows:

> If the principles were infinite in number or form they would not be known.
> The principles must be known.
> ⇒ The first principles must be finite.[53]

This exposition uses the Stoic language of inference. In the long commentary (I.35) Averroes corrects and completes the exposition and

46 *LC Phys.* III.48, Hebrew 118a22. The terms הקדמה and הנחה are found also in the middle commentary (*MC Phys.* VI.2, 68b12).

47 *LC Phys.* III.48, Latin 106B10.

48 On this division, see Aristotle *Topics* I.1 100a25–30, *Sophistical Refutations* I.2. Alexander begins his commentary on the *Prior Analytics* as follows: 'Logic or syllogistic is the study now before us. Under it fall demonstrative, dialectical, and examinatory methods, and also sophistical procedure' (*C An. Pr.* 1.3–5).

49 e.g. Hebrew only I.15, 11a17–18; Hebrew only: I.68, 41a14–5; III.36, 113a22–4; IV.3, 137a19–22; IV.9, 140a15–17; IV.27, 147b21–5; IV.39, 154a24; VII.3, 108a11–16. Latin and Hebrew: I.22, Latin 15G14, Hebrew 13b25 (in the context of Aristotle's accusation of Melissus and Parmenides that 'they reason invalidly from false premises', *Physics* I.3, 186a6–10); IV.89, Latin 174D8, Hebrew 190b11.

50 This example is studied in Hugonnard Roche 2004, 111–12; 2002, 145.

51 *Physics* I.4 187b7–188a18. *MC Phys.* I.2.2.2, 7a19–b15.

52 *Physics* I.4 187b10–13.

53 *MC Phys.* I.2, 7a20–23.

reverts to the Aristotelian style. The main argument, a refinement of the argument of the middle commentary, is presented as a categorical second-figure syllogism, the first premise of which is *sine medio* (מבלתי אמצעי) and the second *cum medio*, (באמצעי), which derives from a second first-figure syllogism.[54]

(1) The first main syllogism is:

Everything composed of infinite first principles in quantity or form—its components and their number are unknown.

Every known composite is composed of principles whose quantity and quality are known.

⇒ Everything composed of infinite first principles is an unknown composite.[55]

(2) The second premise of syllogism 1 is *cum medio* and established by a second first-figure syllogism:

[Everything] which is composed of infinite first principles in quantity and quality is composed of unknown magnitudes or numbers or qualities.

Everything composed of unknown magnitudes and unknown qualities is composed of unknown principles.

⇒ Everything composed of infinite first principles in quantity and form is [composed of] of unknown principles.[56]

(3) The second premise of syllogism 2 is also *cum medio* and established by a third first-figure syllogism:

Everything infinite is unknown.

Everything that is infinite in magnitude or in number or in quality is infinite.

⇒ That which is infinite in number, magnitude, or quality is unknown.[57]

[54] *LC Phys.* I.35, Latin 23D1–2, Hebrew 23a14–15. The Latin is shorter than the Hebrew: 'et iste sermo est syllogismos in secunda figura' (Latin 23C13); 'and the validity (כח) of what he did in this statement is the validity of a categorical syllogism in the second figure' (Hebrew 23a13–14).

[55] *LC Phys.* I.35, Latin 23D6–E1, Hebrew 23a16–20. Because the Hebrew MS Paris 884 is somewhat confused at this point, I consulted Oxford 1388.

[56] *LC Phys.* I.35, Latin 23F1–12, Hebrew 23a25–9.

[57] *LC Phys.* I.35, Latin 23G10–H1. Here I followed the Latin. In the Hebrew, the third syllogism is introduced (Hebrew 23b1–5) but not clearly phrased.

Averroes then remarks that the argument is based on three syllogisms (two first-figure and one second-figure) and six premises, four *sine medio* and two *cum medio*.[58]

Example B

Physics III.5 includes (1) an argument that a body in general cannot be infinite,[59] (2) a short note that number cannot be infinite, and (3–6) four arguments that a physical body cannot be infinite.[60]

(1) Aristotle's argument is: 'If the definition of a body is "that which is bounded by a surface", then there cannot be an infinite body.'[61] The middle term is apparently missing. Philoponus presents (1) as a second-figure syllogism:

Body is that which is determined by a plane.

The unlimited is not determined by a plane.

⇒ There is no unlimited body.[62]

In the middle and long commentaries Averroes adduces a different middle term and constructs a first-figure syllogism:

Every body is bounded by one surface (if it is rotational) or more than one (otherwise).
Everything that is bounded by a surface or by surfaces is necessarily finite.
⇒ Every body is necessarily finite.[63]

In the long commentary he adds a reservation concerning the first premise.[64] As the status of the first premise is doubtful, it is not certain that the syllogism is demonstrative.

[58] *LC Phys*. I.35, Latin 23H1–4, Hebrew 23b5–6.

[59] *Physics* III.5 204b4–9. The argument follows from the definition of 'body'.

[60] Aristotle offers four demonstrations that apply to physical bodies (204b10–205a8). Averroes lists them in MC III.3.4.2. The general argument is in MC 28a5–18. The first demonstration (fo. 28a18–b26) corresponds to *Physics* 204b10–205a8; the second demonstration (fo. 28b26–29b26) corresponds to *Physics* 205a8–24; the third (30a1–6) corresponds to *Physics* 205b24–31; the fourth (30a6–24) corresponds to *Physics* 205b31–206a8.

[61] *Physics* III.5 204b5–6.

[62] Philoponus *On Phys*. 417.1–4.

[63] *MC Phys*. III.3.4.2, 28a10–12; *LC Phys*. III.40, Latin 103B5–C6, Hebrew 114b20–22. The phrasing in the middle and long commentaries is similar, except that 'necessarily' appears only in the former.

[64] Even if one assumes an infinite body, he might not concede that this body has a (polygonal or spherical) shape (Latin 103C6–D4, Hebrew 114b28–115a4). I have

(2) Aristotle's argument is: 'Number is countable. If it is possible to count what is countable it would be possible to traverse the infinite.'[65] The middle and long commentaries expound this in slightly different ways. In the middle commentary:

Every number in act is countable in act.
Everything countable is either odd or even.
⇒ Everything countable is finite.[66]

The argument in the long commentary runs as follows:

Every number is countable
Everything countable, its counting has an end.
If we assume an infinite number, it would follow that its counting would have an end.
But this is impossible.
⇒ There is no infinite number.[67]

This argument can be presented as two syllogisms, one first-figure categorical and the other hypothetical. Averroes adds: 'It seems that this premise is of the type of premises that are self-evident, namely, that every number is countable and that everything potentially countable, when actualized, can be actually counted.'[68] In the Hebrew version he continues: 'It is possible that this statement follows from a *per impossibile* syllogism,[69] and it is possible that it follows from a figure syllogism.'[70]

(3) Aristotle argues that were one element infinite it would have destroyed the others.[71] Averroes does not attempt a formal exposition of this argument in the middle commentary.[72] In the long he presents two syllogisms. The first is of the first figure:
The elements are contraries.

not found Averroes' argument or this doubt about the argument in Philoponus or Simplicius.

[65] *Physics* III.5 204b8–9, Hussey's translation.

[66] *MC Phys.* III.3.4.2, 28a15–17.

[67] *LC Phys.* III.41, Latin 103E14–F5, Hebrew 115a12–15. In the Hebrew he adds: 'and not countable'.

[68] Hebrew 115a15–17, Latin 103F5–11.

[69] At this point he adds והוא נגלה מאמר. Probably should be נגלה מבואר. I ignored these words in my translation.

[70] *LC Phys.*, Hebrew Paris MS 884, 115a19–20; Paris MS 883, 88a18.

[71] *Physics* III.5 204b12–18.

[72] *MC Phys.* III.3.4.2, 28a24–b6.

Contraries are necessarily balanced.[73]
⇒ The elements of which the assumed infinite compound body is composed are balanced.[74]

To this conclusion Averroes adds another premise:

Balanced elements cannot be partly finite and partly infinite.
⇒ None of the elements composing the compound body can be infinite.[75]

Again, there is a question whether this argument is demonstrative or dialectical. All the premises assumed in this argument are self evident, except for the premise that 'the elements are contraries'.[76]

5.3. THE TURNING TO ALEXANDER

The writing of introductions and the logical analysis of arguments are two facets of the formal approach that characterizes the revision of the long commentary on the *Physics*. This approach reflects Averroes' growing interest in the Greek tradition late in his life, most notably in Alexander. This is a major issue in the evolution of Averroes' interpretation of the *Physics* and I shall come back to it several times in Part B. The formal structured introduction is also a Greek stylistic element that Averroes adopted in the late stratum of his long commentaries. In these late-stratum introductions Averroes lists the texts that were available to him with special attention to Alexander:

[Epilogue to the long commentary on *Metaphysics* Z]: It so happened to us when we were writing this commentary that we had none of the commentaries of our predecessors, except for that part of Alexander's commentary on book Λ and that of Themistius [also on book Λ].[77]

[Prologue to *Metaphysics*]: I say there is no commentary (*tafsīr*) by Alexander or by the commentators who came after him on the parts (*maqālāt*) of this discipline [i.e. the fourteen books of the *Metaphysics*] nor any paraphrase (*talḫīṣ*), except on this *maqāla* [namely Λ]; we have found a commentary (*tafsīr*) by

[73] Latin equipotent, Hebrew משתווים. [74] *Physics* II.5 204b13–14.

[75] *LC Phys.* III.42, Latin 103M1–10, Hebrew 115b17–22.

[76] *LC Phys.* III.42, Latin 104B16–C6, Hebrew 116a15–21. The premise in question is controversial and relies on Alexander's compromise that simple bodies are contraries while compound bodies are not.

[77] *LC Meta.* Arabic, vol. 3 1020.13–1021.6; Hebrew, 102b19–24.

Alexander on about two-thirds of this *maqāla* and by Themistius a complete paraphrase according to the signification. I thought it best to summarize what Alexander says on each section of it as clearly and briefly as possible together with Themistius' additions and doubts about it and will also mention our own additions and doubts.[78]

[Introduction to the *Physics*]: The aim of this treatise is to comment upon Aristotle's book entitled the *Physics*, because no complete word-for-word commentary (of the commentators) on this book has reached us. As for what has reached us of Alexander's commentary on this book, part of the first [treatise], the second, the fourth, the fifth, the sixth, the seventh, and part of the eighth[79] is not the words of Alexander.[80] Before [we begin] we should mention, following the custom of the commentators, some of the matters with which they begin [their commentaries on] his [Aristotle's] books. These are, in general, eight.[81]

[Introduction to the *Posterior Analytics*]: We have not found a word-by-word commentary by one of the commentators.[82]

The commentaries by Ibn Bājja, Themistius, and Philoponus that were known to Averroes were not 'word-for-word' commentaries. Averroes refers to the commentary of Themistius as *talkhīṣ* but to that of Alexander as *sharḥ*.[83] He states that he did not have a complete copy of Alexander's commentary on the *Physics*.[84] His copy included only a part of book I and nothing on book III. He next identifies parts of the commentary as spurious,[85] but, owing to the absence of punctuation, the reading of the sentence is equivocal. The spurious text certainly includes parts of book VIII. The references in the long commentary confirm that Averroes had on his desk the complete text of Alexander on books II, IV, V, and VI.[86] I have found no references to Alexander in book III and only a few in book VIII.[87] The one reference to Alexander

[78] *LC Meta*. Arabic, vol. 4 1393.4–1394.2; Hebrew, 139a9–13.

[79] In Paris MS 884 'part of the sixth'. fo. 1a3.

[80] I shall come back later to the punctuation of this sentence.

[81] *LC Phys*., Hebrew 1a1–5, Harvey's translation 71–2. See also Puig 1997, 121.

[82] *LC An. Post.* 7b2–3.

[83] Puig 2002, 333.

[84] Similarly, Averroes was acquainted with only a part of Alexander's commentary on the *Metaphysics*. See Glasner 2007.

[85] On the circulation of Pseudo-Alexandrian writings in the Arabic world, see Fazzo 1997 and 2002.

[86] See above, n. 81.

[87] One reference is explicitly to his treatise *On the Principles* (VIII.4, Latin only, 341K11). In VIII.42 (Latin only) Averroes refers to the commentators Alexander and Themistius, and then again to the commentators (VIII.42, Latin 381I5, 382C2). In

in book VII may be to his commentary on the *Categories*.[88] The three references to Alexander in the late stratum of the middle commentary on book VII all rely, as we shall see, on his *Refutation of Galen* and not on his commentary on the *Physics*. Considering this evidence, I suggest the following punctuation: 'As for what has reached us of the commentary of Alexander on this book: part of the first, the second, the fourth, the fifth, the sixth; [What we have of] the seventh and part of the eighth is not Alexander's words'.

These passages point out an association between Alexander and the late stratum of the long commentary. I will now show that the revision of the long commentary, or at least some of it, was inspired by Averroes' reading of Alexander's commentary. I shall list some noteworthy examples:

Introduction In the eight-point introduction (preserved in the Hebrew translaion), Averroes explicitly refers to Alexander's introduction to his commentary on the *Physics*. Discussing the second point, the utility of the book, he writes: 'Alexander has already explained *in his introduction to this book* how the existence of these virtues follows from a knowledge of the theoretical sciences'.[89] Unfortunately we do not have Alexander's commentary on the *Physics* and cannot confirm that Averroes' discussion of utility indeed echoes Alexander's.[90]

Book I All the references to Alexander in book I are late. They all appear in rewritten passages: I.30–31 (Hebrew only) and I.52 (Latin only).

Comments I.30–31 deal with the concluding passage of Aristotle's attack on Eleatic monism.[91] The two versions differ significantly. The text preserved in Latin is brief and adds little to Aristotle's text. In the text preserved in Hebrew Averroes follows Alexander, referring to him by name,[92] and even quotes an important and otherwise unknown passage

VIII.79, Alexander is mentioned twice, in the form 'Alexander, in some of his treatises' (VIII.79, Latin 426K2, L11; Hebrew 226a14, 22).

[88] *LC Phys*. VII.20, Latin 323I13, Hebrew 123b23.

[89] *LC Phys*. Hebrew 1a25–6, Harvey's edition, 66.8–10, English translation, 75.3–5.

[90] We do not even know whether Alexander's commentary on the *Physics* includes an introduction. Of his extant commentaries, those on the *Prior Analytics, Topics,* and *De sensu* include introductions, while those on the *Metaphysics* and *Meteorology* do not (*CAG* ii.16.13–9.3; ii.2 107.2; iii 1–2.4).

[91] *Physics* I.3 187a1–11.

[92] *LC Phys*. Hebrew I.30, 19b28, 20a14, 23, 20b27.The second and fourth references are to Alexander's rendering of Aristotle's text.

from Alexander.[93] In this case it is clear that the Hebrew preserves the later version and that Averroes rewrote these two comments after he had read Alexander's commentary and gained a better understanding of the subject. The revision of comment I.52 (preserved in the Latin) is also a response to Alexander's commentary.[94]

Book IV In a sentence added to comment IV.77 (Hebrew only), Averroes writes: 'In the words of Alexander, where there is no understanding (השגה), there is no utility.'[95] This may be a reference to what Alexander had said on utility in the introduction to his commentary on the *Physics*, as quoted by Averroes: 'Alexander has already explained in his foreword to this book how the existence of these virtues follows from knowledge of the theoretical sciences'.[96] At IV.27, Averroes comments on Aristotle's statement that it is not possible for a thing to be in itself accidentally.[97] In the version preserved in Hebrew, probably following Alexander who criticizes the logical structure of the argument, he dismisses it as sophistical.[98]

Book V At V.38, in a sentence preserved in both translations, Averroes comments: 'When I wrote this I had not yet encountered Alexander's comment on this chapter, and after having encountered it I found it relevant to this issue.'[99] This remark confirms that Averroes gained access to parts of Alexander's commentary in the course of writing the long commentary and that he revised some of his work after becoming acquainted with Alexander's views.

[93] *LC Phys.* Hebrew 19b29–20a4. On this passage see Glasner 2001.

[94] It concerns Alexander's remark that simple substances can be contraries but compound substances cannot. Averroes responds several times to this remark by Alexander in the late stratum of the long commentary.

[95] *LC Phys.* IV.77 183a25.

[96] In his introduction to the long commentary. See Harvey 1983, 75.

[97] *Physics* IV.3 210b18.

[98] Simplicius informs us that Alexander criticized this argument on the grounds that the middle part is not the same and that Aristotle uses 'being in' in two different senses (*On Phys.* 559.25–31). Averroes writes: 'You should know that these syllogisms are not natural syllogisms, namely that explain that which is unknown by nature in terms of something that is known by nature. Rather these syllogisms are based on that which seems to be true, not on self-evident statements; and these are the sophistical arguments. Such arguments are used in metaphysics and are called "demonstrations by the listener" ' (*LC Phys.* IV.27, Hebrew 147b21–5).

[99] LC Phys. V.38 Latin 231C1–4, Hebrew 28b17–18.

Logical remarks Some of the logical remarks found in the late stratum may reflect Alexander's influence.[100]

In conclusion, while he was writing the long commentary on the *Physics* Averroes looked for sources, mainly for word-for-word commentaries on this text. He made a special effort to get hold of Alexander's commentary and succeeded in obtaining a substantial part of it.[101] Presumably this happened after he had already completed book I of his long commentary and perhaps other parts as well. He was stimulated by Alexander's views and frequently refers to him in books II, IV, V, and VI.[102] He identified book VII and parts of book VIII of the text that he obtained as spurious. At some point after acquiring Alexander's commentary, he wrote his own eight-point introduction and also revised parts of the commentary. In Part B I shall come back several more times to the subject of Alexander's role in the shaping of Averroes' new physics and show that the editing of the long commentary and of a few passages in the middle commentary was inspired by the reading of Alexander's commentary on the *Physics* and of other treatises by Alexander.

100 For example, Alexander insists on a clear distinction between premises that are taken to be true and the hypothesis to be refuted. In the commentary on *Prior Analytics* he distinguishes between 'positing' and 'assuming'. In his commentary on the *Metaphysics* he differentiates 'premises that are primary' from what 'one assumes from himself and posits' or 'what the respondent posits' (*On Meta.* 123.8–14). In the *Refutation of Galen*, Averroes refers to the latter as what 'he supposed in the imagination' (Rescher Marmura 1965, 19.11–20.3). A remark of Averroes suggests that Alexander also addressed the problem of 'why Aristotle was silent' on a certain issue (*LC Phys.* VII.20, Latin 323I13–15, Hebrew 123b23–4).

101 The fact that he opens his introduction by listing the parts of Alexander's commentary to which he had access illustrates the importance that he ascribed to it.

102 See p. 53 above.

PART B

AVERROES' NEW PHYSICS

And when every stone is laid artfully together,
it cannot be united into a continuity,
it can but be contiguous in this world.

John Milton, *Areopagitica*[1]

THE relations between the three commentaries and their different versions, as described in Part A, remain hard to delineate: contrary to initial expectations, it was not possible to determine the chronology of the many different versions on the basis of philological considerations alone. To understand the relations among the versions a close study of their contents is called for.

My study focuses mainly on books VI–VIII of the *Physics*, known in the ancient tradition as the treatise *On Motion*.[2] I have selected three arguments in these books on which *all three commentaries* of Averroes have been significantly revised and have named the selected arguments:

- The succession argument (*Physics* VIII.1): Before any motion there must have been a previous motion or change.
- The divisibility argument (*Physics* VI.4): Everything that is moved must be divisible.
- The moving-agent argument (*Physics* VII.1): Everything that is moved must be moved by something.

For the first argument, all three commentaries exist in two distinct versions. For the second and third arguments, the short and middle commentaries were revised and there are significant differences between the Hebrew and the Latin versions of the long commentary. The heavy revision indicates that these arguments deal with crucial issues on which Averroes changed his mind and which continued to preoccupy him for many years. In all three instances we find the same pattern to which I shall refer as *the turning point pattern*.

The context of the three turning points is a difficult passage in Aristotle, where earlier commentators pointed out difficulties and argued with Aristotle. Averroes charges the commentators with misunderstanding Aristotle's meaning. In book VI 'It is the case that many people had not understood this demonstration and found fault with Aristotle,'[3] 'And Aristotle's intention on this assumption escaped all the

[1] I am indebted to William Kolbrener for this reference.

[2] See Simplicius *On Aristotle's Physics* 6, 923.8–9.

[3] *MC Phys*. VI.184^{a}3–4.

commentators.'[4] In book VII 'Therefore many of those who have not understood this demonstration became angry with Aristotle. Thus Galen wrote his famous treatise and Ibn Bājja . . . followed a way different from Aristotle's and thought that it was Aristotle's [way].'[5] In book VIII 'This [false] understanding of Aristotle started with Philoponus, and [continued with] al-Fārābī and other scholars who lived after al-Fārābī and whose books have reached us.'[6]

Confused by the commentators, Averroes goes through a period of hesitations and intensive study. In book VI 'We, as well as others, thought *for a long time* about what Ibn Bājja argued and approved of what he said, considering it to be the most satisfactory. But a certain objection occurred to me . . .,'[7] 'It so happened that people were much in doubt about this demonstration, so that *we were also confused about it for a long time*. And it was difficult for us to understand the depth of Aristotle's [thought] on this.'[8] In book VIII '*After an intensive inquiry and a long time* it seems to me . . .'[9]

It is the polemical context that leads to 'an intensive inquiry' and to a new original interpretation. It is in the exegetical context that Averroes further develops his interpretation. He undermines the difference between text and comment and presents his solution as Aristotle's own view: 'And since I understood what all the commentators missed and what escaped them I believe that my opinion is more adequate than that of the commentators.'[10] 'After having honestly studied this issue I saw that Aristotle's argument conforms to nature,[11] and there is nothing about it that should cause doubt or perplexity for which one should apologize, as the commentators did.'[12] 'After I started commenting on Aristotle's statement it seems to me that his words work out naturally in all respects and should not be subject to any doubt or demand any apology.'[13]

[4] *LC Phys*. VI.32 Latin 266F11–12, Hebrew 62^{b}22–3.

[5] *MC Phys*. VII.184^{a}3–8. Similarly in the long commentary: 'And it was this premise that escaped Galen and others who have not understood this [Aristotle's] demonstration.' *LC Phys*. VII.1 Latin 307H; Hebrew 107a19–20.

[6] *MC Phys*. VIII.2, 294^{a}24–6.

[7] *MC Phys*. VI.772^{b}14–17.

[8] *MC Phys*. VI.183^{b}25–84^{a}1.

[9] *MC Phys*. VIII.2.2, version A, NY MS 67^{a}8.

[10] *MC Phys*. VI.7, Kalonimus translation 74^{b}7–11.

[11] ירוץ מרוצת הטבע

[12] *MC Phys*. VI.773^{a}2–4.

[13] *LC Phys*. VI.32, 62^{b}2–5.

Averroes, thus, concludes with the praise for Aristotle:

How superior is Aristotle's thought to that of all the others and how far are they all from his understanding, for many things that he understood right away people understood from his accounts after an intensive investigation and a long time. . . . Therefore we say that if his [Aristotle's] accounts of these matters had not been written, discovering them would have been almost impossible or difficult to achieve, or would have taken a long time. . . . And because God has elevated and exalted him, the ancients called him 'the divine'.[14]

'And this accounts for how far is Aristotle's thought from that of everyone [else] and how short is everyone's understanding compared to his understanding. . . . And the [true] meaning of our study of his treatises is different from what was said earlier. This is the case with respect to many issues in his treatises.'[15] 'Blessed be he who distinguished this man with human perfection.'[16]

I shall study the three 'turning-points' in the next three chapters and will show that they are three facets of a systematic revolution in Aristotelian physics, carefully presented as the true interpretation of Aristotle's *Physics*. I shall not proceed in the natural order of the books, but start with book VIII in order to present first what I believe to be Averroes' main motive—his objection to determinism.

[14] *MC Phys*. VI.7 Kalonimus' translation $74^b11–17$, 21–2; Zeraḥya's translation $90^b13–19$, $90^b23–91^a1$.

[15] *LC Phys*. VI.32 Hebrew only $62^b23–25$.

[16] *MC Phys*. VIII.2.2 version A, NY MS 67a26–7.

6

The Turning Point of *Physics* VIII: The Breakdown of Determinism

Physics VIII starts with the *succession argument:* before any motion there must have been a previous motion or change.[1] This argument underlies the thesis of the eternity of the world and paves the way to the thesis of the unmoved mover. Averroes was intensively engaged by this argument. It is the only argument in his corpus for which two separate versions of both the short commentary and the middle commentary are preserved. Similarly two strata of the long commentary can easily be distinguished. This subject thus provides a rare opportunity to follow the different stages of Averroes' writing 'in the making'. Chapter VIII.1 occupied Averroes' mind for many years; he kept coming back to it, and during the years radically changed his interpretation of it. Was Averroes reluctant to accept the thesis of eternity? This does not seem to be the case. Averroes is usually viewed as a steadfast adherent of eternity.[2] The texts show that Averroes was worried not by the central message of the succession argument, that is, the eternity of motion, but rather by its possible deterministic implications. We shall see that Averroes reinterprets the succession argument so as to circumvent these implications.

6.1. THE CHALLENGE OF INDETERMINISM

The question of determinism was a central issue for Averroes because it was one of the issues on which Muslim theologians and philosophers disagreed. Muslim philosophy, most notably that of Avicenna, was strictly deterministic. Determinism was considered to have a sound

[1] See p. 69 below.
[2] Fakhry 1953, 144; 1975, 112, Kukkonen 2000*a*, 331.

scientific basis while indeterminism was not, because the advocates of indeterminism, notably the Greek and Muslim atomists, rejected what was considered to be the very basis of scientific thought: causality. Averroes' agenda was to offer a scientific natural interpretation of indeterminism as an alternative to Kalām's theological one. Establishing indeterminism as a scientific doctrine with Aristotelian foundations was a difficult task. The many versions of Averroes' commentaries on VIII.1 reflect his repeated efforts to avoid the deterministic implications of this chapter, and to reinterpret it to his satisfaction.[3]

Aristotle had no concept of determinism in the sense that we use it today, and the import of his discussions of causality and of chance is not unequivocal.[4] During the centuries that elapsed from Aristotle to Averroes the question of determinism was explicitly stated and, through many discussions and debates, its different aspects and implications became better understood. The question of determinism and the terms of the discussion were consolidated in the Hellenistic period.[5] Deterministic and indeterministic positions were first formulated by the Stoics and by Epicurus.[6] Along with their philosophical positions the Stoic and Epicurean schools developed their respective natural philosophies. The basis of Stoic determinism, we shall see, was the continuous–contiguous structure; that of Greek and Muslim atomism was the interrupted succession. Averroes, trying to steer a middle way between Stoic strong determinism and Epicurean denial of causality, focuses his attention on these structures. His new physics is based on his analysis of contiguity.

6.1.1. The definitions of contiguity and continuity

In the *Metaphysics,* continuity is the defining differentia of magnitude and studied by the science of geometry.[7] In this vein in *Physics* VI.2 Aristotle defines the geometrical concept of continuity: 'By continuous I mean that which is divisible into divisibles that are infinitely divisible.'[8]

[3] See Grant 1978; Grant 1987.

[4] See Sharples 1983, 1–7; Sorabji 1980, ch. 15; Lennox 1984, 52–60. On the differences among Aristotle's ethical writings see Kenny 1979. See also Section 6.2 below.

[5] Bobzien 1998, 2–3.

[6] Sharples 1983, 7. Sorabji (1980, 69) comments that 'it was the Stoics who first connected causation emphatically with necessity and laws'.

[7] *Metaphysics* Δ.13 1020a11.

[8] *Physics* VI.2, 232^{b}24–5. The definition is quoted in *Physics* III.1, 200^{b}19. The notion of continuity is not defined in Euclid's *Elements*, but it is taken for granted

The underlying conception is of division into parts similar to the whole: a line is divisible into lines, a surface into surfaces, and a time interval into time intervals. Aristotle also takes it for granted that it is impossible 'for motion to be composed of something other than motions.'[9]

In *Physics* V.3 Aristotle defines a sequence of concepts that describe *degrees of proximity* between two bodies and lead to the definition of continuity between two bodies:

- Things are said to be *together* in place when they are in one primary place.[10]
- Things are said to be *touching* when their extremities are together.
- A thing is *in succession* (*ephexēs*, يتلو, נלוה נמשך) if it comes after the beginning and there is nothing of the same kind as itself dividing it from that which it succeeds.[11]
- Two successive things are *contiguous* (*ekhomenon*, الشافع, נכרך תכוף) if they are touching.
- They are *continuous* (*sunekhes*, المتّصل, מתדבק) when 'their touching ends coincide and become one'.[12]

These definitions are not geometrical,[13] and are applicable to physical entities.[14] Contiguity pertains to bodies which are spatially joined but essentially different such as air above water.[15] In the case of continuity the two bodies become one and the definition can apply to physical bodies and to mathematical magnitudes alike.

that any line or surface can be cut at random (e.g. propositions II.1–11). In proposition I.10 Euclid proves that any line segment can be bisected.

[9] *Physics* VI.1, 232ᵃ18.

[10] On the difficulties in this definition see Ross 1998, 627.

[11] *Physics* V.3, 226ᵇ33–227ᵃ1.

[12] *Physics* V.3, 227ᵃ9–11. For all the definitions I used White's translation (1992, 23). The Hebrew translators of the three commentaries did not employ the same terms. I follow Kalonimus' translation of the middle commentary, which was the most widespread.

[13] The concept of touch is not a part of Greek geometry. In Euclid's *Elements* (definitions III.2–3), touching means 'tangent to'; i.e., having a point in common. Greek normative geometry had no concept of touching or proximity between distinct magnitudes.

[14] 'It is plain from the definition that continuity is a property of things that naturally form a unity by virtue of their contact with each other. And in whatever way that which holds them is one, so too will the whole be one, e.g. by a rivet or glue or contact or organic union.' *Physics* V.3, 227ᵃ14–16.

[15] White 1992, 27; Furley 1982, 30. Averroes refers to contiguity as 'corporeal continuity', or 'continuity in the body'. *MC De anima*, 22.61.

These definitions apply also to motion.[16] *Successive motions* follow one another and are separated by rests; *contiguous motions* are not separated by rests, but are still distinguishable from one another, while *continuous motions* cannot be distinguished one from another and thus form one motion.

6.1.2. The physical basis of Stoic determinism

Stoic philosophy was a paradigm of determinism and served as a background for discussions of this subject in the Hellenistic and Roman periods.[17] The Stoics have not produced a corpus of canonical texts, and have not been engaged in writing commentaries on the works of the founders of Stoic philosophy.[18] The Arabs were well familiar with Stoic logic, as well as with the basic ideas of Stoic philosophy. They learned about the Stoic school mainly from secondary sources and referred to them as 'the pneumatics' (*rūḥaiyyūn*). Important channels of transmission were the Arabic versions of Alexander and Philoponus, as well as the Arabic translation of Galen and other medical writings.[19] Averroes refers to the Stoics several times.[20]

[16] In *Physics* V.3 Aristotle defines succession, contiguity and continuity of spatial magnitudes, in V.4 he applies these concepts to motion intervals: 'In the torch race we have contiguous but not continuous locomotion: for according to our definition there can be continuity only when the ends of the two things are one. Hence motion may be contiguous or successive in virtue of the time being continuous, but there can be continuity only in virtue of the motions themselves being continuous, that is, when the end of each is one with the end of the other . . . Unity is required in respect of time in order that there be no interval of immobility, for where there is intermission of motion there must be rest, and a motion that includes intervals of rest will not be one but many, so that motion that is interrupted by stationariness is not one or continuous' (*Physics* V.4, 228^{a}20–^{b}6, Oxford translation, modified).

[17] Bobzien 1998, 5; Frede 2003. [18] Snyder 2000, 14–15, 40–41.

[19] See Jadaane 1968, 47; Kogan 1985, 77; Eichner (2002, 286–7); Freudenthal, 1998; Barker and Goldstein 1984. Sharples refers to H. J. Ruland, *Die arabischen Fassungen zwei Schriften des Alexander von Aphrodisias* (Saarbrücken, 1976), which I have not seen.

[20] Jadaane (1968, 94–6) quotes two interesting examples from the middle commentary and from the long commentary on the *Metaphysics*. I shall mention two examples. (1) He refers to the Stoics by name: 'This theory resembles the theory of those ancient philosophers, the Stoics, who say that God exists in everything' (*Tahāfut* 479, English 291–2). (2) He ascribed to 'the learned' the view that 'the world is one and the same existent only because of this one power which emanates from the first principle. And they agree about all this because the heavens are like a single animal . . . and all the potencies and particular parts of this unique animal . . . should be such that there is in them a single spiritual force which connects all the spiritual and bodily potencies and which penetrates the universe in one and the same penetration' (229, English 136–7).

The physical basis of Stoic determinism was the contiguous structure—both spatial and temporal. As Marcus Aurelius puts it,

> What follows is ever closely linked to what precedes; it is not a procession of isolated events merely obeying the laws of sequence, but a rational connection. Moreover, just as the things already in existence are all harmoniously coordinated, things in the act of coming into existence exhibit the same wonderful relation, rather than simply the bare fact of succession.[21]

The adjectives 'close', 'rational', 'wonderful' as describing relations delineate a tight structure. Several modern commentators emphasize this point: 'As physical events are transmitted by nearby action, whether through direct contact of bodies or by the pneuma, this must be true also for cause–effect relations.[22] Contiguity is therefore an essential attribute of causality.'[23] For the Stoics, the contiguous structure underlies and supports deterministic philosophy.

The metaphor of a chain or a rope was used to convey the idea of temporal contiguity: 'The passage of time, like the *unwinding of a rope*, brings about nothing new and unrolls each stage in a turn.'[24] 'All motion is *always linked*, and new motion arises out of old in a fixed order.'[25] 'Things are connected to one another by the latter's being attached to the earlier *in the manner of a chain*.'[26] As all cosmic parts are interconnected, explains Lapidge, so all events are linked to one another. Hence arises the Stoics' notion of a *chain of fate*; and this chain of fate, held together by the pneumatic force, is the basis of the Stoic determinism.[27]

'The learned' in this passage must be the Stoics or some of their followers. Van den Bergh refers several more statements in the *Tahāfut* to Stoic origin. In the Kashf Averroes refers to the Stoic theory of infinite worlds: 'Many of the ancients held with regard to the world, namely, that it arose [after an infinite number of worlds have arisen] one after the other' (quoted in Wolfson 1976, 401). The theory of bodily interpenetration through pores or void spaces is also of Stoic origin. Averroes could have learned about it from Alexander. Todd 1972, 298; Sharples 1992, question 1.6.

[21] Marcus Aurelius, *Meditations* IV. 45. I consulted the translations by Staniforth, Haines, and Long.

[22] Determinism is commonly characterized in terms of 'necessitating causes' or 'necessitating efficient causes'. e.g. Sorabji 1980, ch. 2, 9, 10 (pp. 222–4); Stern 1997, 225–6; Ivry 1984, 161 and n. 7; Marmura, 1991/2, 173.

[23] Sambursky 1959, 53.

[24] Long and Sedley 1987, fragment 55.O, English: i. 338, Latin: ii. 339.

[25] Lucretius, *De rerum natura* II.250–51.

[26] Alexander, *On Fate* XXII, 193.7–8.

[27] Lapidge 1978, 176. Similarly Sambursky (1959, 56–7) uses the expression '*chain of causes* stretching continuously in space and time'.

Particularly relevant to our discussion is the cosmological implication that the stability of the world depends on the contiguity of causal chains. It is the essential linking of causal chains that holds the universe together. As Alexander explains,

Nothing comes to be in the universe in such a way that there is not something else which follows it with no alternative and is attached to it as to a cause; nor, on the other hand, can any of the things which have come to be subsequently be disconnected from the things which have come to be previously, so as not to follow some one of them as if bound to it . . . For nothing either is or comes to be in the universe without a cause, because there is nothing in the things in it that is separated and disconnected from all the things that have preceded it. *For the universe would be torn apart and divided and not remain single, forever ordered according to a single order and organisation, if any causeless motion were introduced.*[28]

It is the contiguity of causal chains that holds the universe together. The Stoics developed their theory of total interpenetration of bodies, striving to conceive the whole universe as one unified entity. This led them to the notion of fuzzy boundaries.[29] According to Plutarch, they eliminated the notion of a boundary as that 'at which the magnitude of a body terminates' and introduced instead a concept of indefinite extension of a body or of gradual merging of bodies into one another. Their notion of continuity and contiguity were not as well distinguished as they were for Aristotle and his followers.

6.1.3. The physical basis of Islamic occasionalism

Islamic atomism was a part of Averroes' intellectual environment. He was familiar with the doctrines of the Muslim theologians and argued with them. He was also aware, at least to some extent, of the differences between Greek, notably Epicurean, atomism, and Muslim atomism.[30]

[28] Alexander, *On Fate* XXII, 192.3–7; English: Sharples 1983, 71; Long and Sedley 1987 fragment 55N, i. 317–18.

[29] See White 1992, 287–93.

[30] 'And the <<mutakallimūn>> <the ancients> of our nation, as they considered division to be division in act, denied that division can go on infinitely and contended that division terminates with something indivisible, and this is what they meant by indivisible parts. But the ancient upholders of indivisible parts accepted infinite division, as this is one of the postulates of geometry, and assumed that this is so *in actu*; according to them there are infinitely many indivisible parts in one finite magnitude.' *MC Phys.*, MS Hamburg 67^b26–68^a7, MS Paris fo. 92b8–15, Zeraḥya's translation 83^a19–b2.

Both these systems were indeterministic and allowed spontaneous uncaused events. In Greek atomism, motion is interrupted by collisions or by spontaneous swerves,[31] in Muslim atomism by direct divine intervention. Both systems were based on discrete, expressly non-Aristotelian physics.[32]

6.1.4. Averroes' agenda

For the Stoics the whole universe is one continuous–contiguous entity penetrated throughout by pneuma. With this strong notion of a unified universe, the distinction between the celestial and sublunar regions does not play a significant role. For Averroes, on the other hand, the clear distinction between the continuous and contiguous reflects the clear distinction between the celestial and the sublunar. He distinguishes two types of motion: 'either multiple motions that succeed one another, or one continuous motion, that is, the motion of the celestial bodies.'[33] The first type of motion is typical of the sublunar region, where different types of changes occur. Averroes refers to these changes also as 'the motions of the parts of the world' or 'motion in genus'.[34] The second type is typical of the celestial region and Averroes refers to it also as 'the motion of the whole world'.[35] The celestial motions are continuous, uniform, and eternal. The continuous structure is fully deterministic. No surprises are to be expected in the celestial realm. What about our sublunar world?

For Averroes chains of sublunar changes were contiguous and not merely successive (as they were for the Theologians) because they are causally linked. By fully subscribing to causality Averroes maintains

[31] The swerve thesis can be used to dismiss determinism, but not to account for ethical indeterminism and free will. See Furley 1982; Englert, 1987.

[32] According to the Muslim atomists the world consists of atoms that are created *ex nihilo* or annihilated by God every time atom. The history of an atom consists of a succession of atomic states. See Wolfson 1976, 518–22, 552; Marmura 1997, pp. xxiii–xxvi; Kogan (1985, 258–9). On time atoms in Islam see Sorabji 1983, ch. 25, Dhanani 1994, 131–3.

[33] *LC Phys*. VIII.1 Hebrew 136^{a}28–^{b}1. See also Puig 1999, 236. Similarly in the commentary on *De animalibus:* 'The existents in motion are of two kinds: Those whose motion is eternal and whose individuals are neither generated not corrupted . . . [And those whose individuals] now exist and now are non-existents.' Quoted from Freudenthal 2002, 120 (Freudenthal's translation).

[34] See pp. 93–95 below.

[35] Averroes borrows these terms from Ibn Bājja, *On Phys*. 154.5–6.

the Aristotelian standards of rational and scientific thinking; by basing his sublunar physics on the contiguous, rather than the continuous structure he believes that he can escape the danger of determinism. We shall see that he eliminates all continuous structures from the sublunar world.

6.2. CONFLICTING MESSAGES IN ARISTOTLE

The main obstacle in Averroes' way to indeterminism was Aristotle's succession argument in *Physics* VIII.1. Several passages in Aristotle bear upon the question of determinism vs. indeterminism.[36] The understanding of the question, however, was at a preliminary stage, the concepts had not yet been consolidated and the terms had not been coined. The discussion was mainly in terms of essential vs. accidental relations. Aristotle's succession argument of *Physics* VIII.1 establishes that sublunar changes are 'chained'. Does this imply that these chains are essentially linked? This question haunted Averroes for years. As against the succession argument of VIII.1, the argument that comes closest to denying essential linking appears in *Physics* V.2, where Aristotle explicitly states that 'change of change' cannot be essential. What he meant by 'change of change' is not so clear, but several commentators have interpreted V.2 as a counter-argument to VIII.1. The tension between these two chapters was brought to light by Philoponus and Ibn Bājja and thoroughly studied by Averroes.

6.2.1. The succession argument (*Physics* VIII.1)

The Succession Argument: Before any motion or change,[37] there *must* (*anankaion*, ضرورة, יחויב) have been a previous change.[38]

[36] Bobzien (1998, 2) mentions *Nic. Ethics* III.1–5, *De int.* 9, *Metaphysics* Δ.2, E.3, Θ.3–4, and *Physics* II and VIII. Balme (1939, 130) contends that in his biological works and in *On Generation and Corruption* 'Aristotle denies that there is any necessity by which one event compels the next to happen.' Balme refers to *De Part. an.* 640^{a}4, *De Gen. an.* 734^{a}25 and *De Gen. et Corr.* 337^{b}15. See also Sharples 1975, 262.

[37] Aristotle uses both terms in the argument.

[38] This is the bottom line of the argument in *Physics* VIII.1251^{a}8–^{b}10, Arabic II. 805. The word *anankaion* or *anankē* is used several times throughout the argument.

Aristotle opens his argument with a basic premise:[39]

> **Premise VIII** (Aristotle): 'It is necessary that there should be things which are able to move (*ta pragmata ta dunamena kineisthai) with* (*kath'* + accusative) each kind of motion'.[40]

He claims that the premise follows from the definition of motion and from experience.[41] His definition of motion as 'the actuality of the movable qua such'[42] asserts the presence of a movable body, and thus the premise indeed follows from it. The premise as Aristotle states it is weak and Aristotle later uses a stronger assumption: 'There must be something burnable *before* (*prin*) it is burnt and something able to burn things *before* it burns them'.[43] Commentators could thus find in Aristotle either a weak or a strong statement of the premise:

> **Weak statement:** *With* any motion there must be a moved thing.
>
> **Strong statement:** *Before* any motion there should be a moved thing *and* a mover.

Aristotle claims to derive the succession argument from the definition of motion but, in fact, he uses the strong statement of the premise which leans not only on the definition of motion but also on the argument of *Physics* VII.1, that is, that a motion-situation necessarily involves a distinction between something that moves and something that is being moved. It also states explicitly the temporal priority of the moved body and the potential mover to the motion, which the weak statement does not. We shall see that the precise statement of the premise was a major issue for Averroes and that he revised it several times.

The argument opens with the presentation of two mutually exclusive alternatives: 'These things [whose existence is asserted by premise VIII] must either (i) come to be at some time, or (ii) they must always exist'.[44]

(i) In the case of generated things 'the given motion *must* have been preceded by another change and motion, in which the thing able to be moved or to cause motion itself came to be'.[45]

[39] Averroes refers to it as مقدمة. *SC Phys*. (Arabic 129.7).
[40] *Physics* VIII.1, 251^{a}10.
[41] Presumably the experience that motion exists, that the Eleatics denied.
[42] Aristotle quotes the definition in VIII.1 251a8. The definition is given in III.1 201a10.
[43] *Physics* VIII.1, 251^{a}15.
[44] *Physics* VIII.1, 251^{a}17.
[45] *Physics* VIII.1, 251^{a}17–20.

(ii) In the case of an eternal mover and an eternal moved thing 'if the motion did not continue always, clearly the objects were not in a condition such that the one was able to be moved and the other able to cause motion, but one of them had to undergo change.'[46] The conclusion of the argument is: 'Before the first change there will have been a previous change'.[47]

In the same vein Aristotle argues that motion is imperishable.[48] The bottom line follows: 'There was not, nor ever will be a time when there was not, or when there will not be, motion'.[49]

In order for motion to occur, both a mover and a movable thing must be present and, conversely, if a mover and a movable object are present, either a certain motion or rest must result.[50] Does this mean that the resulting motion or rest is uniquely determined by the previous situation? Aristotle does not say so and Averroes, we shall see, answers in the negative. Puig has shown that his interpretation of the famous future sea battle argument,[51] is also indeterministic.[52]

[46] *Physics* VIII.1, 251^{a}20–^{b}9. The passage 251^{b}1–8 is a short excursus on causality: Aristotle distinguishes between things that can produce a single motion (such as heating by fire) and things capable of producing contrary motions (such as heating or cooling by the doctor or the cook). This is a step towards the important distinction between necessitating and non-necessitating causes. Ross (1936, 688) comments that Aristotle makes no use of this. This passage might be an interpolation.

[47] *Physics* VIII.1, 251^{a}27–8; 251^{b}9–10; Arabic ii. 806.8.

[48] *Physics* VIII.1, 251^{b}28–31. [49] *Physics* VIII.1, 252^{b}5.

[50] Both motion and rest require a cause. Avicenna unequivocally states that *existence or non-existence* of a possible existent 'are both due to a cause'. Quoted in Belo 2004, 29. See discussion in Graham 1999, 43–4.

[51] In the famous discussion of the sea battle Aristotle concludes: 'It is necessary for there *to be or not to be* a sea battle tomorrow; but it is not necessary for a sea battle to take place tomorrow, nor for one not to take place' (*De Int.* 9, 19a31–3, trans. Ackrill). In a similar context in the *Metaphysics* he uses again the either–or construct. After telling a long story about a man who will die by violence (*Metaphysics* E.3 1027^{b}1–5) he concludes: 'But *this is either the case or not.* So *of necessity he will die or not die.*' The outcome, however, is not deterministically decided: 'the process goes back to a certain starting point but this no longer points to something further. This, then will be *the starting point for the fortuitous,* and will have nothing else as cause of its coming to be' (*Metaphysics* E.3 1027b11–14, trans. Ross). In his commentary on *De Interpretatione* al-Fārābī discusses the sea battle problem. See Zimmermann's edition of this commentary and Adamson 2006.

[52] See Puig 2005*a*, 99. I quote from a lecture in English (2005*b*), in which he somewhat expands on this point: 'Aristotle said that we cannot know which alternative event will take place (*De int.* 19a 33) and this meant for Averroes that we cannot have a determinate knowledge. This subjective imprecision is an exact reflection of an imprecision in the very nature of future events. However, he is interpreting Aristotle

6.2.2. Accidental succession (*Physics* V.2)

VIII.1 is a key chapter that leads to the climax of Aristotle's *Physics*. V.2 is of secondary importance and plays a relatively minor role in the *Physics*. In this chapter Aristotle deals with a complex concept: 'change of change'. The context is the question whether 'motion of motion, becoming of becoming, or, in general, change of change' are possible.[53] In this context Aristotle follows what Bostock calls 'the narrow ontology of the *Categories*', according to which only substances can undergo change.[54] Change must be studied in its relation to substance, which is the subject of change. Change of change is a secondary kind of entity that depends on the primary change, and is therefore accidental:[55]

Even this [motion of motion] is possible only *in an accidental sense* (*kata sumbebēkos*) . . . So, if there is to be motion of motion, that which is changing from health to sickness must simultaneously be changing from that change to another. . . . It is *only accidentally* that there can be change of change, e.g. there is a change from remembering to forgetting only because the subject of this change changes at one time to knowledge, at another to ignorance.[56]

The statement that attracted the attention of the commentators is 'change of change is possible only accidentally',[57] which they interpreted to mean that 'change can be *consequent upon* change only accidentally.' I use the expression 'consequent upon' to translate the Arabic تابع ال, Hebrew נמשך ל, which is frequently used by Averroes.

from the opposite direction: whereas Aristotle departed from the concrete limbs of the disjunction, Averroes proceeds from the global construction. But no general ideas or truth values are under discussion. Real existents are the issue. Since they have not acquired existence yet, truth and falsity have neither acquired existence.' I am grateful to Prof. Puig for sending me the lecture.

[53] *Physics* V.2, 225^{b}14–16. On the meaning of this passage see Bostock 1991, 204–5.

[54] Bostock 1991, 205. See also Graham 1987, 35–6.

[55] Aristotle suggests two possible senses. The first is the more precise logically: 'the motion of which there is motion might be conceived as subject' (*Physics* V.2, 225^{b}16). The second is the more relevant in the present context: 'that some other subject changes from a change to another mode of being, as e.g. a man changes from falling ill to getting well' (*Physics* V.2, 225^{b}21–33). The secondary change from the change F–T to the change T–R is induced by the primary changes from F to T and from T to R. Aristotle recapitulates this conclusion at the end of the discussion, 226^{a}19–22.

[56] *Physics* V.2, 225^{b}23–33. If, for instance, a subject changes from F to T and then back from T to F, a 'secondary change' from the change F–T to the change T–F is induced.

[57] Lettinck 1994*a*, 402–3.

The implication of V.2 is that change should be studied in its relation to substance (the changing subject) rather than to other changes, because these relations are accidental.[58] Essential linking between changes is denied. In *Physics* VIII.1, however, Aristotle studies the dynamics of changes in relation to other changes and argues that a change *must* be preceded by one change and succeeded by another. Philoponus, a shrewd critic of Aristotle, was quick to point out the contradiction.[59] As Lettinck observes, Philoponus' argument is not offered in support of Aristotle's argument in V.2, but rather as a refutation of his argument in VIII.1.[60] Ibn Bājja argues that V.2 conflicts not only with VIII.1 (the succession argument) but also with III.1 (Aristotle's definition of motion).[61] Averroes finds in this chapter support for his contention that the chains of sublunar changes are not essentially linked.

To sum up, Aristotle does not offer an unequivocal statement on determinism in the *Physics*. Chapter VIII.1 can be interpreted as supporting the deterministic interpretation and V.2 as denying it, but both messages are rather vague. Let us see now how Averroes' handles this rather complex situation.

6.3. THE STORY OF THE MIDDLE COMMENTARY

6.3.1. Preview

Averroes, the devout Aristotelian, could have easily ignored or dismissed Philoponus' reading of V.2 as a counter-argument to VIII.1 and defended the succession argument. At first this is indeed what he

58 Bostock 1991, 205.

59 'If there were motion of motion it would follow that a present motion must be preceded by another motion . . . If this series of motions were infinite and did not have a beginning, then a present motion would not exist, because it can exist only because the first one has existed.' Philoponus, *On Phys*. 520.5–10, English: Lettinck 1994*b*, 37.

60 Lettinck (1994*b*, 11). Philoponus' argument from the impossibility of infinite past generations is aimed at the succession argument of *Physics* VIII.1: Socrates could not have been born, because 'when the first term does not exist, the following ones cannot exist either'.

61 'One may raise an objection and say: the transition from capacity to actuality (الفعل) is a change, while motion is a perfection (كمال). A thing thus moves potentially (بالقوة) and then moves in perfection (بالكمال)' (Ziyada 52.3–5). The argument is difficult. Perhaps Ibn Bājja points out to the essential linking between capacity and perfection that leads to infinite regression. See also Lettinck 1994*a*, 419.

does, but eventually his interpretation of VIII.1 undergoes a radical transformation. I shall refer to the early interpretation that is preserved in version A manuscripts as interpretation A and the late one, that is preserved in version B manuscripts, as interpretation B.[62]

Interpretation A is straightforward; Averroes more or less follows Aristotle's text and defends Aristotle's argument against Philoponus.[63] At a certain stage he adopts a more critical approach and re-examines the argument thoroughly. I shall refer to it as the turning point stage. This is the stage of the formation of Averroes' new ideas. Interpretation B is an attempt to save Aristotle's argument by a new construal. Interpretations A and B are present in all three commentaries. In the short commentary we find the two interpretations in different manuscripts and there is no linking between them. In the middle and long commentaries we find 'turning point passages' that explain the transition from interpretation A to B. These 'turning point passages' are naturally the most interesting parts.

I begin with the turning point of the middle commentary and will proceed to that of the long commentary in Section 6.4. To facilitate reading, I shall start with a brief outline of the argument and would like to draw the reader's attention to the fact that the turning point passage of the middle commentary (paragraphs MA4 and MA5) appears in version A manuscripts, not in version B manuscripts. This fact, we shall see, complicates matters.

The middle commentary—an outline:

Version A
[MA1] Premise VIII: strong statement.[64]
[MA2] The answer to Philoponus.[65]
[MA3] The succession argument: interpretation A.[66]

Turning Point Passage
[MA4] The linking question.[67]
[MA5] Interpretation B suggested.[68]

[62] On the different versions see Ch. 4 above.

[63] See Appendix 4, p. 89 below.

[64] *MC Phys.* VIII.2.1 version A, $65^{b}12$–22.

[65] *MC Phys.* VIII.2.1 version A $65^{b}22$–$66^{b}5$. Premise VIII is valid in both types of motion situations: after generation and after rest.

[66] *MC Phys.* VIII.2.2 version A, $66^{b}5$–30.

[67] *MC Phys.* VIII.2.2 version A, $66^{b}30$–$67^{a}15$.

[68] *MC Phys.* VIII.2.2 version A, $67^{a}15$–28.

Version B
[MB1] Premise VIII: intermediate statement.[69]
[MB2] The succession argument: interpretation B.[70]
[MB3] The views of the mutakallimūn and of the sages.[71]
[MB4] The argument with al-Fārābī.[72]

6.3.2. The onset of the turning point: the linking question

The turning point passage opens a new chapter in Averroes' study of change and motion. He introduces a more precise tool of analysis: the terms for measuring proximity that Aristotle defines in *Physics* V.3, namely succession, contiguity, and continuity.[73] Using these terms, the study of motion becomes more scientific and Averroes can offer a better analysis of Aristotle's argument and find where the difficulty lies. With this new tool Averroes can remove the threat of determinism on the one hand and of occasionalism on the other. The Stoics did not pay due attention to the distinction between continuity and contiguity and thus failed to note the 'times of the possible' in sublunar processes. The mutakallimūn did not pay due attention to the difference between contiguity and succession and thus failed to appreciate the scientific order that governs sublunar processes. Averroes' idea was ingenious and can be considered as showing a scientific approach to physics. We cannot say how original it was. In his no longer extant treatise *On Changeable Beings* al-Fārābī analyses types of successions,[74] presumably in order to defend Aristotle's argument against Philoponus.[75] It was most probably

[69] *MC Phys.* VIII.2.1 version B, 92^b5–15.
[70] *MC Phys.* VIII.2.2 version B, 92^b16–94^a5.
[71] *MC Phys.* VIII.2.2 version B, 94^a6–19
[72] *MC Phys.* VIII.2.2 version B, 94^a19–26.
[73] See p. 64 above.
[74] Davidson tried to reconstruct al-Fārābī's argument and showed that it concerned possible and impossible modes of infinity: 'Al-Fārābī and Avicenna had tried to explain why arguments against the existence of certain kinds of infinite do not exclude others . . . The explanation given by both al-Farabi and Avicenna was that the existence of an infinite number of objects is impossible only when two conditions are met, only when the objects exist together at the same time, and when they also have a relative "position" to one another or are essentially ordered. Arguments against the infinite would not apply to infinite past and past events' (Davidson 1987, 128–30, 367–70, quotation from 367–8).
[75] Little has been preserved of Philoponus' commentary on *Physics* VIII, but in his commentary on *Physics* V.2 he argues that an infinite succession that has no first argument is impossible: 'When the first term does not exist, the following ones cannot exist either' (*On Phys.* 523.12–15, English: Lettinck 1994*b*, 38). In his commentary on *Physics* V.3

the reading of this treatise that suggested to Averroes the analysis of the succession argument in terms of degrees of proximity.

The turning point passage opens with *the linking question*: what is the relation between a given motion and the motion that must have preceded it, continuity, contiguity, or mere succession?[76]

[Turning point passage, paragraph MA4] . . . it has not been explained in what sense motion is said to be perpetual: as being in succession,[77] or contiguous,[78] or continuous.[79] This is because the infinite contiguity of movements is possible in one respect and impossible in another, and this can be imagined in different respects (which al-Fārābī had already studied in his *On Changeable Beings*), distinguishing between the possible and the impossible aspects.[80]

Thinking in these terms, Averroes notes that Aristotle proves less than he endeavours to prove. Aristotle argues that there must be motions of the same kind before an assumed first motion and after an assumed last motion. This is precisely the meaning of succession.[81] Aristotle establishes the existence of successive chains of sublunar changes, but does not show that these chains are contiguous. *In itself*, thus, the succession argument is not sufficient to establish the stability or the eternity of the world. The core of the turning point is the understanding (achieved after an intensive inquiry) that the source of the stability of the sublunar world and of the perpetuity of sublunar motion must be in the celestial region.

he deals with Aristotle's definitions at length and points out several difficulties. In this context he distinguishes between successions of things that have position and of things that do not have position (e.g. 548.15–20, 549.11–15, English ibid. 50–51), which, according to Davidson, is a criterion for possibility.

76 The terms are explained in section 6.1.1 above.

77 Anonymous translation: המשכה; Zeraḥya's translation: תתאלי, which is the Arabic term.

78 Anonymous translation: תכיפה; Zeraḥya's translation: הזדווגות.

79 Anonymous translation: דיבוק; Zeraḥya's translation: דבקות.

80 *MC Phys*. VIII.2.2 version A, Anonymous translation: New York MS $66^{b}30–67^{a}6$, Oxford MS $96^{a}16–22$; Zeraḥya's translation: $112^{a}5–13$.

81 The qualification 'of the same kind' (ממינה) appears twice in the argument. It is not explained and does not seem to be correct. It is not mentioned in the parallel passage in the long commentary. Perhaps Averroes adds 'of the same kind', in order to conform to the definition of succession.

[Turning point passage, paragraph MA4, concluded] From what the sage [Aristotle] says,[82] it seems that the argument he presents here[83] implies that it [the cause of perpetuity] is one continuous eternal motion.[84] *After an intensive inquiry and a long time,*[85] it seems to me (and this can, perhaps, be inferred from the words of the sage[86]) that the sage indeed argued that every newly generated motion necessarily succeeds a previous motion of its kind,[87] and this goes on *ad infinitum* into the past and also into the future, i.e. that every motion assumed to be the last[88] is indeed succeeded by another motion of the same kind. And this, according to the definition of the infinite, is one of the possible rather than of the impossible aspects.[89] The argument seems to imply, however, that 'this possible' must be contiguous[90] and that the non-contiguous must be contiguous *because of [the existence of] a motion that is itself continuous.*[91]

It took Averroes 'an intensive inquiry and a long time' to reach this interpretation, and it took me in turn 'an intensive inquiry and a long time' to understand it, especially the last sentence.[92] The meanings of the whole passage and the use of the expression 'this possible' are easier to understand from the parallel passage in the long commentary:

This statement—that the motion which we assumed to be first must be preceded by another [i.e. the succession argument]—does not imply that the second be contiguous to the one preceding it, but [only] that it be in succession,

[82] Anonymous translation 'the sage', Zeraḥya translation 'Aristotle'.

[83] Or: 'which led him here'.

[84] The first sentence heralds the solution that is suggested in the last sentence.

[85] 'A long time' is in Zeraḥya's translation only, and not in the anonymous translation.

[86] Following the anonymous translation: והוא אשר ראוי שיובן מכח זה המופת. Zeraḥya translates (both MSS): יהוא אשר לפיהו המצלתי בעבור דברי ארסטו. Perhaps should be המלצתי, which means in medieval Hebrew 'I expressed by words'.

[87] See note 11 above.

[88] Following the anonymous translation. Zeraḥya's translation reads: איזו תנועה שהונחה חלקים.

[89] Perhaps Averroes is thinking of Aristotle's definition at the end of *Physics* III: 'Time, change, and thought are infinite things of the kind in which what is taken does not persist throughout' (*Physics* III.8208ª20).

[90] The word used is *dibbuq*, which is the common word for continuity, but here it must mean contiguity, as distinguished from mere succession. Such loose uses of this word are common.

[91] *MC Phys.* VIII.2.2 version A, Anonymous translation: New York MS 67ª6–14, Oxford MS 96ª21–ᵇ2, Zeraḥya's translation 112ª12–23.

[92] אלא רבכש הארי הזמ רמאמה הזש ירשפאה אוה הנה בייוחמ קובדה קובדהו סנמא היהי בייוחמ יתלבב סיקבדתמה ינפמ העונת איה המצעב תקבודמ. See note 90 on the translation.

I mean that there be a time of rest between it [and the preceding motion]. And this is the time in which *the possible* is.[93]

Averroes finds support for this interpretation in the 'indeterministic chapter' *Physics* V.2. In his long commentary on this chapter he explains:

It has been established that a motion cannot be from motion essentially. It is thus necessary that *a motion be generated from motion accidentally.*[94] Motion is a passage of existing things from one resting form to another resting form, and one such passage cannot follow another *unless accidentally.*[95]

According to Averroes Aristotle proved that there must be infinite successions of sublunar events, and that the linking between successive motions cannot be essential. Therefore the time between two consecutive motions is the time of *the possible*. The argument, however, is not yet complete. The structure of a successive chain is too loose. It remains for Averroes to 'close the gaps', that is, to establish that this succession must be contiguous, without giving up 'the times of the possible'. To this end he turns to the heavens: the contiguity of sublunar chains is not essential but consequent upon another motion that is truly continuous, namely the celestial motion. This point is recapitulated two chapters later, in VIII.2.4: 'And because the succeeding motion is not necessarily always continuous, *unless due to a continuous motion*, there is a perpetual continuous motion that is the reason why the successive is perpetual.'[96] The celestial motions are truly continuous and in the celestial region everything is fully determined. The continuous celestial motions guarantee contiguity in the sublunar world, which does not entail determinism and allows times for 'the possible'.

[93] *LC Phys.* VIII.6 Latin 342D14–E7; Hebrew 139^b18–21. In his philosophical lexicon, Aristotle uses the same term, (*dunamis*, قوة) for both potentiality and possibility (*Metaphysics* Δ.121019^b31–2). Isḥaq Ibn Ḥunayn uses a different word for possible— ممكن (*Physics*, Arabic 805,11–12), which is rendered in the Hebrew of the long commentary as אפשר. The Latin translator uses *potentia* for both potential and possible. See Wolfson 1929, 692–3.

[94] *LC Phys.* V.17 Latin 220C5–9, Hebrew 17^b15–17.

[95] *LC Phys.* V.12, Latin 217 C13-D4; Hebrew 15a24–6. See also *LC Phys.* V.13 Hebrew only 16^b13–14.

[96] *MC Phys.* VIII.2.4.95^b4–6.

6.3.3. The vertical natural order

The idea of inferring the persistence of sublunar processes from the continuity of celestial motions is by no means new.[97] It goes back to Aristotle's *De generatione et corruptione*.[98] Sublunar processes are ontologically dependent on the celestial motions: both the perpetuity and the variation of change in the sublunar world are caused by the celestial motions.[99] The new point that Averroes makes in the turning point passage is not that the eternity and stability of the sublunar world can be derived from vertical considerations but rather that they *cannot* be derived from horizontal considerations—that is, from the causal structure of sublunar chains of motions—as Aristotle tries to do in *Physics* VIII.1. Averroes tacitly dismisses the 'horizontal' approach and restates the succession argument in vertical terms:

[Middle commentary version B] [According to the sages] the motion that is induced by a primordial mover is necessarily eternal and a mover cannot be affected by a mover except via this motion which is, on the one hand, newly generated[100] but, on the other, eternal and primordial. It is newly generated because its parts change place and because of its *proximity to or distance from* the generated beings. It is eternal because it never ceases. Without the assumption of such a motion it would be impossible to derive newly generated motions from an eternal mover and it would necessarily follow that either there is no generation at all, or that every generation is the outcome of a newly generated mover.[101]

[Long commentary] Because when we assume [a] that this order is natural and [b] that *no other order is possible* (namely that all motions terminate at the

[97] This subject is studied in Freudenthal 2002, 120–28 and Freudenthal 2006.

[98] 'Since it has been proved that movement by way of locomotion is eternal, generation also, these things being so, *must take place continuously*, for the locomotion will produce the generation perpetually by bringing near and then removing the generating body.' *De Gen. et Corr.* II.10, 336ᵃ14–18, Williams's translation.

[99] Averroes explains that 'the efficient cause of *the continuity of generation and corruption*, according to Aristotle, is the primary, continuous motion, while the efficient cause of generation and corruption is the motion of the sun in the inclined circle.' *SC De Gen. et Corr.* Hebrew 121.67–122.78, English 133. See Freudenthal 2006, 32.

[100] מתחדשת. The Arabic root is حدث.

[101] *MC Phys.* VIII.2.2 version B, 94ᵃ12–19.

celestial body), and [c] that the celestial body is near to some of the things and remote from others[102]—then [this assumption] is the cause that some things rest for a while and some move for a while, and that motion is followed by another motion. And he explained that it is impossible for motion to vanish for a while.[103]

'The sages' to whom Averroes attributes this cosmology are, probably, Alexander and his followers. Alexander develops the vertical system in his *On the Principles of the Universe*, a treatise with which Averroes was acquainted.[104] Alexander emphasizes that the stability of the sublunar world follows from vertical considerations, not from the succession argument, and cannot rely on 'horizontal considerations':

Therefore it is not at all to be feared that the world might perish, since it has acquired stability and duration from such principles. For it originates from and is connected with the non-perishability of the divine body and its circular motion, and the eternity in species of the material bodies which are in generation follows its course according to the continuity of their variation.[105]

The continuity of things that come to be has a cause and it is on account of this that the universe is one and eternal, always organised in one and the same way.[106]

Alexander uses the vertical argument in his campaign against the Stoics' 'horizontal', non-hierarchical universe, held together by pneuma:[107]

Surely it is absurd to claim that the whole of a substance is unified by pneuma . . . For they do not know the fundamental explanation for the unification of the whole—this is the nature of the divine body, which moves in a circle and is composed of ether, which *holds together and preserves the whole* by surrounding the whole enmattered, passive and alterable substance [i.e. the sublunar world] with continuous and everlasting motion, and by causing in a fixed order the interchange of bodies that come to be by its *different states towards them at different times*.[108]

102 I slightly corrected the syntax of [c].

103 *LC Phys.* VIII.9 Latin 345F15–G11, Hebrew 142^b28–143^a1.

104 Averroes could probably have found Alexander's statement also in the commentaries on the *Physics* and on *De Gen. et Corr.*, which are no longer extant. Unfortunately, the parts of the latter recently discovered by Emma Gennagé do not include chapter II.10.

105 Alexander, *On the Principles* 73, # 57.

106 Alexander, *De fato* XXV, 195.23–5. Quoted from Freudenthal 2006, 41.

107 Freudenthal 2006, 37–8, 48–9.

108 Alexander, *On Mixture* 223.6–14, Todd's translation with few modifications, 133–5.

Therefore, it is not at all to be feared that the world might perish, since it has acquired stability and duration from such [celestial] principles.[109]

Freudenthal suggests a strong interpretation: Alexander 'identifies sublunar nature with the effects of the motions of the heavenly bodies'.[110] The contiguous structure is the sublunar image of the continuous structure that is possible only in the celestial region.

For eternity [in the sublunar world] cannot exist in number, but only *in species*, preserved by the body which is like the nature of all bodies devoid of all opposites, through the intermediacy of the things moved in a circle around the earth.[111]

Their permanence and duration are eternal only *in species*, corresponding to the eternity in number of the others.[112]

The true eternity of the celestial individuals can induce only 'eternity in species' or 'broken eternity' on earth.

Averroes follows Alexander almost verbatim:

. . . the movement of the heaven is *numerically one*, and one can apply such an expression only [in a derivative sense] to the transitory movements of the sublunar world; for these movements, since they cannot be numerically one, are one in species and lasting through the movement which is numerically one.[113]

The idea of a vertical unique natural order is stated several times in the *Tahāfut al-Tahāfut*:

That from their [the heavens'] movements there follow well-defined acts from which this sublunary world, its animals, vegetables and minerals *receive their subsistence and conservation* is evident from observation, for, were it not that the sun in its ecliptic *approaches the sublunary world and recedes* from it, there would not be the four seasons . . . Those actions which the sun exercises everlastingly *through its varying distance* from the different existents are also found in the moon and the stars.[114]

The infinite movements are infinite *in genus only* because of the one single continuous eternal movement of the body of the heavens.[115]

The eternity of motion is not a corollary of its being motion, as the horizontal argument implies, but is due to something outside it, namely the celestial motion. Therefore the perpetuity of sublunar motion is not essential. The succession argument no longer threatens indeterminism,

109 Alexander, *On the Principles* 73 # 57.

110 Freudenthal 2006, 40.

111 Alexander, *On the Principles* 73, # 58

112 Ibid. 85, # 80

113 *Tahāfut* 487.5–8. See Freudenthal 2002.

114 *Tahāfut* 188–9.

115 *Tahāfut* 283.

but actually supports it. This is the crux of the new interpretation and Averroes repeats it many times in version B texts:

[Long commentary] Eternity and perpetuity are essential in the continuous and accidental in the contiguous.[116]

[*Questions in Physics*] But this conclusion follows necessarily from the assumption of an eternal motion, for it is not something that follows from the nature of motion itself, *but is accidental to motion* because there is an eternal motion.[117]

[Short commentary version B] And since [the fact that] any motion except the first [i.e. celestial] motions is preceded by another motion is accidental and consequent upon the first motions, it is impossible for a newly generated (الحادثة) motion to be preceded by another newly generated motion essentially.[118]

[Middle commentary version B] This is how Aristotle's argument at the beginning of this book should be understood; namely, that there is an eternal motion, numerically one or more than one . . . [The situation that] before any motion there is a motion and after it a motion is due to its [the motion's] being *an accident of the essential motions* [i.e. the celestial].[119] This necessarily implies that what seems to be the case—namely, that some of them [the sublunar motions] are the causes of others—*has no basis at all.*[120] Since sublunar motions depend ontologically on the celestial, the attempt to deduce the eternity of sublunar motion from 'horizontal' considerations is absurd.

Averroes' strategy, which he uses time and again, is to interpret a problematic chapter in Aristotle in the light of other chapters which offer a different, even conflicting message. In *Physics* VIII.1 Aristotle attempts to derive sublunar eternity and stability from horizontal considerations. In *De generatione et corruptione* II.10 he derives the same results from vertical considerations. Averroes tries to reinterpret the argument of

[116] *LC Phys.* VIII.56 Latin 397G2–4, Hebrew 197^b27–8.

[117] *Questions in Physics* VII, 18–19, # 15, trans. Goldstein (modified).

[118] *SC Phys.* Arabic 133.8–134.3; Hebrew 40^a28–31.

[119] The sentence is somewhat difficult: כי יראה שקודם כל תנועה תנועה ואחריה תנועה, אחר שהיה בו מקרה מהתנועות בעצם. It is not clear what the word בו refers to. I checked Hamburg and Paris manuscripts.

[120] *MC Phys.* VIII.2.294^a19–24. Zeraḥya's translation is not available for version B passages.

VIII.1 as vertical: the contiguity of motion in the sublunar world is due to the existence of *another* continuous motion. With sublunar chains dependent on something external to them, their contiguity cannot be essential and does not imply determinism.

6.3.4. The revision of Aristotle's argument

Having arrived at the conclusion that stability and eternity are accidental to sublunar motions, it remained for Averroes to correct or to reinterpret the succession argument. 'Fortunately' this argument is vague enough to allow different interpretations. His strategy was to turn it into a *per impossibile* argument: instead of applying it to an arbitrary motion, as Aristotle does, he applies it to the motion of the outermost sphere, that is, the first motion 'in nature', or in nobility, whose existence was proved in VII.1.[121] If a notion of temporally first motion is at all possible,[122] then this motion should be the natural candidate. If it is shown that before this specific motion there must have been another change or motion, it will follow, *per impossibile*, that the notion of a temporally first motion is untenable. The motion of the outermost sphere which is first in nature must have always existed. This revision of the succession argument completes and concludes the turning point passage:

[Turning point passage, paragraph MA5] And when this [what is stated in VIII.1] is taken together with what has been said in the seventh book [VII.1], namely that things that are in local motion terminate at[123] that which is itself moved by an unmoved mover[124]—it follows that this mover is eternally moving and that whatever is moved by it is moved eternally. Had we assumed that the

121 See Wardy 1990, 100.

122 Philoponus rightly comments that temporal priority is not well defined in the case of infinite motion. It is thus taken for granted that the motion which is assumed to be first is finite, i.e. sublunar.

123 תעלה אל literally 'ascend to'. In some contexts the word used is תכלה which means terminate. A similar sentence appears in the *Questions in Physics*, too. I translate 'terminate at' following H. T. Goldstein.

124 This sentence has been emended slightly. Anonymous translation: יעלו אל מתנועע מאליו בו מניע לא יתנועע; Zeraḥya's translation: יעלו אל מתנועעים מעצמו במניע בו לא יתנועע. Perhaps the original sentence was corrupt.

first mover began to move at a certain time, it would have followed [according to VIII.1] that another motion must have preceded it, and then that which was assumed to be first is not first. And when [it is established] that the first is that which is not preceded by a motion, it follows that its motion is eternal, and that the motion of whatever is moved by it is eternal. *Therefore the first motion and the first moved body must be eternal.* This is why the argument concerning the first mover in book VII precedes the present argument.[125]

This is the general idea of interpretation B and the conclusion of the turning point passage.

Let me summarize the analysis of the turning point passage of the middle commentary. For the Stoics continuity and contiguity are close concepts. The whole world is a contiguous structure in place and in time and this structure guarantees determinism.[126] Averroes carefully distinguishes between continuity and contiguity. The former governs the celestial region; the latter governs the sublunar region. Averroes associates contiguity with possibility.[127] Necessity is instantiated in continuous structures, which are typical of the celestial realm; possibility is instantiated in contiguous structures, which are typical of the sublunar world.[128] The continuous structure is deterministic, the contiguous structure is not: the points of contact in a contiguous chain are the times of 'the possible'.[129] True continuity is possible only in the heavens. Contiguity is 'continuity in body' (الاتصال في الجسم) or, as Ivry translates, 'corporeal continuity'.[130] It is the closest approximation to continuity that can be achieved in the lower world.

125 *MC Phys*. VIII.2.2 version A, anonymous translation: New York MS 67^{a}13–22, Oxford MS 96^{b}1–15; Zeraḥya's translation: 112^{a}20–^{b}7.

126 See pp. 66–7 above.

127 Avicenna and Averroes understood necessity and possibility differently (Belo 2007, 125, 143–5, 151–2, 168–73, 179–184). As Belo notes (ibid. 96), the former neatly pairs necessity with existence and possibility with inexistence; the latter pairs necessity with eternity and possibility with changeability (ibid. 138–9).

128 Compare Kukkonen (2000*a*, 347): 'the theory of potentiality and actuality, of natural possibilities and impossibilities, is an essential tool that cannot conceivably be given up without at the same time destroying all possibility of human rationality'.

129 See p. 78 above.

130 'The notion of corporeal continuity is that its parts meet at common termini.'*MC De anima*, Arabic and English 22.61. On Averroes' distinction between mathematical and physical continuity see Murdoch 1964, 423–5.

6.3.5. The blaming of Al-Fārābī

When he was working out his interpretation B of *Physics* VIII.1, Averroes' strategy was to blame al-Fārābī (instead of Aristotle) for interpretation A, and to ascribe his own new interpretation B to Aristotle. Using this strategy, Averroes 'saved' Aristotle from error and could continue to rely on his authority. This strategy reflects also his reservation regarding the main stream of Islamic philosophy.

[Short commentary version B] This is what al-Fārābī thought in his treatise *On Changeable Beings* [that Aristotle's intention was to establish that before any motion there is a motion and that he adduced the definition of motion], as did others who followed him, such as Avicenna and Ibn Bājja. Philoponus saw this before them and endeavoured to answer Aristotle, because he assumed that a motion is preceded by a motion *essentially*.[131]

He [al-Fārābī] thought that Aristotle deduced from the definition of motion that every motion is preceded by another; but this is false.[132] [Middle commentary version B] This [false] understanding of Aristotle [i.e. interpretation A] started with Philoponus, and [continued with] al-Fārābī and other scholars who lived after al-Fārābī and whose books have come down to us.[133]

[*Questions in Physics*] You ought to know that the method *we have followed* [i.e. interpretation B] in establishing the eternity of motion is the method of Aristotle himself at the beginning of the eighth book, not the method that Philoponus understood to be Aristotle's ([Philoponus' understanding] being identical with the method that al-Fārābī in his book *On Changing Things* understood to be Aristotle's). For this reason, the inquiry [undertaken] in this book [Physics VIII] about establishing [the existence of] an eternal motion was confused.[134]

Al-Fārābī is faulted three more times in the long commentary.[135]

In these texts Averroes' technique seems rather dissonant: he shifts the 'blame' for the straightforward interpretation of the succession argument to al-Fārābī, and presents his own, far from straightforward,

131 *SC Phys.* Arabic 134.7–135.2, Hebrew $40^{b}11$–18.

132 *SC Phys.* Arabic 135.7–8, Hebrew $40^{b}23$–5.

133 *MC Phys.* VIII.2.$294^{a}24$–6. Zeraḥya's translation is not available for version B passages.

134 *Questions in Physics* 18, # 15 (trans. Goldstein).

135 *LC Phys.* VIII.1 Latin only, VIII.4 Latin only, VIII.9 both versions.

interpretation B as revealing the true meaning of Aristotle's text. His intention is, nevertheless, clear: to mark the beginning of the history of determinism with al-Fārābī, rather than with Aristotle. Determinism is not a part and parcel of Aristotelian philosophy but of its interpretation by the Muslim philosophers, which was 'contaminated' by Neoplatonism. This is the message of interpretation B that was so important for Averroes.

6.3.6. The versions of the short and middle commentaries

As mentioned at the beginning of this chapter Averroes repeatedly revised his interpretation of the succession argument. Trying to date various versions we can rely mainly on the differences among them. The precise statement of premise VIII, as well as of the conclusion, turn out to be a good criterion for the sorting and dating of the different versions. I shall summarize here, as briefly as possible, the variants that are found in the short and middle commentaries and turn to the long commentary in section 6.4.

Interpretation A Interpretation A develops through an argument with Philoponus.[136] As we have seen, Aristotle's text can give rise to a strong statement and to a weak statement of premise VIII.[137] Philoponus takes for granted the strong statement,[138] and Averroes, in the A versions of his commentaries, follows Philoponus' words: *strong premise VIII* (intepretation A) 'The capacity for motion must be *temporally prior* to the motion, and the capacity of each part of it [the motion][139] must be *temporally prior* to this part.'[140] His argument more or less follows

[136] See Appendix 4 below. [137] See p. 70 above.

[138] Simplicius, *On Phys.* 1130.12, English: Wildberg 1987*a*, 123. Such understanding is not taken for granted by Themistius (*On Phys.* 210.4–5) or Simplicius himself (*On Phys.* 1127.3–4). Philoponus introduces the term 'capacity' which is not in Aristotle: *to dunamei* (ibid. 1130.30–1131.1, English 124), or *dunamis* (1130.13, 1133.23, English 123, 125). Puig (1999, 232) comments that Philoponus, following the Neoplatonic tradition, conceives of capacity as a force independent of the subject.

[139] The feminine gender attests that 'it' refers to the part of motion, not the part of body.

[140] *SC Phys.* version A, Arabic 131.10–11, Hebrew 41^a22–4. Similarly in the middle commentary: 'The capacity for motion must be temporally prior to the motion and the capacity for *every part of it [the motion] is also prior to every part that is generated from it.*' *MC Phys.* VIII.2.1 version A, anonymous translation 65^b20–22; Zeraḥya's translation 110^a16–18. On the two notion of priority see Puig 1999, 235.

Aristotle's and leads to the *strong conclusion*: '*Whatever* motion was assumed to be newly generated is consequent upon a previous motion of the same kind'.[141]

Interpretation B (middle)[142] Averroes does not argue that before any motion assumed to be (temporally) first there must have been a previous change but, rather, that before the motion of the first celestial sphere, which was shown in VII.1 to be first in nature, there could not have been another change. Since temporal priority is meaningless in the case of infinite motion Averroes assumes natural priority, rather than temporal priority. I shall refer to this as the *intermediate premise*: the capacity for motion is naturally prior to the motion.[143]

The argument is *per impossibile*: The celestial bodies must be either (i) generated or (ii) eternal.[144] The first alternative is ruled out.[145] As for case (ii), Averroes (following Aristotle) shows that the celestial motion could not have started at a certain time.[146] The argument leads to the *weak conclusion* 'The first moved body and the first mover are eternal,'[147] 'there are eternal motions'.[148]

141 *MC Phys*. VIII.2.2 version A, 66^{b}29–30.

142 See also Twetten 1995, 112–14; Puig 1997; 1999, 242.

143 Instead of temporal priority Averroes asserts natural priority. The statement of premise VIII meets the needs of the argument that is restricted to the celestial motions: 'Where there is motion there should be things whose nature is to move; namely, if motion exists the things that are actually moved are prior *in nature* to the motion' (*MC Phys*. VIII.2.1 version B 92^{b}9–11).

144 *MC Phys*. VIII.2.2 version B 92^{b}16–21.

145 'If the celestial bodies were generated, there should have been other prior locally moved things, so that the assumed celestial bodies would be dependent on them. This process would either (i.a) be infinite or (i.b) would be terminated at locally moved eternal bodies, such as the celestial bodies. In case (i.a) the existence of an infinite number of moving and moved bodies which are causes of one another is (i.a.a) impossible essentially and accidentally if they are assumed to be simultaneous; (i.a.b) impossible essentially but possible accidentally if they are not assumed to be simultaneous' (*MC Phys*. VIII.2.2. version B, 92^{b}25–93^{a}11). Possibility (i.b) remains. Averroes presumably relies on al-Fārābī's analysis of possible and impossible successions in ruling out i.a.a and i.a.b.

146 This argument follows Aristotle. If the mover and moved are eternal but the first motion began at a certain time, there must have been a previous change in the mover or the moved body that brought about a change in the relation between the two; hence the motion assumed to be first cannot be first (*MC Phys*. VIII.2.2. version B 93^{a}17–^{b}1).

147 *MC Phys*. VIII.2.2. version A, 67^{a}20–21.

148 *MC Phys*. VIII.2.2. version B, 94^{a}21–3.

Interpretation B (short) B (short) seems to be a generalized and improved version of B (middle). Averroes assumes 'a first motion prior to all motions *either in time or in nature*'. Thus posited, the first motion can be either (i) in a generated moved body or (ii) in an eternal one.[149] The first alternative is ruled out.[150] The assumed first motion must, therefore, be in an eternal body.[151] At this point the argument is reduced to the case of infinite-type motion and leads to the weak conclusion: 'The first motion has never ceased and will never cease.'[152] Most important about interpretation B (short) is the *weak premise*: 'Motion can exist only *in* a moved thing.'[153] I shall refer to this weak statement of the premise as the *axiom of Inherence*.[154] We shall see that this is the last step in the evolution of Averroes' interpretation of *Physics* VIII.1.

One advantage of interpretation B (short) is that the strong statement of the premise does not follow from the definition of motion but the weak statement does. In the *Questions in Physics* Averroes makes this point: 'Aristotle presented the definition of motion only to establish that every motion is *in* the moved body.'[155] This version of the premise is not about temporal priority but about inherence. Averroes retreats

[149] *SC Phys.* Arabic 130.6–131.1, Hebrew 39^{b}15–23.

[150] Assumed to be in a generated body, the first motion cannot be first *either in nature or in time*, because (i.1) a first motion cannot be a property of a generated body and (i.2) if the first moved bodies were newly generated there should have been a motion prior to them *either in time or in nature* (*SC Phys.* Arabic 131.1–4, Hebrew 39^{b}23–8). The beginning of the first sentence (six words) is missing in the Arabic.

[151] *SC Phys.* Arabic 131.6–132.12, Hebrew 39^{b}30–40^{a}16. The first sentence of the answer is corrupt and there is a difference between the Arabic (132.2) and the Hebrew (40^{a}5–6).

[152] *SC Phys.* Arabic 132.16–17, Hebrew 40^{a}16–18. The weak conclusion is stated also in the *Questions in Physics* VII 18, # 13 Vatican MS 104^{b}28–9. The text is not good and there are differences between manuscripts.

[153] *SC Phys.* Arabic 129.7, Hebrew 39^{b}8–9. In the middle commentary on VI.4, Averroes refers to motion as being *in* something—תנועה בדבר מה (*MC Phys.* 75^{a}10, 17, 23), where Aristotle talks of motion *of* something—*kinesis tinos* (*Physics* 234^{b}27–33). Ibn Bājja comments that the capacity that precedes the motion is either said of an object or not (Ziyada 154.3–6, Lettinck 1994*a*, 595).

[154] Alexander uses a similar statement in order to distinguish time from motion: 'movement is in the moving thing and in the place in which it moves whereas time is neither in the moving thing nor in the place in which it moves', *On Time* 60.

[155] *Questions in Physics* 19, # 18, I have modified Goldstein's translation slightly in the interests of uniformity.

to the narrow ontology of *Physics* V.2: motion is not an independent entity, in some sense it exists in the moved body. Chapter 8 below will further elucidate the meaning of turning point of book VIII and its relation to the turning point of book VI.

APPENDIX 4: AVERROES' ARGUMENT WITH PHILOPONUS

The defence of Aristotle's succession argument against Philoponus' criticism stands at the centre of Averroes' early interpretation of *Physics* VIII.1. It occupies a major part of the A versions of all three commentaries. Philoponus' criticism focuses on premise VIII on which Aristotle's argument depends.[156] He proceeds from a strong statement of the premise—the capacity for motion is temporally prior to the motion—which is more susceptible to criticism than Aristotle's rather ambiguous statement and easier to disapprove of. This premise, he argues, conflicts with the conception of natural motion as the 'immediate accompaniment' (*euthus sunepomenēn*) of body: 'Some generable things are no sooner generated than moved with [their] natural motion . . . Fire, assuming that it is generated in the lower region, at the same time both becomes fire and, *concurrently with its essence, possesses upward locomotion*.'[157] Here, with Philoponus' criticism, actually starts a long discussion on the status of the boundary points of the motion interval, which was a major issue in Averroes' physics. According to Aristotle a part of fire starts its upward motion as soon as it is generated. The question is about the beginning point, namely the generation. For Philoponus the generation and the upward motion of a part of fire are two distinct processes: the capacity for the generation of fire is in the wood, the capacity for its upward motion is in the fire.

It was not the wood that possesses the capacity of spatial movement upwards. For the change of wood into fire is generation. Therefore, if locomotion upwards is motion and not generation, [while] the change of wood into fire is generation and not motion—even though there is no generation without motion—then the upward locomotion of fire was not the actuality of the wood's capacity. For things moving within each species of motion move in such a way that they remain the same substance and are not destroyed, but the wood does not remain wood when it moves upwards . . . From this [it follows] that it is not true that the capacity for motion pre-exists the motion, which was the basis for the proof of the eternity of motion. For wood pre-exists the upward movement of

[156] See p. 70 above.

[157] Simplicius, *On Phys.* 1133, 24–7, English: Wildberg 1987*a*, 125. See Puig 1999, 233. The relevant contexts in Aristotle are *Physics* II.1, *De caelo* I.2, III.2.

the fire because it also pre-exists the fire which is generated out of it. But fire is no sooner fire than [it is] on the move upwards.[158]

According to Philoponus the motion starts *after* a part of fire is generated from wood.[159] According to Averroes the motion of a part of fire starts *together* with its generation from wood. Averroes adopts the solution rejected by Philoponus[160] and suggested by al-Fārābī and Ibn Bājja;[161] namely, that the capacity for the motion of fire is in the wood or oil.[162]

[Short commentary version A] the capacity prior to such motion [the upward motion of fire] is necessarily in the wood or in other [bodies] that can become fire. Generally speaking, where there is a capacity for the existence of fire, there is [also] a capacity for its motion. This [concomitance] follows a certain order, namely, it has the capacity for motion through having the capacity for being fire.[163]

[Middle commentary version A] And of the things that started their motion at the time that generation started, it is also clear that the capacity that is prior to the motion, as well

[158] Simplicius, *On Phys.* 1133.31–1134.14, English Wildberg 1987*a*, 125–6 (trans. Wildberg with slight changes).

[159] Ibn Bājja raises a similar question about the beginning of motion after rest (*On Phys.* 160.13–14; Lettinck 1994*a*, 598). In this context Averroes distinguishes two types of beginnings: the beginning of motion when the body is generated, e.g. when wood or oil turns into fire, and the resumption of motion after a pause, e.g. the motion of a living creature after being at rest *SC Phys.* Arabic 131.11–132.15; Hebrew $41^{a}24$–$^{b}1$; *MC Phys.* VIII.2.1 version A, New York MS $65^{b}20$–26; Zeraḥya's translation $110^{a}10$–111.5. *LC Phys.* VIII.4 Latin 340L8–M3, 341A2–11, Hebrew $138^{b}3$–6, 10–14. I shall quote the middle commentary: 'The capacity for motion must be *temporally prior* to the motion and the capacity for every part of it [the motion] is also prior to every part that is generated from it. This is because those things that move naturally are of two kinds: either [*a*] they move after rest, as in the case of the local motion of an animal after rest, and many of the changing things after not changing, or [*b*] things that start their local motion as soon as they start their generation, and when their generation is completed their local motion would also be completed, unless [their motion] is impeded by some impediment.'

[160] Philoponus' argument was known to the Arabic philosophers and they responded to it (Puig 1999*a*, 151). On the argument between Philoponus and Simplicius see Puig 1999, 232–234, 1999a, 146–150. It seems that Averroes was not acquainted with Simplicius' side, but he was acquainted with Philoponus' (Puig 1999*a*, 158).

[161] Ibn Bājja notes that the capacity for the upward motion is already in the heavy object from which the light object is generated, namely the oil (*On Phys.* 172.10–13; Lettinck 1994*a*, 602). He ascribes this point to al-Fārābī's *On Changeable Beings*.

[162] In the middle commentary, Averroes 'shifts' from the wood example to the oil example. In the long commentary he mentions 'either the burning wood or the flaming oil' (*LC Phys.* VIII.4, Latin 341A10–11, Hebrew $138^{b}13$–14). The former originated in Philoponus, the latter probably in al-Fārābī's lost treatise *On Changeable Beings*. Oil is mentioned several times by Ibn Bājja in close association with al-Fārābī's treatise (Lettinck 1994*a*, 602, 606, 608, 614).

[163] *SC Phys.* Arabic 130.16–132.15–17, Hebrew $41^{b}1$–6.

as the capacity for each of their parts, is indeed in the matter in which the capacity for the form of the generated thing is.[164]

[Long commentary] And the capacity for this motion is not in the subject, which is the fire *in actu*, but in the subject from which fire is generated, such as the burning wood or the flaming oil.[165]

For Averroes the coexistence of body and motion starts with the beginning point, the generation. In the middle and long commentaries he carries the idea of coexistence a step further: body and its motion not only start together but also end together: the fulfilment of the two capacities is simultaneous:

The perfection of motion [i.e. the natural place] is achieved together with the perfection of the form.[166]

Every part of the form that acquires perfection reaches also a part of the [natural] place, unless impeded by some impediment, just as the parts of all other accidents that are consequent upon the form are achieved. For example, when the oil is turned into fire, each part of it that achieves 'fireness' also achieves a part of the [natural] place.[167]

In Averroes' scheme the natural motion of a part of fire includes its generation from wood, its upward motion and its coming to rest at its natural place. His answer to Philoponus—that the capacity for the motion of fire is in the wood—looks somewhat strained. It seems that he thought up this solution in order to brush off Philoponus' criticism and to defend Aristotle's argument (interpretation A).[168] Yet this solution became the beginning of a lifelong interest in the question of the boundaries of the motion interval. Should the beginning of a motion interval or its end be considered to be a part of the motion? Averroes deals with this question in the early A versions of his commentaries, but it became even more important for him later, after he abandoned interpretation A. We shall see in the next chapter how important was the subject of boundary entities in the formation of Averroes' new physics. This may well be the reason why (luckily for us) he did not discard the A versions of the short and middle commentaries on *Physics* VIII.1 after he wrote the B versions.

[164] *MC Phys.* VIII.2.1 version A, anonymous translation 66^a1-3, Zeraḥya's translation 110^b3-9.

[165] *LC Phys.* VIII.4 Latin 341A7–11, Hebrew 138^b12-14.

[166] *MC Phys.* VIII.2.1 version A, anonymous translation 65^b25-6, Zeraḥya's translation 110^b1-3. The argument is repeated twice.

[167] *MC Phys.* VIII.2.1 version A, anonymous translation 66^a3-6, Zeraḥya's translation 110^b9-12. Similarly in the long commentary: *LC Phys.* VIII.4 Latin 341A2–7, Hebrew 138^b10-12, see also 168^b22-3.

[168] The capacities for the form of fire and for its motion are both temporally prior to the form and motion themselves, because they are already present in the wood.

6.4. THE RIDDLE OF THE LONG COMMENTARY

The story of the middle commentary seems rather simple: The fact that the turning point passage is part of version A implies that turning point occurred when Averroes was writing the middle commentary, that is, about 1170. Version B, which was written later, is a revised version of the argument. Let me turn now to the long commentary which tells an altogether different story. In the long commentary the succession argument is covered by the first nine texts and comments. Some of these comments include added and rewritten passages that appear only in the Latin translation. I shall refer to the main text that appears in both translations and which probably reflects the original writing of the long commentary as *stratum A,* and to the added and rewritten passages as *stratum B.*

The long commentary on *Physics* VIII with its two strata is an enigmatic text. *The first riddle* concerns stratum A: the problem is noted right at the beginning. In comments VIII.1–5 Averroes follows the old interpretation A as if the turning point had not occurred earlier. The turning point 'occurs' again in comment VIII.9. The attentive reader who has read the middle commentary carefully knows that the turning point was a major event in Averroes' intellectual biography and a major step in his indeterministic campaign. This event is assertively announced already in version A of the middle commentary, which is dated some fifteen years or so before the long commentary. How is it possible that Averroes ignores in the long commentary what he achieved in the middle commentary and was undoubtedly very important for him? *The second riddle* concerns stratum B: in this parallel text Averroes, by contrast, strongly advocates the new understanding that he had achieved in the middle commentary (interpretation B). Stratum B, thus, explicitly and expressly conflicts with stratum A. The two riddles are connected and both lead to the inevitable question of when the turning point really occurred.

Stratum A of the long commentary and version A of the middle commentary proceed along parallel lines. Both begin with a conventional interpretation of Aristotle's text and culminate in the turning point. The impression given is that in the long commentary Averroes is working out the turning point all over again. We shall see that also in books VI and VII the turning point is 'announced' in both the middle and long commentaries. When did these turning-points actually 'occur'? Which is the 'real-time report', that of the middle commentary or that of the long? There are two possible accounts which will be examined in this and the following chapters:

Account I: The turning point occurred when Averroes was writing the middle commentary.

Account II: The turning point occurred when Averroes was writing the long commentary or the turning point was a process that consolidated while he was writing the long commentary.

Deciding between these two accounts is crucial to the understanding of Averroes' intellectual biography: In what period in his life did he develop his 'new physics'? Was it before or after his public debates with the mutakallimūn around 1180?[169]

Averroes' middle commentaries are often referred to as paraphrases, though this conception has been challenged recently.[170] The middle commentary on the *Physics*, as it came down to us, definitely does not fit this description. It is a 'revolutionary text' that announces and presents three significant 'turning-points'. Did these indeed occur while Averroes was writing the middle commentary? If so, the period around 1170 (when Averroes was employed by the Caliph Abu Yaᶜqūb and served as a qādi in Seville) was a very significant period in the development of his ideas. If Account II is correct, though, the development of Averroes' ideas may have been a more gradual process, based on more sources and greater knowledge. Furthermore, it may have been a response to the arguments with al-Ghazālī and the theologians, which deeply engaged Averroes' mind.

In the next four sections I shall deal with the two riddles. I shall first adduce the textual evidence and then consider the pros and cons.

6.4.1. The first riddle: evidence

Comment VIII.1

From the very first sentences of the eighth book it becomes clear that this is a pre-turning point text. The long commentary on book VIII opens with the main question whether motion *in genus*—that is, finite-type,

[169] Harvey 1997, 105. [170] See p. 11, n. 10 above.

sublunar motion[171]—has always been.[172] This issue is debated in the two versions of the short commentary using the same term *in genus* (بالجنس).[173] In version A of the short commentary the argument leads to the strong conclusion: 'Motion is never absent *in genus*, neither in the past nor in the future';[174] in version B the argument leads to the weak conclusion: 'The first motion [i.e. of the outermost sphere] has never ceased and will never cease.' In version B of the short commentary Averroes explicitly denies what he himself said in version A: 'This is how Aristotle's statement at the beginning of this book should be interpreted, and not, as people thought, that he intended only[175] to establish that motion *in genus* is never absent, because what he says pertains to the whole world whereas the motion that is not absent in genus is in a part of the world.'[176]

Contrary to the reader's expectations, in the long commentary Averroes follows version A of the short commentary which was written about three decades earlier, ignoring the turning point passage which is a part of version A of the middle commentary, which was written some fifteen years or so years earlier:

Since his first intention <and the goal of this book> is to inquire about the first mover, he started to inquire whether motion is generated in time or [whether it is] eternal, *in genus* . . . Saying, 'Did motion come into being at some time without having existed before?'[177] he does not ask about a particular motion, but rather asks whether *the motions that are in the parts of the world* were generated after [a period] when the part of the world was not in motion

[171] 'And the motion that is not absent *in genus* is in a part of the world' (*SC Phys.* Arabic 133.5–134.3; Hebrew 40a24–31). 'It should be examined here what he intended in this book, whether he intended that there always was motion *in genus* or he intended that there is eternal motion, one in species'(*LC Phys.* VIII.9 Latin 345C11–345D1, Hebrew 142b10–12). This use may go back to Alexander who distinguished between eternity in number of the celestial and in species (في النوع) of the sublunar (*On the Principles* 73, # 58, 85, # 80). The terms 'in species' and 'in genus' are sometimes confused.

[172] *LC Phys.* VIII.1 Latin 338F6–10, Hebrew 136a20–22.

[173] The expression 'motion in genus' appears six times in version A of the short commentary: Arabic 129.8, 129.11, 129.12, 130.12, 130.13, 135.19–20; Hebrew 41a1, 41a5, 7, 11, 12, 42a3.

[174] *SC Phys.* Arabic 135.19–20, Hebrew 42a3–4.

[175] The word *innamā* can be translated as 'rather' or as 'only'. Ibn Tibbon translates it to Hebrew as *omnam* (which adds nothing to the meaning), Puig translates it to Spanish as *solamente*.

[176] *SC Phys.* Arabic 133.5–8, Hebrew 40a24–8.

[177] *Physics* VIII.1, 250b11.

at all, and whether they [the motions] will all perish so that no part of the world moves at all, or whether these *motions in the parts of the world* have not deviated from their present pattern and will not deviate in the future. This inquiry is necessary because it is clear that there are only two alternatives in the world: *either many successive motions or one continuous motion*, which is the motion of the celestial body. Concerning these two perceptible types of motion we should ask whether it is possible for them to start after one of them was absent, [whether] one of them started before the other, or [whether] they started together (namely, motions that are perceived as *continuous* and those that are perceived as *contiguous)*, and whether these two types [of motion] may perish until nothing moving is left at all.[178]

In comment VIII.1 of the long commentary Averroes follows version A of the short commentary and seems unaware of version B and of the turning point that he himself had announced in version A of the middle commentary.[179]

Comment VIII.4

Comment VIII.4 is very conspicuously a pre-turning point text. It deals with the crucial passage *Physics* VIII.1251^{a}8–17, in which Aristotle derives premise VIII from the definition of motion. This is precisely the issue on which Averroes changed his mind. Correcting the statement of the premise is the most notable outcome of the turning point. According to interpretation A premise VIII claims that the capacity for motion has temporal priority to the motion itself; according to all the variants of interpretation B, it does not. It is thus very surprising that in the long commentary Averroes still, without the slightest hesitation, understands premise VIII in terms of temporal priority, as in interpretation A:

The moved things must be prior to the motion for each kind of motion. Just as the moved things are prior to the motion, so is the capacity prior to the motion. It should be understood that the moved thing is *temporally prior* to the motion in one of two ways . . .[180]

The capacity for motion is *temporally prior* to the motion.[181]

178 *LC Phys*. VIII.1 Latin 338F6–H9, Hebrew 136^{a}20–^{b}4.

179 This is also the case in comment VIII.5. *LC Phys*. VIII.5 Latin 341M1–13, Hebrew 139^{b}2–7. The two versions differ somewhat.

180 *LC Phys*. VIII.4 Latin 340L3–8, Hebrew 138^{b}1–2; see also Latin 340K3–8, Hebrew 138^{a}25–7.

181 *LC Phys*. VIII.4 Latin 341G1–2, Hebrew 139^{a}15.

Comment VIII.9: the turning point

Stratum A of the long commentary starts as a pre–turning point text and gradually leads to a turning point passage in comment VIII.9.[182] I shall offer a summary of the turning point passage of comment VIII.9 as compared to that of the middle commentary.

[LA1] An apology for having followed interpretation A up to this point.[183]

[LA2] The main question: 'Did he mean that [*a*] motion *in genus* has always been,[184] or did he mean [*b*] that there is an infinite motion, one *in species*.'[185] This question was first raised in comment VIII.1, the answer there was [*a*].

[LA3] Al-Fārābī's question: which types of infinite succession are possible and which are not.[186]

[LA4, compare MA4] The linking question and the turning point. The linking question is the onset of the turning point.[187] The announcement of the turning point is similar to that found in the turning point passage of the middle commentary: '*After an intensive inquiry it seems to me that what is argued here implies the existence of one continuous motion.*'[188] The answer to the main question is now [b].

[182] The text is *Physics* $251^{b}5$–9, which concludes, 'therefore there will be change previous to the first change.'

[183] 'The fact that this demonstration, which he [Aristotle] advanced here, pertains to any mover, whether a rational force [i.e., a separate intellect] or a non-rational one [i.e. a body], is what compelled us <<at first>> to interpret [this demonstration] the way we did.' *LC Phys*. VIII.9 Latin 345C6–11, Hebrew $142^{b}9$–10.

[184] Following the Latin. The Hebrew is confused.

[185] *LC Phys*. VIII.9 Latin 345C11–D1, Hebrew $142^{b}10$–12. The question was first raised in comment VIII.1.

[186] 'In this there is a certain difficulty: if he intended that motion not be absent *in genus* at a certain time, it can be thought that it is impossible for it to be continuous *in genus*, no matter how it [the motion] was assumed to be. These are, however, impossible and possible assumptions. And what follows necessarily from the premises he assumed—namely, that capacity is *temporally prior* to the actuality—is possible. Therefore what he [i.e., the person who raised the difficulty] intended is contradictory (*diminutum*, סותר)' (*LC Phys*. VIII.9 Latin 345C11–345E6, Hebrew $142^{b}10$–20).

[187] p. 76 above.

[188] *LC Phys*. VIII.9 Latin 345I4–7, Hebrew $143^{a}8$–9.

[LA6, compare MA5] Interpretation B. The interpretation is similar to that of version B of the middle commentary.[189]

After comment VIII.9, interpretation B ideas appear several more times in the main body of the long commentary on book VIII:

It has already been explained in the seventh [book] that there is a first mover in which all local motions terminate . . . and when we combine that with what was explained in this book, that before and after every motion there is a motion, it follows that this first moved body is eternal and its motion is eternal.[190]

The contiguous [things] are not eternal by essence, but only by accident. Hence there must be one motion that is eternal by essence: this is the motion that is local continuous motion, which is truly one, since eternal continuity should be first in that which is always continuous, and when it is in that which is not continuous it is consequent upon its being in the continuous. This is because the accidental cannot be always unless its cause is eternal by essence.[191]

6.4.2. The first riddle: discussion

Summa VIII.2 of the middle commentary (version A) and comments VIII.1–9 of the long commentary (stratum A) describe two parallel routes that lead to 'turning point passages'. Which of the two is the real-time report? Above, I have stated two possible accounts. According to Account I, the turning point occurred when it is first mentioned, namely, when Averroes was writing the middle commentary (version A), about 1170. According to Account II, the turning point occurred when Averroes was writing the long commentary or, alternatively, it was a process that consolidated while he was writing the long commentary, probably in the 1180s.[192] Stratum A, from comment VIII.1 to VIII.9, reflects the 'real-time' process that culminated in the turning point.

[189] 'And because it is established that there is a change that is first *in nature* and that it is impossible for there to be a change that is first in time, it necessarily follows that there is one continuous motion, on account of which every change is preceded by another.' *LC Phys*. VIII.9 Latin 345L3–M2, Hebrew 143ª17–21.

[190] *LC Phys*. VIII.21 Latin 356H10–I7, Hebrew 154ª1–5.

[191] *LC Phys*. VIII.49, Hebrew only 189b20–25.

[192] On the order of the writing of the middle and long commentaries see Ch. 2 above.

Argument for account I

- We know that the middle commentary was written before the long,[193] so this is the simple straightforward account. No additional assumptions about revising the middle commentary are necessary.

Objection to account I

- Account I obliges us to assume that Averroes started to write the long commentary before he completed the middle commentary. This assumption expressly conflicts with Averroes' own testimony that the long commentary on the *Physics* was written after the middle.[194]

Arguments for account II

- The first riddle is solved.
- The presentation of the long commentary is more 'historical' and illustrates the course of Averroes' thought better than the briefer and more formal presentation of the middle commentary does.[195] For instance, in the long commentary the linking question is raised twice,[196] most probably as a response to al-Fārābī's question. In the middle commentary, the turning point passage opens, rather abruptly, with the linking question.

Objections to account II

- Account II obliges us to assume that (i) version B of the short commentary, (ii) version B of the middle commentary, and also (iii) parts of version A of the middle commentary[197] were written contemporarily with or after the long commentary.

[193] See Ch. 2 above. [194] See Ch. 2 above. [195] See Section 6.4.1 above.

[196] The question comes up in comment VIII.6 (Latin 342E7–F4, G3–13; Hebrew 139b21–6, 29–140a3). The approach is horizontal. Averroes raises the question again in VIII.9: '<Then he took> another question: in what manner any motion is preceded by another motion' (Latin 345F7–9; Hebrew 142b25–6, the two translations differ). This time he turns to the vertical solution. (Latin 345F7–I4, Hebrew 142b25–143a8.

[197] Paragraphs MA4 and MA5 of the turning point passage which concludes chapter VIII.2.2, and the concluding paragraph of chapter VIII.2.4, which relies on the turning point passage.

Are these assumptions plausible? The first two assumption are not only plausible but almost certainly true. Puig argues that version B of the short commentary is later than the long commentary and in what follows we shall see several more instances of evidently late passages in the short commentary and of associations between the short commentary and the long. Version B of the middle commentary, like version B of the short commentary, seems to be a late revision.

The third assumption is more difficult. A plausible explanation is that the turning point passage, that is, the concluding paragraphs of version A (MA4 and MA5) actually belongs to version B. Paragraphs MA4–MA5 do not naturally continue paragraphs MA1–MA3, but version B seems to continue the turning point passage. Version B seems to take up the argument exactly where version A left off.[198] The argument of MB2 follows MA5 quite smoothly and there is no break between the two versions. The break is between paragraphs MA3 and MA4. In MA3 Averroes offers the pre-turning point interpretation A, in MA5 the post-turning point interpretation B;[199] in MA4 he mentions a period of hesitation: '*After an intensive inquiry and a long time* it seems to me . . .'[200] This strongly suggests that chapter VIII.2.2 of version A was not written in a single session, and that paragraphs MA4–MA5 are indeed later than MA1–MA3. We have seen that end-of-comment additions are common in the long commentary.[201] The suspect passages in both VIII.2.2 and VIII.2.4 appear precisely at such junctures. It is not unlikely that a copyist copied at the ends of the chapters some glosses that were written in the margin.

So far II seems to be the more plausible of the two accounts. It depends, however, on the assumption that the middle commentary was revised. I shall adduce some more evidence that it indeed was.

198 Version A concludes: 'And when one takes into account what has been said in the seventh book, namely that the things that are in local motion terminate at that which is moved by itself, in which there is an unmoved mover, then it will become clear that this mover is eternally moving and that which is moved by it is eternally moved' (note 125 above). The argument of version B opens by restricting the discussion to 'these bodies [whose motion] is prior to all other motions, and that at them all other motions terminate, namely the celestial bodies and particularly the outermost sphere' (*MC Phys.* VIII.2.1, 92^{b}17–20.).

199 See outline, pp. 74–75 above.

200 'Long time' appears only in Zeraḥya's translation.

201 See pp. 33 and 30–35.

- We have seen that Kalonimus' translation is based on a text later than Zeraḥya's,[202] and the Arabic outline is even more updated than the outline in Kalonimus' translation.[203]
- Chapter III.3.3. In *Physics* III.4 Aristotle lists four senses of 'infinite'.[204] The Greek commentators list five.[205] Averroes lists two in the short commentary,[206] four in the middle commentary (Zeraḥya's translation),[207] and five in the long commentary.[208] The middle commentary in the version translated by Kalonimus seems to be an incomplete or interrupted text of the version translated by Zeraḥya.[209] The correction, presumably, follows a new source, perhaps Philoponus or Alexander.[210] The original argument in the middle commentary may have relied on Themistius or Ibn Bājja.[211]
- Chapter VI.4 of the middle commentary was most likely revised and chapter VII.1 was certainly revised. These chapters will be studied in Chapters 7 and 8 below.

Conceding that paragraphs MA4–5 belong to version B of the middle commentary, rather than to version A, all problems are solved. This

[202] p. 30 above.

[203] In Kalonimus' translation we find version B and the outline of version A, listing five points. In the Arabic BL manuscript we find the outline of version B that lists six points. See al-Masumi 1956, 79–80; Harvey 1982, 573.

[204] *Physics* III.4, 204^{a}1–7.

[205] Both Philoponus (*On Phys.* 409–13) and Simplicius (*On Phys.* 469–71) list five meanings.

[206] *SC Phys.* Arabic 35.10–15, Hebrew 10^{a}23–7.

[207] *MC Phys.* Zeraḥya's translation III.3, 333^{a}18–19.

[208] *LC Phys.* III.34, Latin 100F4–I5, Hebrew 111^{b}3–29.

[209] Averroes announces that there are five meanings but lists the same four that he listed in the early version, counting the last as fifth (so that the fourth is missing) (*MC Phys.* Kalonimus' translation III.3, 327^{a}4). This is so in all the Hebrew manuscript that I compared, as well as in Mantino's Hebrew–Latin translation.

[210] Averroes was not acquainted with Simplicius' commentary. It is likely, however, that Simplicius followed Alexander in his five-meanings interpretation.

[211] Two examples that are mentioned in the middle commentary are not taken from Aristotle. The example of the point that illustrates the first meaning appears in both versions of the middle commentary and in the long commentary (*MC Phys.* Zeraḥya 33^{a}20, Kalonimus 27^{a}5, *LC Phys.* Hebrew 11^{b}9). We find this example in Themistius (*On Phys.* 82.32), Simplicius (*On Phys.* 469.32–470.2), and Philoponus (*On Phys.* 409.21–4). The example of the sea that illustrates the third meaning appears in both versions of the middle commentary (*MC Phys.* Zeraḥya 33^{b}1–3, Kalonimus 27^{a}8–10). This example is also found in Themistius (*On Phys.* 83.4–5) and Philoponus (*On Phys.* 410.6). Both examples are mentioned by Ibn Bājja, but he lists only three senses and associates the point with the second and the sea with the third (Lettinck 1994*a*, 249).

'solution' is not unlikely because there is reasonable independent evidence that the middle commentary was indeed revised.[212] The detailed study of stratum B of the long commentary on VIII.1 as well as of chapters VI.4 and VII.1 of the *Physics* in the following chapters will throw more light on the revision of the middle commentary and on the plausibility of Account II.

6.4.3. The second riddle: evidence

In the previous section I dealt with the first riddle: in stratum A of the long commentary Averroes sticks to the early interpretation A that he has already dismissed in version A of the middle commentary. Now let me address the second riddle: stratum B of the long commentary is a very strong, uncompromising presentation of interpretation B and thus explicitly and expressly conflicts with stratum A.

Stratum B consists of three added passages, all of them beginning with the word *dico* (I say)—found at the end of comments VIII.1, 4, and 5, in the Latin redaction only[213]—and of the rewritten version of comment VIII.7, again only in Latin. Together these texts form a parallel text that covers Aristotle's argument in which we are interested (*Physics* VIII.1251^{a}8–28). Apparently the three *dico* passages are not part of the original text.[214] They do not have the typical structure of comments in the long commentary and seem to form an independent interpretation. All three *dico* passages open with the words *hec expositio* ('this exposition'), apparently referring to the stratum A text that preceded the passage. In VIII.1 and VIII.4 Averroes expressly rejects 'this exposition', namely what he himself wrote in these two comments. It is only in comment VIII.9 that interpretation B first merges with the main text. Let us look at the stratum B parallel text.

[212] More evidence may turn up when a critical edition is prepared.

[213] I am very grateful to Horst Schmieja who confirmed that the three *dico* passages appear in all the Latin manuscripts that he examined.

[214] In comments VIII.1 and VIII.5 the *dico* passages interrupt the original connection between the comment and the following text. The common part of comment 1 ends with the statement that the opinion discussed 'can be viewed in two ways, each of which was upheld by one of the ancients, and he said:' (LC Phys. VIII.1 Latin 339A3–5, Hebrew 137^{a}9–10). This sentence leads directly to the discussion of the views of Empedocles and Anaxagoras in texts 2 and 3. The common part of comment VIII.1 ends '& d. Si igitur', text VIII.2 opens 'Si igitur . . .'. Similarly, the common part of comment VIII.5 ends 'incoepit declaratre ipsum' (341M12–13), which leads directly to comment VIII.6. In both cases the Hebrew text flows directly, while the Latin is interrupted by *dico* passages.

Comment VIII.1

Whereas in stratum A Averroes follows Interpretation A, in stratum B he unequivocally and assertively supports Interpretation B, rejecting what he himself wrote in the main part of this comment. This opening passage of stratum B can be considered to be a third turning point passage; in fact, it follows a similar pattern.[215]

I say that this exposition (*hec expositio*), as I said, is what is understood at first sight, and so understood al-Fārābī, as he said in his book *On Changeable Beings*, and so understood Avicenna and Ibn Bājja the Spaniard, namely, that Aristotle's intention in his first chapter[216] is to establish that before any motion there is a motion and before any change there is a change and that motion *will never be absent in genus* [339B]—in order to proceed from here to establish that motion is primary, eternal, and all-encompassing, either one or many. And there is a difficulty in this statement (*declaratione*). For this reason al-Fārābī, in his treatise *On Changeable Beings*, intended to complete the statement (*sermone*) by inquiring into how many ways one can imagine that before every change there is a change, and what may be true about it and what may not; therefore his inquiry is included here. As for myself, I was somewhat mistaken in what I believed to be the explanation here [339C] namely, that Aristotle's statement is a contradictory statement (declaratio diminuta). I continued to study this statement until I discovered the sense of his inquiry. I found statements (*sermones*) of his that agree with this intention of his, rather than with the first explanation [interpretation A] as it was conceived first.

Here Aristotle intended to inquire whether [*a*] the first motion that encompasses the world—or the first motions, if there were more than one—were newly generated, in such a way that there had been no motion at all before them, so that motion would consequently be new [339D] *in genus* and everything would start to be moved after nothing had been moved; or whether [*b*] the first motion that encompasses all and exists in the first moved body—or in the first moved bodies, if there were more than one motion—may be eternal, having never ceased nor will it ever cease. . . .[217] And he derived this statement from[218] the definition of motion in order to show that there is a moved body. He did not bring up the definition of motion in order to show that any motion is preceded by another motion, as al-Fārābī and [339E] others believed. For the inquiry he intended here is universal [and applies to] the whole world.

215 *LC Phys*. VIII.1 Latin only 339A5–F7.

216 The word used is *tractatus*, but it should be *capitulum* as in comment VIII.4. The reference is clearly to the first chapter of book VIII.

217 The last part of the sentence is not clear.

218 Here I render *de* as 'from', though it is usually used in the Latin translation in the sense of 'about', because this is the only way to make sense of the sentence.

Nor is it true that, in Aristotle's opinion, there must be a motion before the all-encompassing motion or a change before the change, which is the first change.

The passage concludes with the charge against al-Fārābī and his followers, a theme that appears in all B versions of VIII.1.

Comment VIII.4

The second of the three *dico* passages is appended to the Latin redaction of comment VIII.4, which deals with premise VIII. Averroes again refers to stratum A of the same comment as 'this exposition' and to the presentation of stratum B as 'our exposition'.

I say that al-Fārābī and others understood this chapter in line with *this exposition*, namely, that he [Aristotle] introduced the definition of motion in order to establish that the capacity is before the act . . . but according to *our exposition*, he introduces the definition of motion in order to establish that *motion is in the moved body*, since, according to his definition, it is the perfection (*entelecheia*) of the moved body and must be *in the moved body*. Every perfection (*perfectio*) must necessarily be *in* the thing that is being perfected. And indeed in this matter we find that Alexander, in his book *On the Principles*, introduced the definition of motion in order to establish that motion is eternal.[219]

In stratum A of this comment, Averroes quoted the strong statement of premise VIII. In stratum B he expressly denies the strong statement and subscribes to the weak:

He derived this statement from the definition of motion in order to show that there is a moved body. He did not bring up the definition of motion in order to show that any motion is preceded by another motion, as al-Fārābī and others believed.[220]

According to our exposition, he introduces the definition of motion in order to establish that motion is *in* the moved body.[221]

[219] *LC Phys*. VIII.4 Latin only 341I9–K13. The ascription of the erroneous interpretation to Alexander, instead of al Fārābī, may be a slip of the pen, going back to Averroes himself. I am very much indebted to Dr Horst Schmieja, who examined all the available Latin manuscripts. He found three manuscripts in which 'de principijs' was missing and two which read 'de principio'. None of the Latin manuscripts read 'al-Fārābī' instead of 'Alexander'. I have not found this statement in Alexander's *On the Principles*. On the contrary, Alexander, like Averroes, argues: 'The first mover is the principle and the cause of this eternal motion belonging to these things, I mean that the eternity of the first mover and of the first object moved is the cause of the eternity of the whole world as well' (Alexander, *On the Principles*, 70–71 # 52).

[220] *LC Phys*. VIII.1 Latin only 339D9–E1. Quoted in section 4.3 comment VIII.1.

[221] *LC Phys*. VIII.4 Latin only 341K3–6. Quoted in section 4.3 comment VIII.4.

Comment VIII.5

In text VIII.5, Aristotle presents two alternatives: that the assumed first motion is (i) in generated bodies or (ii) in eternal bodies. The third *dico* passage is appended to the Latin translation of comment VIII.5. Here Averroes does not object to what is said in stratum A: 'I say that this is a true exposition'.[222]

Comment VIII.7

In comments VIII.6 and VIII.7 Averroes deals with alternatives (i) and (ii), which were presented in text VIII.5. The differences between the Hebrew and Latin translations of VIII.6 are relatively minor, whereas the two versions of VIII.7 are altogether different. Comment VIII.6 followed by the Hebrew VIII.7 is a stratum A text. The Latin comment VIII.7 is a stratum B text and replaces the old VIII.6 and VIII.7. It is closer to B (short) than to B (middle).[223]

Comment VII.1

Interpretation B appears in book VII of the long commentary, too—again only in the Latin. It seems to belong to the same revision as stratum B of book VIII. The context is Themistius' contention that the argument of VII.1 is redundant. The answer preserved in the Hebrew translation does not rely on interpretation B; the one preserved in the Latin does:

> Here [in VII.1] he intended to establish the existence of a first mover. At the beginning of the eighth [book] he assumes that there are a first mover and a first moved body and asks whether this motion is eternal or newly generated. Therefore those who contend that this argument [of VII.1] is superfluous and that the argument of the eighth [book] is sufficient, like Themistius, are wrong.[224]

222 *LC Phys.* VIII.5 Latin 341M14–15.

223 Relying on the seventh and fifth books Averroes proceeds to inquire 'whether a motion of such disposition can be first in time and in motion or whether it cannot be first unless in nature' (*LC Phys.* VIII.7 Latin only 342L9–M10). This is followed by the refutation of both possibilities: (i) that the moved body is generated and (ii) that it is eternal.

224 *LC Phys.* VII.9 Latin 312B5–C7.

6.4.4. The evidence of the sources

The argument so far relied solely on the texts of the three commentaries. I shall turn now to Averroes' use of the sources, trying to find some external evidence on the order of Averroes' writing. The turning point of *Physics* VIII is associated with the reading of two texts: al-Fārābī's treatise *On Changeable Beings*,[225] now lost,[226] and Alexander's *On the Principles of the Universe*.[227]

It was Averroes' critical reading of al-Fārābī's *On Changeable Beings* that triggered the turning point.[228] All the 'turning point reports' start with a reference to al-Fārābī's study of possible and impossible successions.[229] Averroes refers to al-Fārābī's analysis in the turning point passage, and in all version B texts.[230] When did he acquire this text? There is no evidence that he was acquainted with it when he

[225] See pp. 75–6 above.

[226] Mahdi (1967, 236) thinks that it contained al-Fārābī's response to Philoponus, notably to the sixth book of *Against Aristotle*. Lettinck (1992, 2, 260, 265) on the other hand suggests that it might be al-Fārābī's commentary on the *Physics*, referred to once by Averroes.

[227] See p. 80 above.

[228] 'This is because the infinite contiguity of movements is possible in one respect and impossible in another, and this can be imagined in different respects (which Al-Fārābī has already studied in his *On Changeable Beings*), distinguishing between the possible and the impossible aspects.' *MC Phys*. VIII.2.2 version A, 67^a5–6.

[229] Middle commentary turning point passage paragraph MA4, long commentary stratum A comment VIII.9 paragraph LA3, long commentary stratum B comment VIII.1 Paragraph LB1. See pp. 75, 96 and 102 above. *MC Phys*. VIII.2.2 paragraphs MA4, MB5. *LC Phys*. comments VIII.9 paragraph LA3, Comment VIII.1 stratum B, paragraph LB1, Comment VIII.4 stratum B. *SC Phys*. VIII version B.

[230] '[The doubts concerning Aristotle's argument] led al-Fārābī to write his treatise *On Changeable Beings*, in which he attempted to investigate the conditions in which motion before motion is possible and distinguished between the impossible and the possible [conditions]' *SC Phys*. Arabic 135.3–6, Hebrew 40^b19–22. 'Therefore al-Fārābī, in his book *On Changeable Beings*, attempted to list the possible manners in which a motion can be preceded by another, in the mover and in the moved thing. He then distinguished between the possible and the impossible and [asked] whether the possible is necessitated by the definition of motion.' *LC Phys*. VIII.9 Latin 345D14–345E6, Hebrew 142^b17–20. A similar statement in stratum B of the long commentary, *LC Phys*. VIII.1 Latin only 339B5–13. 'Al-Fārābī, in his book *On Changeable Beings*, had to investigate all the manners in which motion after motion exists, so that the manners in which this is possible could be distinguished from those in which it is impossible.' *Questions in Physics* 19, # 17, Goldstein's translation with modifications.

wrote version A of the middle commentary (*c*.1170),[231] and there is no mention of it in the polemical works of the early 1180s.[232] It is referred to in the short commentary on the *Metaphysics*,[233] but because the date of this commentary is not certain,[234] and because this commentary was revised,[235] this reference provides no decisive evidence.

On the Principles of the Universe is Alexander's major cosmological treatise.[236] Averroes relied on it when he developed his vertical cosmology in the turning point passage of the long commentary.[237] Genequand finds 'echoes' of this treatise in *De substantia orbis* and in the long commentary on *Metaphysics* Λ, and explicit references to it in the short commentary on *Metaphysics* (which cannot be used for dating).[238] The earliest certain reference to Alexander's treatise seems to be in the *Tahāfut al-Tahāfut*, where it is explicitly mentioned twice.[239] There is, thus, no evidence that can support the dating of the turning point before 1180. About this time, in the *Tahāfut al-Tahāfut* we find a clear statement of his 'vertical' cosmology, but not yet of the distinction between continuity and contiguity.

Both Neoplatonic philosophers and Kalām theologians adhered to theories of eternal generation, but their respective theories were very different from each other. For the former, eternal generation was a strictly deterministic continuous process,[240] for the latter a voluntary and interrupted one: at every moment the world is generated anew by God. Perhaps Averroes started to entertain the idea of eternal generation in the *Tahāfut*. The evidence of the polemical books must be used with care. Yet Averroes considers the view of the theologians that the world is in the process of eternal creation, and thus conceived as 'God's product':

[231] Besides the references in book VIII (one in the turning point passage of version A and one in version B) Al-Fārābī is mentioned by name once more in book IV. This reference may be second-hand (relying on Ibn Bājja) and does not help much. Averroes' answer to Philoponus, which appears in the A versions of all three commentaries—that the capacity for the upward motion of fire is in the wood—goes back to al-Fārābī's treatise, but Averroes could have found it in Ibn Bājja.

[232] In the *Tahāfut*, *Kashf*, or the *Faṣl al maqāl*.

[233] *SC Meta*. German, 107.

[234] Al- ᶜAlawi (1986, 57) suggests 1161 with a question mark.

[235] See Glasner 2007, 144–5.

[236] The treatise is extent in Arabic and has been edited and translated into English by Genequand. Pines (1963, p. lxvii) describes it as Alexander's 'most ambitious attempt to systematize Aristotle's physical as well as some of his metaphysical doctrines'.

[237] *LC Phys*. comment VIII.9, See Section 6.4.1 above. He explicitly refers to comment VIII.4 stratum B, but this reference seems to be a mistake.

[238] Alexander, *On the Principles*, 25–6.

[239] *Tahāfut* 421, 495.

[240] 'Not only that a cause will always produce its proper effect, but also that whatever comes to be always has a cause which necessarily produces it'. See Belo 2004, 35.

If the world were by itself eternal and existent, not insofar as it is moved (for each movement is composed of parts that are newly generated), then indeed the world would not have had an agent at all . . . in this way the world is God's product and the word 'generation' (الحدوث) is even more suitable to it than the name 'eternity' (القدم).[241]

The influence of Kalām cannot be denied. Is this lip service to traditional Islam?[242] I do not think so. Averroes disagreed with much of the teaching of the mutakallimūn, mainly with their occasionalism and denial of natural order, but he recognized the great advantage of their dynamic cosmology. Stripped of its strong religious underpinning, the theory of eternal generation could be turned into a scientific basis for indeterminism. There is noting arbitrary in Averroes' theory of eternal generation. God endowed the heavenly bodies with continuous motions which guarantee the continuity of creation:

He endowed [the heavens] with the capacity to move without cessation or weariness. Nor is there any fear that [they] might collapse like the ceilings of lofty buildings . . . so much so that were one of the heavenly bodies to stop for a single moment, let alone all of them, everything on earth would perish.[243]

The celestial bodies subsist *through their movement* . . . The existence of the celestial bodies attains its perfection only through their being in motion . . . thus the philosophers do not mean by the term 'eternal' that the world is eternal through eternal constituents, for the world consists of movement . . . Therefore the term '*eternal generation*' (الحدوث الدائم) is more appropriate to the world than eternity (القدم).[244]

God, the author of goodness and kindness, has compensated for the imperfection attached to these things . . . by making the process of generation eternal. For this is the only way in which it is possible for the being of these things to be continuous, since continuity of becoming is the nearest approach to continuity of being, which belongs to things that are eternal in their being.[245]

241 *Tahāfut* 162.

242 For a few recent studies on Averroes' attiude to traditional Islam see Taylor 2005, Wohlman 2004, Canova 2007, Campanini 2007.

243 *Al-Kashf*, 82. Averroes repeats this point 'that our existence and the existence of whatever exists [on earth] are preserved by them [the celestial bodies]; so much so that were one to imagine that one of them were removed or were imagined to be in a different position, to have a different magnitude or a different speed from that determined by God, then all existing things on the face of the earth would perish'. It should be noted that the *Kashf* was even less philosophic than the *Tahāfut*, and was written for a popular audience. It is thus less reliable.

244 *Tahāfut* 172.

245 *MC De Gen. et Corr.* Hebrew 91.75–92.81, English 104. Kurland's translation. See also Kukkonen 2002*a*, 409–12.

By no means in his *Tahāfut* does Averroes simply side with the falāsifa.[246] Politically Averroes belonged in the philosophers' camp, but it is no easy task to define his position between the philosophers and the theologians. The traditional picture of the conflict between Averroes and the theologians is oversimplified.[247]

6.4.5. The second riddle: discussion

The second riddle concerns the difficult-to-understand relationship between the two strata of the long commentary. According to account I, the turning point occurred when Averroes was writing the middle commentary and, therefore, both strata of the long commentary are post-turning point texts. This means that strata A and B present two sides of a mock dialogue: in stratum A Averroes claims to follow interpretation A, while in stratum B he puts forward his own view. This account is rather strange. Account II is simpler: the turning point actually occurred when Averroes was writing the long commentary (stratum A), while stratum B introduces corrections inserted into the main text. Account II offers a better picture of the turning point 'in the making'. In the previous section we saw some evidence that the 1180s, during and after the public debates with the theologians, was a formative period in Averroes' life. He treated Kalām's theories critically and with reservation; nevertheless these theories played an important role in the development of his ideas. The ideas that started to ripen at this period were examined and processed by Averroes when he worked on the long commentary and, after a period of hesitations, incorporated into his physics.

[246] Kogan (1985, 34) remarks that Averroes 'leaves no doubt that he differs with al-Ghazālī far more than with the philosophers.' Yet he admits that Averroes' defence of the philosophers is 'decidedly ambiguous' (ibid. 49) and that on several issues he 'has moved toward al-Ghazālī's view' (ibid. 37). In his 1984 paper, Kogan suggests that Averroes wishes to undermine the differences. Puig (1986, 219) argues that Averroes changed his mind regarding the Kalām.

[247] Several recent studies present a more complex picture of the subject. e.g. Griffel 2002, Stroumsa 2005.

7

The Turning Point of *Physics* VI: The Breakdown of Motion

In the previous chapter we saw that Averroes regards chains of changes in the sublunar world as contiguous structures. We shall see now that he does not hesitate to interpret even the single motion, the exemplar of a continuum for Aristotle, as a contiguous structure. Aristotle addresses the concept of motion in *Physics* III, V and VI from different perspectives, and offers three different definitions or construals of this concept.[1] Despite the differences, motion is conceived as a continuous entity in all three books and throughout the *Physics*.[2] I shall show how Averroes reworks all three definitions and in fact tears down completely Aristotle's concept of motion as a continuous entity. It is typical of him that he does not admit a conflict with Aristotle but, consistently and systematically, reinterpets the latter's statements, leading in a new direction. I shall argue that his new concept of motion, later termed *forma fluens*, was one of Averroes' greatest achievements.

[1] I shall not deal here with the concept of change in *Physics* I.7.

[2] In *Physics* VI Aristotle takes it for granted that motion is continuous, in *Physics* V he defines it as a continuous change, and in *Physics* III he remarks that 'motion is thought to be (*dokei de*) something continuous' (*Physics* III.1 $200^{b}16$). One of the early attempts to define the spatial magnitudes was by the 'flux definitions': a line is generated by the motion of a point, a surface by the motion of a line etc. See Heath 1925, I.159. Aristotle quotes these definitions in *De anima* I.4, 409a4. These definitions imply that the continuity of motion is even more basic than that of the spatial magnitudes.

7.1. INTRODUCTION: THE VARIOUS CONCEPTS OF MOTION IN ARISTOTLE'S *PHYSICS*

Note on translation

The two terms change and motion are used interchangeably in *Physics* VI,[3] but are carefully distinguished from one another in V. In some recent translations of Aristotle there has been a tendency to use the English term 'change' for both *kinēsis* and *metabolē*. In the present study it is important to maintain the distinction between the two terms and to be faithful to the sources as far as possible. I have thus translated them as well as their Arabic, Hebrew, and Latin equivalents as 'motion' and 'change' respectively, trying to keep to the words of Aristotle and Averroes. Sometimes, therefore, my use of these terms may seem confused.

7.1.1. The definitions of motion

The conceptual basis of *Physics* V and VI is *Premise V/VI*: Every change is from something to something.[4] The approaches of these two books are, however, very different.

The approach of *Physics* VI is geometrical.[5] Motion is an essentially continuous and homogeneous entity and is presented by a line interval.[6] The Greeks conceived of a spatial interval as an entity of type 'length',[7] bounded by entities of type 'point'.[8] Midpoints of a line have no actual existence. In analogy with the spatial interval the change interval is an entity that is time-dependent,[9] and is bounded by two endpoints, the

[3] On the use of these terms in Physics VI see Glasner, forthcoming.

[4] *Physics* II.1, 193^{b}18; IV.11, 219^{a}10; V.1, 224^{b}1, b35; V.2, 225^{b}30, 226^{a}14; VI.4, 234^{b}10; VI.5, 235^{b}7; VI.6, 237^{a}19; Γ.8, 239^{a}23; VI.10, 241^{a}28; VII.1, 242^{a}30–b4; VIII.2, 252^{b}10. The premise is mentioned once in *De caelo* I.8, 277^{a}15, in *Metaphysics* IV.8, 1012^{b}28, and twice in *Metaphysics* K.12, which is a summary of *Physics* V.2.

[5] See Glasner, forthcoming.

[6] The distance traversed and the motion are two distinct entities, described by two distinct line segments (ABC and DEF respectively). *Physics* VI.1 231^{b}22–4.

[7] Al-Fārābī regards length as absolute extension; in this sense it underlies the notion of a line. See Freudenthal 1988, 137–9.

[8] In Euclid's *Elements* definitions I.2 and I.3 'A line is a breadthless length', and 'the boundaries (*perata*) of a line are points'.

[9] Premise V/VI is common to books V and VI. In VI Aristotle introduces a second premise: Every motion is in time (*Physics* VI.2, 232^{b}20; VI.6, 236^{b}19; VI.7,

point of departure (*terminus a quo*) and the point of arrival (*terminus ad quem*), which are actual stops.[10] There is no arrival or departure at a midpoint:

Any point between the extremes of a straight line is potentially the middle but not actually, unless it divides the line here when the moving body has come to a standstill and begins to move again . . . But when it travels continuously, A is not able *to have arrived at* or *to have departed from* point B . . . But if someone claims it has arrived and departed—A will always be at a standstill when it is travelling.[11]

Since change is conceived as an interval, a notion of instantaneous change is foreign to *Physics* VI. Even generation and corruption are regarded as continuous changes.[12] Premise V/VI asserts that change is from something to something, and Averroes explains that this premise was introduced to assure that motion in an instant is impossible.[13]

In *Physics* V Aristotle adds a logical structure to the geometrical presentation of *Physics* VI: the two 'somethings' should be of the same genus: either contraries or contradictories. Motion is defined as a change between contraries (e.g. the cooling of water). Between contraries all the intermediate states are present and therefore motion must be a continuous temporal process. Between contradictories, however, there are no intermediate states. The typical examples are generation and corruption (e.g. the corruption of the form of water and the generation of the form of ice). The notion of instantaneous change that is foreign to *Physics* VI can, thus, be integrated into *Physics* V. Aristotle had not pursued the notion of instantaneous change, but in *Physics* VIII he remarks that alteration may occur in an instant, as in freezing.[14] A

237^b23; VI.8, 239^a23). The whole argument of *Physics* VI proceeds from these two premises.

[10] See also Simplicius, *On Phys.* 1281.7–10. Averroes remarks on this analogy: 'Motion is continuous and velocity in motion is analogous to division in the continuous. As the division of the continuous [magnitude] can be carried on infinitely so velocity in motion' (*LC Phys.* VI.15 Latin 255K3–8, Hebrew 53^a12–14).

[11] *Physics* VIII.8 262^a22–4, 28–33, Graham's translation. See also Simplicius *On Phys.* 1283.9, English McKirahan 2001, 58; 1281.20, 1282.13–1283.20.

[12] *Physics* VI.6 237^b10–21. See also *Metaphysics* E.3 1027^a29–32; Kirwan 1971, 195–6.

[13] *LC Phys.* VI.15 Latin 255K11–13, Hebrew 53^a15–16, a part of the Latin sentence is missing.

[14] *Physics* VIII.3 253b25. See Waterlow's thorough analysis in 1982, 131–58, especially 154–8.

concept of instantaneous change was, thus, available and examples such as the curdling of milk or the lighting of a room were common in Greek and medieval texts.[15]

The concept of motion of *Physics* III assumes a stronger philosophical underpinning and is conceptually richer than the geometrical concept of book VI. Motion (*kinēsis*) is defined as 'the perfection (*entelekheia*) of that which potentially is (*tou dunamei ontos*) as such'; in III.2 Aristotle adds that 'motion is thought to be a kind of actuality (*energeia*), although an incomplete (*atelēs*) actuality'.[16] Through the notion of *dunamis* Aristotle tries to capture the elusive dynamic nature of motion; through the notion of *entelekheia*, its progressive nature and end-orientation.

7.1.2. The ontological perspective: *forma fluens* vs. *fluxus formae*

One of the major issues of medieval scholasticism was the ontological question to which category motion belongs; that is, what kind of entity is motion? Albertus Magnus deals with this question and offers several ways to look at motion. According to one such way motion is identical in essence with the end that it attains. This is the conception of motion as *forma fluens*, that is, the form of the motion, which Albertus ascribes to Averroes. Another way to view motion is as the way to a certain category. This is the idea of *fluxus formae*, that is, the flow of a form, which Albertus ascribes to Avicenna.[17] In her important article '*Forma fluens* oder *Fluxus formae*?' Anneliese Maier distinguishes the two ways of regarding motion. It can be conceived of as 'merely the way'. The way is an entity in itself and, as such, it should belong to a particular

[15] For instance Simplicius *On Phys.* 968.23; Averroes *MC Phys.* VI.7 73a20–b7. Ibn Bājja ascribes a concept of instantaneous change to Aristotle. See Lettinck 1994*a*, 486.

[16] *Physics* III.2, 201^b32–3. See Wisnovsky 2003, 26. The two terms, *entelekheia* and *energeia*, are used interchangeably in some manuscripts. In the *Metaphysics*: 'Motion is the actuality (*energeia*) of that which potentially is as such' (*Metaphysics* K.9 1065^b16). The definition is cited in *Physics* VIII.1 251^a9–10, where some manuscripts read *energeia*, some *entelekheia* (Kosman 42 n. 8). For instance, in *Physics* VIII.1, Philoponus' manuscript reads *entelekheia* (Simplicius, *On Phys.* 1130.8; English: Wildberg 1987, 123 n. 172) while Isḥaq Ibn Ḥunayn's translation reads فعل which is the common translation of *energeia*. On the meaning of the two terms see Blair 1967.

[17] Quoted in McGinnis 2006, 190–91.

category. The two candidates are quantity[18] and passion.[19] It also can be conceived of as a 'gradual *part-for-part and part-after-part*' generation of the final category—substance, quality, quantity, or place.[20] Murdoch and Sylla define the dilemma concisely: Is motion a process or is it 'the loss or acquisition of various *termini* or forms'?[21] The former is an entity of the type process or flow, the second of the type form.

Aristotle, as is often the case, is equivocal. White remarks that 'the *fluxus formae* better captures the anti-reductionist dimension of Aristotle's conception of motion, but perhaps this does not quite do justice to Aristotle's emphasis on the essential connection between motion and its actual *terminus ad quem.*'[22] Indeed passages that support both conceptions of motion are 'there' in Aristotle for his commentators to find.

The interval model of *Physics* VI is a suitable basis for the *fluxus formae* conception: motion is an entity in itself, continuous and homogeneous. The definition of motion as perfection in *Physics* III.1, on the other hand, can serve as a basis for the *forma fluens* conception. In fact, Aristotle comes near to this conception in III.1: 'There is no motion apart from actual things . . . There is nothing to be found as a common item superior to these.'[23] Averroes concludes that '*the genus of motion is the perfection* of that which is potential.'[24] The following two passages quoted by Maier sum up his *forma fluens* ontology:

> *We say* that motion differs from the perfection towards which it proceeds only in degree. Motion is therefore necessarily of the same genus of the perfection towards which it proceeds, as it is nothing but the *generation, part after part,* of the perfection towards which the motion is until this perfection is actually achieved.[25]

18 Aristotle lists motion as an instance of quantity in his philosophical dictionary (*Metaphysics* Δ.13 1020^{a}29–32) and in the *Physics* (IV.12 220^{b}25–6).

19 Aristotle's very brief statement about the category of passion in *Categories* 9 was interpreted by Avicenna and Averroes as implying that motion belongs to this category. See Maier 1958 61–2 (and n. 1), 72; Murdoch and Sylla 1978, 213–14; Weisheipl 1982, 527–8. Aristotle's statement that the elements have a principle of being acted upon (*Physics* VIII.4 255^{b}29–31) could have contributed to this interpretation.

20 Maier 1958, 63–4. Substance, quality, quantity, and place are the categories in which change is possible (*Physics* V.1 225^{a}4–19, 225^{b}7).

21 Murdoch and Sylla 1978, 215.

22 White 1992, 114.

23 *Physics* III.1 200^{b}33–5 (Hussey's translation). This is the strongest allusion found in Aristotle. The argument in *Physics* V.1, that motion is possible in four categories, also contributes to this interpretation.

24 *LC Phys.* III.6 Hebrew only 96^{a}16–17. The Latin text 88A14–B4 does not mention the genus.

25 *LC Phys.* III.4 Latin 87C11–D4, Hebrew 95^{a}11–15. Quoted by Maier.

The intermediate between the potential and the actual in the same genus must necessarily be of the same genus as the actual which is the perfection, and differs only in degree, because the path to the hot is hot to a certain degree and similarly the path to the cold.[26]

It was Maier who noted the significance of these passages.[27] Thanks to her work Averroes has been recognized as a forerunner of the conception of motion as *forma fluens*.[28] This conception was introduced into Western thought in the thirteenth century by Albertus Magnus and was used by fourteenth century nominalists, notably by William of Ockham, to support their ontological convictions.[29]

Of the several passages in his writings that bear upon this theory only those which Maier quotes drew scholarly attention. Other important passages remained mostly unnoticed. In these passages we see that Averroes not only alluded to this new conception of motion but actually developed it to its minute details.

7.2. ARISTOTLE'S DIVISIBILITY ARGUMENT: A CRACK IN THE INTERVAL MODEL OF MOTION (*PHYSICS* VI.4)

The three turning points with which I deal here (in books VI, VII, and VIII) have the same structure: Averroes starts from a debate among the commentators on a difficult passage in Aristotle, offers a bold new solution and presents it as the true interpretation of that passage. This structure is most explicit and emphasized in book VI. Averroes plays with the 'data'—the difficult passage in *Physics* VI, the remarks of the

[26] *LC Phys.* V.9 Latin 215A1–8, Hebrew 13^{a}28–31. Quoted by Maier.

[27] She traces the '*Forma fluens* or *Fluxus formae*' question back to Avicenna and Averroes, who introduced these two basic positions: Maier 1958, 61–73; Murdoch and Sylla 1978, 214–15. The terms were coined neither by Averroes nor by Avicenna. Maier ascribes them to Albertus Magnus (1958, 68).

[28] Being a conscientious and cautious commentator, Averroes introduces his *forma fluens* model without totally discarding the *fluxus formae* model. 'Motion can be considered in two manners: qua matter it belongs to the genus of that towards which the motion is [*forma fluens*]; but qua form, namely qua a change associated with time, it is in the category of passion [*fluxus formae*].' *LC Phys.* V.9 Latin 215B1–7; Hebrew 13^{b}2–3. See also Maier 1958, 66. He ascribes more importance to the former, however, and regards it (the view of the *Physics*) as *truer*, while the latter (the view of the *Categories*) is commonly accepted. *LC Phys.* III.4 Latin 87D13–E2, Hebrew 95^{a}19–22.

[29] Maier 1958, 100; Murdoch and Sylla 1978, 216, McGinnis 2006.

commentators, and several other relevant passages in *Physics* III, V, VI, and VIII—and comes up with his new theory of motion.

The difficult passage in this case is the divisibility argument of *Physics* VI.4: 'everything that changes must be divisible'. *Physics* VI, as already mentioned, is Aristotle's most geometrical book, and motion is conceived as a continuous interval-like entity.[30] The divisibility argument does not stand up to the geometrical norms of book VI, and conflicts with the interval model of motion. The reasoning is dubious and, according to Bostock, it 'must be dismissed as worthless'.[31] I quote the full text.

The divisibility argument

[1. The statement] Everything that changes must be divisible.

[2. The premises] Since every change is from something to something [premise V/VI], and when a thing is at that towards which it changes it is no longer changing, and when it and all its parts are at that from which it changes it is not changing as that which is in whole and part in an unvarying condition is not in a state of change,

[3. The conclusion] it follows that part of that which changes must be at the starting point and part at the goal.

[4. An added explanation] (Here by 'that to which the thing changes' (*eis ho metaballei*) I mean the first thing changed into (*to prōton kata tēn metabolēn*): for example, in the process of change from white the goal in question will be grey, not black: for it is not necessary that that which is changing should be at either of the extremes.)

[5. Q.E.D.] It is evident, therefore, that everything that changes must be divisible.[32]

The main argument (sentences [2] and [3]) is that when a body changes from a *terminus a quo* to a *terminus ad quem*, part of it must still be at the former and part of it already at the latter. Two difficulties were raised by Aristotle's followers:

The first difficulty is that the argument is obviously false: when a man walks from Athens to Thebes, it is not the case that a part of him is in Athens and a part of him is in Thebes.[33] Apparently the presentation of the journey from Athens to Thebes as a single motion between two

[30] See pp. 63–4 above. [31] Bostock 1991, 201.

[32] *Physics* VI.4, 234^b10–20 (Oxford translation with a few modifications).

[33] The example is taken from *Physics* VI.1. The difficulty is noted by Bostock 1991, 201.

endpoints must be revised. Sentence [4] offers a correction: 'Here by "that to which the thing changes" I mean the *first* thing changed into.'[34] But the notion of 'first thing changed into' expressly conflicts with the conception of motion as a continuous entity that underlies *Physics* VI.[35]

The second difficulty is that the argument is not applicable in the case of an instantaneous change that occurs all at once. If the change is instantaneous it is impossible that a part of the changed body will be at the *terminus a quo* and a part at the *terminus ad quem*. This difficulty illustrates the basic discrepancy between the interval model of motion and a notion of instantaneous change.[36]

Of the two difficulties it was the second that first attracted attention. It was noted by Theophrastus and became a subject of a lively debate among the commentators. Mainly Alexander and Ibn Bājja's solutions are relevant for us.[37] Alexander denied the possibility of instantaneous change and contended that all changes are temporal.[38] Ibn Bājja offered a clear distinction between geometrical and physical divisibility.[39] The former, *divisibility by boundaries*, is applicable to homogeneous magnitudes: lines are divided by points, surfaces by lines and bodies by surfaces.[40] The latter, *divisibility by attributes or by contraries*, is applicable only to physical entities.[41] A physical attribute can provide a 'scale' for the division.[42] Ibn Bājja's answer to Theophratus is that the argument

[34] Sentence [4] is put in parentheses in Ross's Greek text and in most translations. It may be an interpolation.

[35] Bostock (1991, 201) points out the problem: 'There need not be any such "first" state, and there cannot be if, as with motion, the states intermediate between A and B form a *continuum*, as Aristotle himself contends in the next two chapters.'

[36] See *MC Phys.* 72^{a}20–22; Simplicius, *On Phys.* 966.15–27 (English: Konstan 1989, 62–3).

[37] Averroes mentions also Thenistius' solution (*MC Phys.* 72^{a}25–b4), but this solution did not play an important role in the formation of his own ideas.

[38] I follow Averroes' report in *MC Phys.* 72^{a}23–5.

[39] He distinguishes four types of divisibility, two of which are relevant in the present context.

[40] 'Continuity is of several kinds. The first and the better known is division in boundaries (الانقسام بالنهايات). This [division] is the opposite of continuity. And in this division the one becomes many; and the many in continuity become one. And by the division by boundaries the continuous loses its continuity and thus other magnitudes are produced in delimited bodies, which are either adjacent or encompassed by different places. Thus the one disappears and is replaced by many beings, or else it becomes one by a different type of unification.' Ibn Bājja, *On Phys.* 99.14–20 (Lettinck 1994*a*, 486–7).

[41] Ibn Bājja *On Phys.* 99.20–100.4 (Lettinck 1994*a*, 487). Heterogeneity defines a 'scale'.

[42] For instance, a body can be divisible by an attribute if a part of it is hot and another part cold.

is about divisibility between contraries, and thus instantaneous changes are excluded from the discussion.[43]

Commentators pointed out, as I mentioned above,[44] two major difficulties concerning Aristotle's divisibility argument. Following Theophrastus' question, the second difficulty became widely known. The first difficulty, though more serious, attracted less attention. Averroes was the first who seriously tackled it and who dared to dismiss the conception of motion as a continuum. I shall follow Averroes from his solution to the second difficulty to his solution to the first difficulty, from the polemical context to the exegetical context. He was apparently stimulated by debate among the commentators on the second difficulty and regarded his new answer to Theophrastus as a 'turning point'. Having made this first step he turns to Aristotle's argument and to the first and deeper difficulty.

7.3. *PHYSICS* V REINTERPRETED: FROM HOMOGENEITY TO HETEROGENEITY

The breakdown of the concept of motion as a continuous entity starts from the endpoints. The first step towards the new concept of motion is the replacement of Aristotle's *premise V/VI*—change is from something to something—by *premise V/VI′*—Change is from rest to rest.[45] What is the advantage of the new version? Averroes answers this question in great detail in both the middle and the long commentaries on *Physics* VI.4, but the answer pertains mainly to *Physics* V. In *Physics* V change must be either between contraries or between contradictories.[46] Averroes switches from V/VI to V/VI′ in order to circumvent the logical infrastructure of *Physics* V and thus to escape commitment to homogeneity.

[43] Following Averroes: *MC Phys*. VI.7 72b4–9; *LC Phys*. VI.32 62a25–9.

[44] pp. 115–6 above.

[45] 'What he meant by "from something to something" is "something at rest to something at rest" or, generally, "from an opposite rest to an opposite rest".' *MC Phys*. Kalonimus VI.7 $73^{a}13$–14, Zeraḥya $89^{a}1$–13. Averroes carefully uses the more general term 'opposite', instead of 'contrary'. Both translations use הפך for 'contrary' and סותר for 'contradictory'. For 'opposite' Kalonimus uses מקבל and Zeraḥya מנגד. See also *LC Phys*. VI.32 Latin 266C12, Hebrew $62^{b}6$, $63^{a}1$–2.

[46] 'Aristotle's statement that everything that changes is from something to something cannot mean from contrary to contrary. For if it were so this statement would not comprise all temporal changes, among which are changes from contradictory to contradictory, such as generation and corruption.' *MC Phys*. Kalonimus $73^{a}4$–8.

Changed beings are of two kinds: the kind that exists essentially (this is the change from rest to rest) and the kind that does not exist essentially but is rather the end of another change . . . It is clear that these [latter] changes are atemporal because they are the ends of changes and an end is indivisible . . .[47] Therefore if these are said to be changes it is only equivocally, because they are not from rest to rest, but are rather the ends of such changes, namely [of changes] from rest to rest.[48]

Averroes makes this point several more times: what happens in an instant is not a true change but, rather, a boundary of one.[49] Consequently all changes are temporal:

This being so, the true essential changes are of two types: either the end of the change [is] of the genus of the change or it is of a different genus. Each of these two types is a temporal change, so that part of the change is in the *terminus a quo* and part in the *terminus ad quem*.[50]

The difficult concept of change between contradictories, which may be instantaneous, is eliminated and Theophrastus' question is satisfactorily

[47] *LC Phys.* VI.32 Latin 266C8–D5, Hebrew $62^{b}5$–10.

[48] *MC Phys.* Kalonimus $73^{b}8$–10, Zeraḥya $89^{b}10$–12.

[49] 'I wish I knew which are the changes that occur atemporally, whether they are changes *per se* or ends of changes that are from rest to rest. And it becomes clear that *they are ends of changes* since they are atemporal and are not from rest to rest, and that the term *change* truly pertains to this *motion*, to which the end of change is an end . . . The term generation (and corruption) indeed designates the change from the resting subject of being to the resting newly-generated motion, and it [generation] is atemporal because it is an end of a change. Thus, for example, it is the change from the resting form of milk to the curdling that occurs to it in the stomach that deserves to be called change, and it is clear that it is a temporal process. But the curdling itself is the end of this change in the same way that the acquisition of the form of the newly generated is the end of the motion of generation, and this occurs instantanously because it is the end of the motion of generation, not the motion itself' (*MC Phys.* Kalonimus $73^{a}20$–b10; Zeraḥya $89^{a}18$–b12). See also *LC Phys.* V.51 Latin 238H8–9, Hebrew $36^{b}2$–3; *LC Phys.* VII.18 Latin 320K8–10, Hebrew $120^{a}27$–8.

[50] *LC Phys.* VI.32 Latin 266D 7–14, Hebrew $62^{b}11$–13. This point is made also in the middle commentary. The middle commentary, however, was revised: 'Aristotle's statement that everything that changes is divisible and every change is from something to something pertains to two types of changes: [1] those in which the end of the change is of the same genus as the change and [2] those [in which it is] of another genus. And these changes, if [they can be] called changes, <are included in these [changes of the second type] in the same way that a part of a thing is included in the thing or the boundary of a thing is included in the thing. *According to this [interpretation] every change is temporal*>.' *MC Phys.* Kalonimus $74^{a}1$–5, Zeraḥya $90^{a}5$–7. Kalonimus $74^{a}3$–6 is missing in Zeraḥya's translation (evidently a copyist's error). Part of the sentence that Kalonimous translates in the plural Zeraḥya translated in the singular.

answered.[51] The 'price' is that some changes involve a change of genus at the end. Change can no longer be considered as a homogeneous entity. The typical example of heterogeneous change is a change in quality followed by a change in substance,[52] such as from hot water to ice. Averroes insists, however, that this is not the only instance of heterogeneous change.[53] In principle, change should be conceived as a heterogeneous entity.

The reader may feel that this analysis is a mere play on words, but Averroes most emphatically describes it as a turning point in his thought. Why was this seemingly minor revision in the statement of premise V/VI so important for him? Evidently Averroes was challenged by Theophrastus' question and this 'play on words' provides an answer. The issue, however, is much deeper: conceived as *fluxus formae,* motion is basically a homogeneous entity; conceived as *forma fluens*, it is essentially heterogeneous. The turning point is a first step towards the conception of motion as *forma fluens*. This process starts with the endpoint, the *terminus ad quem*, and continues, as we shall see, with working out a new notion of intermediate terminus.

51 'For the changed things are said to be divisible insofar as they are subject to temporal change, not insofar as they are subject to the end of change, which is temporal.' *MC Phys.* VI.7 $74^{a}5$–9. Similarly in the long commentary: 'everything that has changed in no time has also changed in time; and the former change, insofar as it is consequent upon the latter, is accidental, and insofar as it has changed in time it is divisible.'

52 'The motion of coming to be and passing away is composed of a change in quality and a change in substance, and the change in substance is a-temporal, I mean the acquisition of the substantial form by that which comes to be' (*LC Phys.* VI.59, Latin 284H10–I2, Hebrew $81^{b}24$–5). Similarly the generation of flesh from blood is the end of a change and is instantaneous (ibid. Latin 284L3–7, Hebrew $82^{a}31$–b6; the Latin is incomplete). 'In some the end of change is of the same species as the motion; these are changes from contrary to contrary. In some the end of change is not of the same species as the motion; these are changes from privation to being, like generation and other changes of this sort.' *MC Phys.* Kalonimus $73^{b}10$–14, Zeraḥya $89^{b}13$–16.

53 'I shall be utterly surprised if the commentators conceded that (i) generation and corruption belong to those changes that are from something to something and (ii) that the change is not numerically one from the beginning of the motion to its end [i.e. that generation and corruption belong to the non-homogeneous changes], and would not concede this in the case of [other] changes that are of the same type as generation and that undoubtedly do not differ from generation and corruption because they are from not being to being and from opposite rest to opposite rest. And the reason for their [the commentators'] error is that they considered the end of a change as a change because it [the end of change] differs from the thing of which it is an end. This error did not occur to them in [the case of] generation and corruption because the name [generation] in this case corresponds to the change as a whole, not to the end of the change' (*MC Phys.* Kalonimus $73^{b}14$–23, Zeraḥya $89^{b}16$–$90^{a}1$).

Interpreting *Physics* VI.4, Averroes proceeds from the second difficulty raised by Aristotle's argument to the first, more difficult one.[54] It was the polemical context, the debate between the commentators, that drove him to engage in a deep study of the structure of the endpoints of change. We shall see in the next section that it was the word-by-word study of Aristotle's argument that led him to a deeper study of the problematic notion of 'first thing changed into' that eventually culminated in the new understanding of motion as *forma fluens*.

7.4. *PHYSICS* VI REINTERPRETED: FROM A CONTINUOUS INTERVAL TO A CONTIGUOUS CHAIN

Physics VI is the bastion of the interval model of motion. Yet the notion of 'first thing changed into' or first terminus which is introduced in *Physics* VI.4, conflicts with the interval model and with the rest of book VI. Is it a true point of arrival at which the body actually stops? This can be inferred from the argument, but Aristotle does not explicitly say so.[55] The Greek commentators did not try to resolve this difficulty, but Averroes did.[56] If his aim as commentator had been to 'save' the integrity and coherence of *Physics* VI, he could have easily avoided the problem as he did in the short commentary.[57] In the middle and long commentaries, however, he is definitely interested in the problematic concept of intermediate terminus.

7.4.1. Averroes' futile attempt to save the divisibility argument (middle commentary)

In the middle commentary Averroes maintains the concept of motion as an interval.[58] He analyses the divisibility argument carefully, and tries to explain it, but not yet to 'correct' it:

[54] See pp. 115–6 above.

[55] It can be implied from sentences [2] and [4]. See Section 7.2 above. It is easier to draw this conclusion from the Arabic translation: Aristotle's says 'when the thing is at that towards which it changes' (234^{b}11–12); Isḥaq Ibn Ḥunayn translates 'when the thing *stays* (لبث, *manet*, התעכב) in this manner (امر).'

[56] e.g. Philoponus, *On Phys.* 649.2–22 (English: Lettinck 1994*b*, 91).

[57] *SC Phys.* Arabic 96.11–97.9, Hebrew 29b12–30a1.

[58] 'The one continuous motion is that in which the moved body is one and the *terminus ad quem* is one and the time in which the motion [takes place] is one.' *MC Phys.*

Everything changed must necessarily be divisible. This is because every change is from something to something. [*a*] When the changing body is at the first *terminus ad quem* it is not changing, because it is at rest. Similarly, when it is at the *terminus a quo* [it is not changing] because there, too, it is at rest. It follows necessarily that the changing body changes in act[59] when part of it is at the *terminus a quo* and part of it is at the first *terminus ad quem*. This is because it cannot be as a whole in either of them and it is also impossible for it not to be in one of them, because [*b*] between *terminus a quo* and the first *terminus ad quem* there is no intermediate [state];[60] for if there were an intermediate [state] the first *terminus ad quem* would not be first. But [*c*] there is an intermediate [state] between the *terminus a quo* and the final *terminus ad quem*, and the motion to the final *terminus ad quem* is possible only via the first *terminus ad quem*. For example, if the change is from white to black, it first changes from white to yellow.[61] Since for everything that changes, part of it is at the *terminus a quo* and part at the *first terminus ad quem*, it follows that whatever changes is divisible.[62]

This description implies that the change from the *terminus a quo* t_0 to the *terminus ad quem* t_n is divided by one or more termini $t_1 \ldots t_{n-1}$. The quoted passage rests on three assumptions:

Assumption [a]: at t_1, the first *terminus ad quem*, the body is at rest.

Assumption [b]: there is no intermediate state between t_0 and t_1.

Assumption [c]: t_1 is an intermediate state between t_0 and t_n.

Assumption [*a*] confirms that Averroes was still thinking of the intermediate termini as stops at which the body comes to rest.[63] Using Ibn

VIII.5.3, 107^{b}2–4. The only designated points are the stops where the body comes to a rest: 'Because it is well known that when the moved body comes to a stop an actual point is generated, *I say* that the opposite also follows: when an actual point is generated on the path, the moved body has come to rest.' *MC Phys.* VIII.5.3, 108^{a}20–22.

59 In *Physics* VI Aristotle does not yet distinguish between an actual and a potential division.

60 Kalonimus אמצעי, Zeraḥya ממוצע. The Arabic was perhaps توسّط. See *Physics* VI.1 231^{b}12; *LC Phys.* VI text 3, Latin 248D5–6, Hebrew 46^{b}2.

61 Aristotle refers to the intermediate colour between black and white as *phaion*, namely grey (*Physics* 234^{b}18), Isḥaq Ibn Ḥunayn has ادكن, namely, a blackish dark colour. Kalonimus refers here to this colour as yellow (צהוב), the translator of the long commentary and Gersonides use a different word for yellow (קמלי) (*LC Phys.* VI.32 61^{b}24; Gersonides *On MC Phys.* 111^{b}1). Yellow and green were often confused in medieval Hebrew, so one often finds both in this and similar contexts. The use of yellow or green as intermediate colours between black and white can be explained by the Aristotelian theory of the generation of colours. See Fontaine 1998, p. viii.

62 *MC Phys.* VI.7, 72^{a}5–19.

63 Each stop defines two new points: the endpoint of an interval and the beginning point of the next interval. Thus the intermediate termini define a sequence of motion

Bājja's terms, Averroes was still thinking of division by boundaries.[64] The original motion-interval is replaced by several intervals, but the interval model is maintained. The structure of the whole and that of the parts is the same. This is no longer so in the long commentary.

7.4.2. Averroes' new interpetation (long commentary)

At first sight, the long commentary's presentation of the divisibility argument looks similar to that of the middle commentary. A closer reading, however, uncovers the very significant difference: Assumption [*a*], that the intermediate termini are actual stops, is omitted in the long commentary.[65] This is the vital step towards the new concept of change. Averroes concedes that change is from rest to rest, that is, bounded by actual stops, but introduces also a concept of intermediate change, whose boundaries are not actual stops.

> When he says that every change is from something to something he means from something in which it rests <to something in which it rests>. This, as we said, is the change that is *essential*, namely from rest to rest. But the *change that is consequent upon a change* is not from something at rest to something at rest and therefore is not a change that exists essentially.[66]

The *complete change* or *essential change* is 'from rest to rest', that is, a true interval between two true endpoints. The change that is 'consequent upon a change' is not separated by a rest from the change

intervals $[t_0,t_1]$ $[t_2,t_3]$ $[t_4,t_5]$ . . . $[t_{n-1},t_n]$; each $[t_i,t_{i+1}]$ is a single change-interval in the geometrical sense of *Physics* VI.

[64] See pp. 116–7 above.

[65] Tenets [*b*] and [*c*] are listed in *LC Phys.* VI.32, Latin 266I2, K4, Hebrew 63^{a}16, 22–3. Tenet [*a*] is not listed and this omission is intentional. In comment VI.40 Averroes emphasizes four times that at t_0, the *terminus a quo*, the body is at rest, but does not say that at t_1, the *first terminus ad quem*, it is at rest. 'He means that since any change is from something at rest to something at rest [premise V/VI] and change is between two things at rest, and between the first change $[t_1]$ and the rest at the *terminus a quo* $[t_0]$ there is no intermediate [tenet b], it necessarily follows that the first to be changed is that which has just departed from the *terminus a quo* $[t_0]$ and has just arrived at the *first terminus ad quem* $[t_1]$, not the second. Because when the thing at rest departs from the *terminus a quo* $[t_0]$ to the *first terminus ad quem* $[t_1]$, this change is necessary' (*LC Phys.* VI.40 Latin 272B11–C10, Hebrew 69^{a}10–14). 'Since between the rest $[t_0]$ and the first change $[t_1]$ there is no intermediate [tenet b], it follows that the changed thing, when departed from the rest $[t_0]$, is necessarily at the beginning of the *terminus ad quem* $[t_1]$' (ibid. Latin 272D8–13, Hebrew 69^{a}25–7). The context is *Physics* VI.5 235^{b}6: 'that which has changed, at the moment when it has first changed, is in that to which it has changed.'

[66] *LC Phys.* VI.32 Latin 266F12–G6, Hebrew 63^{a}1–4.

that precedes it. I shall refer to it as *intermediate change* and to its endpoints, which are not true stops as *intermediate boundaries*. The fine structure of a true change is a contiguous chain of intermediate changes. This is a non-geometrical model: the structures of the whole and of the part are different: the whole is bounded by true boundaries, the parts by intermediate boundaries. Change (or motion) is not a homoeomerous, interval–like entity. In the long commentary there are several more passages which expand and elaborate on the new concept of intermediate change/motion.

- In *Physics* VIII Aristotle argues that contrary or contradictory changes must be separated by stops.[67]

In this context Averroes again puts forward his new theory: complete essential change is between actual stops, but is composed of intermediate changes which are not separated by stops. In the Latin redaction of the long commentary he mentions examples of situations in which 'there is no time between all of these [motions] and *none of them is a complete motion*, with [both] beginning and end.'[68] The end of one intermediate change is the beginning of the other. In an added passage in the Hebrew redaction he carries his new theory another step forward: the intermediate termini are due to the physical heterogeneity of the motion interval which is divided by different natures:

And *we say* that two contiguous motions must necessarily be one with respect to time, because the 'now' which is the beginning of the one and the end of the other necessarily has an extra-mental potential existence, insofar as the 'nows' in time exist. This being so, the two contiguous motions fail to be continuous *because of their different natures*;[69] and there is no time interval between them, because one is the end of the other.[70]

This passage explains why continuity is possible only in the celestial region where nature is perfectly uniform. The term 'continuous' in

[67] *Physics* VIII.7 261^{a}32–^{b}7.

[68] The situations that Averroes mentions are that of successive motions in many moved bodies, like strings (chorda) when struck together and that of successive motions in the same moved body so that one is the perfection of the other. These motions are contiguous and must not be separated by stops. LC Phys. VIII.62 Latin only 402D7–E6.

[69] Averroes apparently adopts Ibn Bājja's notion of divisibility by attributes.

[70] *LC Phys*. VIII.62 Hebrew only 202^{b}24–8. Averroes continues that 'of the two contrary motions, however, one can be neither the end (*takhlit*) nor the perfection (*shelemut*) of the other, and therefore there must be time between them.' The argument applies equally to the case of contradictory motions (*LC Phys*. VIII.62 Hebrew only 202^{b}28–203^{a}3).

Physics VIII is stronger than in VI and also includes the meaning of everlasting.[71] A linear motion cannot be continuous because it is bounded by endpoints.[72] Continuous motions are possible only in the celestial realm.[73]

- In another passage in the long commentary on *Physics* VIII Averroes further explains the role of the medium in sublunar motion. The context is the question of the thrown stone. Aristotle's answer is that after leaving the hand the stone is further pushed by successive layers of air. In this context both Aristotle and Alexander mention 'successive movers':

[This motion] is not continuous though it appears to be. For it occurs either in successive things or in things in contact; for there is not a single mover but a series of contiguous ones.[74]

For if the mover were not itself something one in number, motion would then not remain one and continuous, but would become manifold and discontinuous because of the difference between the things moved.[75]

Since antiquity this account has been considered one of the weakest links of Aristotle's physics and was criticized by Philoponus, Avicenna, and many others. Here Averroes once again uses his familiar strategy: he builds his own unconventional interpretation on an atypical and problematic passage in Aristotle. He turns Aristotle's controversial account of the motion of the thrown stone into a general model of motion: *Any motion* in a medium involves a multiplicity of movers and therefore intermediate termini:

He means that the motion (by pushing), in which the mover and the moved body are not separated, is not continuous, because it is in air or water. But

[71] *Physics* VIII.7 261^{a}27–^{b}16.

[72] Two things or two motions cannot be said to be continuous, because continuity means divisibility and extremes are indivisible. Qua indivisible entities, extremes cannot be even contiguous (*Physics* VI.5, 236^{b}11–14, VI.6, 237^{a}33, VI.6, 237^{b}8).

[73] In this vein Averroes argues that time, qua continuous and eternal, must be circular (Kogan 1984, 209–10).

[74] *Physics* VIII.10, 267a 12–14 (Graham's translation). In *De caelo* Aristotle suggests that this mechanism may be relevant to any motion in a medium: 'Were it not for a body of the nature of air there could be no such thing as enforced motion. By the same action it assists the motion of anything moving naturally.' *De caelo* III.2 301b 28–30, Guthrie's translation.

[75] Alexander, *On the Principles*, 67.47. It should be noted that the passage on chapter VI.4 from Alexander's lost commentary on the *Physics* that was discovered and studied by Marwan Rashed (1997) deals with different aspects of the interpretation of this chapter, notably the motion of the soul.

because air and water are <<frequently>> apt to division and affection (הפעלות, passion), their own motion imparts to whatever is moved in them a motion that is <non-uniform and> unequal but of diverse modes, because their aptitude to division and affection is not equal in all their parts. *This statement seems to apply to everything that moves in a medium* whether or not the pushing agent and the pushed body are separated.[76]

Being produced through successive interactions with a physical medium, motion cannot be continuous. Furthermore, the natural motions of the elements can no longer be conceived as natural or essential. Averroes does not hesitate to draw this conclusion:[77]

those motions of simple bodies in the media of water and air are not natural motions, as might appear at first sight. For if this were the case, natural motions[78] would exist which have not yet been observed and which will never be observed, unless it were possible for these bodies to move without a medium.[79]

Furthermore, a thing moved essentially does not exist at all, and if it were [moved] it would have necessarily been moved in no time by any random mover.[80]

The bottom line is that only the motions of the spheres are uniform and truly continuous. Averroes states it explicitly several times in the long commentary: 'He [Aristotle] wants to state in this chapter that the continuity of motion implies that the mover is not a body';[81] 'continuous motion can only be the product of a completely unmoved mover.'[82] The celestial movers are incorporeal and the celestial region is homogeneous enough to allow the geometrical interpretation of motion as a continuous entity; the sublunar region is not. Owing to the heterogeneous structure of the medium, sublunar motion cannot be continuous.

- The following example shows that it is not only the nature of the sublunar medium but also the dynamic nature of motion itself that involves generation and corruption of parts that excludes the

76 *LC Phys.* VIII.85 Latin 433C6–D6, Hebrew 232^{a}6–11.

77 The context of the following passages is the frequently quoted comment IV.71 of the long commentary. This comment was translated into English by Edward Grant.

78 'For . . . motions' missing in Hebrew.

79 *LC Phys.* IV.71, Latin 161G13–I3, Hebrew 178^{a}22–5 (English Grant 1974, 261a).

80 Ibid., Latin 161K15–L11; Hebrew 178^{b}11–14, English 261b–262a (Grant's translation).

81 *LC Phys.* VIII.85 Latin 432M1–3, Hebrew 231^{b}15–17. On the subject of celestial vs. sublunar matter see Belo 2007, 173–4.

82 *De substantia orbis* IV.20, Hebrew 48, English 115.

possibility of continuous motion. In a surprising passage in the long commentary on *Physics* V, Averroes expressly denies that continuous motion exists in the sublunar world: what seems to be one motion is actually a contiguous chain.

The context is Aristotle's question whether a succession of motions separated by rests (e.g. Socrates' walking yesterday and today) can be considered to be numerically one.[83] This question is too easy and the answer is obviously in the negative. Averroes aims at a stronger statement and takes Aristotle's question one step further: 'It seems that by this question he intended to arrive at the question *concerning continuous motion*.'[84] He answers this question also in the negative:

How can it [continuous motion] be one when a part of every motion is destroyed and a part generated? Because the destroyed [part] is irretrievable the motion is not numerically one . . . If that which was corrupted could come back and be numerically one, a numerically one motion would be possible; but if it is impossible there cannot be any numerically one motion.[85]

If we conceded that whatever is generated after being corrupted is numerically one, it would follow not only that continuous motion is numerically one, but [also] that the motions interrupted by rests[86] are (when the subject is numerically one and that in which the motion is also numerically one). It seems that if this question is understood as concerning continuous motion, then the difference between parts of continuous motions and motions that are generated one after the other is that the generated and corrupted motions are distinguished from one another by the intervening rests between them while [in the case of] the continuous motions, the generated [motion] can neither be distinguished from the corrupted nor can be pointed to, but is <mixed in it. And it is possible that this is what he meant when saying that continuous motion> is numerically one.[87]

It is not only the natural heterogeneity of the sublunar world, but also the dynamic nature of motion itself, that leads Averroes to his new model of motion as a contiguous chain.[88]

83 *Physics* V.4 228a3–5.

84 *LC Phys*. V.36 Latin 229G10–12, Hebrew 27a7–8.

85 Ibid., Latin 229G12–H1, Hebrew 27a8–12.

86 Latin 'sed etiam motus inter quos est quies', Hebrew: אבל התנועות אשר תמנעום מנוחה. The Hebrew translation is loose. The verb מנע means to impede, but not to interrupt or to step in, which seems to be the meaning here.

87 Ibid., Latin 229H15–K3, Hebrew 27a14–22.

88 Averroes assumes (without explanation) that the celestial motions do not involve generation and corruption of parts.

It is possible that in his analysis of motion in the long commentary Averroes was stimulated by Avicenna's discussion of motion in the Shīfā'. Motion qua continuous entity, according to Avicenna, is perceived only when that which is moved is at the endpoint, but at the endpoint motion qua continuous entity no longer exists.[89] Motion in act is in the moved body. In this context Avicenna introduces the term 'intermediate terminus'. When the body is neither in the *terminus a quo* nor in the *terminus ad quem* it is in an intermediate terminus 'in such a way that it does not exist in even one of the instants that occur in the duration of its passage into act as something fully realized at the limiting point.'[90]

7.5. *PHYSICS* III REINTEPRETED: FROM DIMENSIONAL ENTITY TO BOUNDARY ENTITY

In his long commentary on the *Physics* Averroes gives up the conception of motion as a continuous entity. The basic structure of change and motion in the sublunar world is the contiguous chain. Averroes' next step is very surprising: he associates motion with the sequence of intermediate termini, i.e. the *termini ad quem* of the intermediate motions.[91] This means a dramatic change in the conception of the entity 'motion', and the last step towards its conception as *forma fluens*. Motion is not a dimensional entity but a sequence of boundary entities. Let us follow his steps.

In *Physics* III Aristotle defines motion (*kinēsis*) as 'the perfection (*entelekheia*) of that which potentially is qua such'. Is motion, thus defined, an interval-like entity? The answer depends on the meaning of perfection. Starting with Aristotle himself two interpretations of the notion of perfection evolved: as a dimensional entity and as a boundary entity. In *De anima* Aristotle distinguished two senses of *entelekheia*: 'first as knowledge, second as contemplation'.[92] These senses have often

89 Avicenna, *Phys*. II.1 p. 84; McGinnis 2006, 198.

90 Avicenna, *Phys*. II.1 p. 84; McGinnis' translation, 2006, 201.

91 Following Aristotle Averroes uses in his commentaries on Physics III the term motion.

92 *De Anima* II.1 412^{a}22 (Hamlyn's translation). Wisnovsky (2003, 26–32) compares the use of *entelekheia* in the two definitions.

been referred to as actuality and actualization,[93] or as 'a state of being' and 'a process of becoming.'[94]

These two notions of *entelekheia* are clearly distinguished by Philoponus: the first is 'when the thing is already in its complete state and has rid itself of all potentiality', the second is 'when having changed from its potential state, it undergoes mutation according to its potentiality, and is being turned into its form.'[95] *Perfection I* is a final state, free of potentiality, *perfection II* is 'in the making', mixed with potentiality.[96]

It is the presence of potentiality that distinguishes a dimensional entity from a boundary entity. Thought of as perfection I, motion is a boundary entity. The interpretation of motion as perfection I better explains the end-orientation of motion, but seriously conflicts with *Physics* VI and with our intuition of motion as a process. Thought of as perfection II, motion is an open-ended interval. The interpretation of motion as perfection II was easier to accept, but not free of difficulties. Open-ended interval was not a properly defined entity in Greek geometry. The main problem is the relation between motion, interpreted as an open-ended interval, and its endpoint. Kosman remarks that motion is the actuality of the potential toward another entity, which he regards as 'auto-subversive, for its whole purpose and project is one of self annihilation'.[97] Waterlow remarks that if motion is interpreted as 'tending', then it cannot be commensurate with the state of actuality

[93] In *Metaphysics* Θ actuality is ended while motion is unended *(atelēs)*. 'Of these processes we must call the one set movements, and the other actualities. For every motion is unended—making thin, learning, walking, building; these are movements, and unended at that' (*Metaphysics* Θ 6 1048^{b}29–30).

[94] Wisnovsky 2003, 25. I refer the reader to Wisnovsky's thorough and complete analysis of the developments of these notions in the Greek tradition (2003, chs. 2–4).

[95] Philoponus, *On Phys.* III 342,17–20, English: Edwards 1994, 14. The two perfections are presented in the opposite order in Themistius (see Philoponus ibid. 351.10–14, English 22) and in most of the Arabic commentators. See Hasnawi 2001*b*, 224–6; Wisnovsky 2003, 52, McGinnes 2006, 197. Avicenna followed the presentation of Themistius, while Averroes that of Philoponus. So the former's first perfection was the latter's second perfection.

[96] On the two interpretations see Wisnovsky 2003, 25 and nn. 6 and 7. Philoponus also distinguishes two corresponding meanings of *dunamis*: *dunamis* I is the contrary of *energeia* and thus the contrary of *entelekheia* I, *dunamis* II is coexistent with motion, which is *entelekheia* II. See Simplicius, *On Phys.* 1130.30–1131.2, 1131.5–6 (English: Wildberg 1987, 124–5).

[97] Kosman 1969, 57–8.

towards which it tends, because they are different kinds of entities and differently structured.[98] Averroes sees this difficulty and insists that motion is a heterogeneous entity whose endpoint does not have to be commensurate with the process which led to it.[99] The common understanding of motion as perfection II, that is, as a process, was already challenged by Avicenna.[100] Averroes, we shall see, follows a similar route.

In the short and middle commentaries, Averroes keeps the interpretation of motion as perfection II. The enduring presence of potentiality in perfection II guarantees the continuity and homogeneity of motion.[101]

[Middle commentary] As perfection is either [I] a resting perfection in which there remains no capacity at all insofar as it is perfection, *and this is the end of motion*, or [II] it is a deficient incomplete perfection, and this [type of perfection] preserves that which is potential *and this corresponds to motion*.[102]

It follows that it is in the nature of motion to be continuous because when the moved thing rests, its motion is annihilated and there is no potentiality left in it, because it is already at rest.[103]

[Short commentary] Perfection, as we said, is of two types: either [I] it is complete perfection, in which there is nothing potential at all, and it is the end of motion . . . or [II] it is perfection that preserves that which is potential, and can exist only when the potentiality is attached to it, and this is called motion. It follows that motion is one of the continuous entities.[104]

The parallel passage in the long commentary has been modified by Averroes and is different from the Hebrew.[105] The crucial step is described in an unexpected context: in the short commentary on *Physics* V.2. In this passage Averroes redefines perfection I and perfection II

98 'For if one says only that a change tends towards some eventually actual end-state, one is left with no basis for maintaining that the tending itself is real while it continues and of an ontological status commensurate with that of the actuality brought about.' Waterlow 1982, 112. McGinnis (2006, 197–8) argues that this definition of motion is circular.

99 See p. 119 above.

100 Avicenna *Phys.* II.1 83; McGinnis 2006, 198.

101 *MC Phys.* III.2.2 $23^{b}20$–22; LC Phys. III.6 Hebrew $96^{a}30$–b1, quoted below in n. 105.

102 *MC Phys.* III.2.2 $23^{b}10$–13.

103 *MC Phys.* III.2.2 $23^{b}19$–20.

104 *SC Phys.* III, Arabic 31.10–14, Hebrew $9^{a}4$–10. In III.1 while Aristotle only assumed that 'motion is thought to be something continuous', Averroes tries to derive the continuity of motion from its definition.

105 'From this definition is seen also the continuity of motion, <because perfection—as something potential is attached to it—is not distinguished from what keeps

in order to support his new interpretation of motion. The passage is undoubtedly a late addition to the short commentary. It includes new ideas that are not even alluded to in the middle commentary on this chapter. It summarizes and even carries further the ideas that were developed in the long commentary. There is plenty of evidence that this passage was revised: there are lacunae and many differences between the manuscripts.[106] Since it is so important I am translating it in full, relying on all the available sources.[107]

We say that perfections (كمالات, שלמויות), as [already] said, are of two kinds. [I] One is the end and perfection of motion, that is taken in its definition. Because this perfection is *actual and divisible*, its existence is qua divisible by motion. [II] The second perfection does not exist in actuality. It is the perfection of motion <but is consequent upon another previous motion>.[108] It is not

the motion continuous>. And when the motion comes to rest the potentiality will be separated from the actuality' (*LC Phys.* III.6 Latin 88C5–8, Hebrew $96^{a}28$–b1). The phrase in angle brackets appears only in the Hebrew redaction and is syntactically difficult. Later Averroes acknowledges that an apparent continuity is not always a true one: 'What you see is that the motion of growth and that of alteration are *multiple motions*. Therefore we cannot say that the growing object has one motion from the beginning of its growing to its end <because> its motion takes place in a perceptible time period. Similarly in many alterations. It is impossible for it to be, throughout its time of growing, in a motion that cannot be perceived by the senses, <as Aristotle fancied (כפי שיבדאהו ארסטו). This being so> the motion of growing, from its very beginning to its end, is composed of many movements and many rests. <But>, the continuity of that which is moved locally in one motion from beginning to end, [and] not interrupted by rests, is more manifest. <<We believe that>> <and indeed> this is <not> so in the cases of growing and alteration, because we see many of the things growing the size of one finger in a year, and it is improbable that this finger is divided through the whole year' (*LC Phys.* III.6 Latin 88C8–D13, Hebrew $96^{b}1$–10). Averroes recapitulates this point in comment VIII.23: 'This statement is not true of growing and alteration, namely that there is always motion in them, even if imperceptible' (VIII.23 Hebrew $155^{b}19$–20, the Latin in 358H is different).

106 Differences between manuscripts usually mean that the text was meddled with. The new ideas that are found in this passage are suggested in the long commentary but are not mentioned at all in the middle. The notion of accidental succession appears twice in the short commentary: in the passage with which we are dealing and in the late version B chapter VIII.1.

107 Puig's critical edition of the Arabic text, Puig's Spanish translation, exemplars of the two main variants of the Hebrew translation (Riva di Trento printing and MS Vatican Urb. 39/1) and Shem-Tov ben Yosef Ibn Falaquera's Hebrew translation of this passage in his encyclopedia *Dèot ha-Filosofim*.

108 The words in angle brackets appear only in the Hebrew translation, but not in the Arabic manuscripts or in *Dèot ha-Filosofim*. The sentence is apparently 'patched'. Perhaps

necessary that this perfection[109] be actualized in motion, because it has no actual existence.

Averroes begins by defining two perfections. Interestingly his distinction does not coincide with the common distinction that he himself follows in his commentaries on *Physics* III.1. In this passage Averroes identifies motion with Perfection I, while in other contexts he identifies it with Perfection II. The rest of the passage confirms that Averroes offers here a new definition of the two notions of perfection. According to the commonly accepted distinction, perfection I is a boundary entity, perfection II is a dimensional entity: 'a state of being' and 'a process of becoming'. Unexpectedly, in the quoted passage both perfections are boundary entities: the first of the complete change, the second of an intermediate change.[110]

[Case I. Perfection I] If it were the perfection of an actualized motion,[111] namely [of] the first type[112] of motion, its relation to the motion that precedes it [would be] the relation of the final perfection of motion to the motion. It would follow that there is motion to the motion essentially so that perfection exists in actuality.[113]

[Case II. Perfection II] And if it is not the perfection of an actualized motion (whose relation to the motion that precedes it[114] is the relation of the final perfection of the motion to the motion), as is apparent from its manner [i.e. it is not perfection I], since [this] motion has neither beginning (as we shall explain later[115]) nor is [this] motion actual perfection—it follows that *the existence of the motion that is preceded by another motion is accidental* and due to its being newly generated (حادثة).[116]

the revised sentence should read: 'the second perfection does not exist in actuality, but is consequent upon another previous motion.'

109 In Riva di Trento edition 'to this perfection', which is read as the conclusion of the previous sentence.

110 pp. 122–3 above.

111 From 'because' in the previous quotation to this point is missing in Falaquera's quotation.

112 Literally 'the first part'.

113 On the meaning of 'motion of motion' see p. 72 above.

114 From 'the relation of the final perfection' to this point is missing in several Hebrew manuscripts.

115 This is explained in *Physics* VI.5.

116 *SC Phys.* Arabic 76.7–15, Hebrew 23ᵃ2–12, Spanish 177.

In the long commentary on the same chapter (V.2), perfection II also describes an accidental relation between intermediate motions:

> He [Aristotle] means that it is impossible that <the generation of>[117] motion follows essentially <the generation of> another motion in the same way as <the generation of> static forms[118] follows the motion [i.e. in the same way as perfection I]. But, if it happens, it is *by accident.*[119]

Averroes offers two new notions of perfection to describe his new model of motion. He redefines perfection I as the final terminus, the telos of the complete motion; e.g. white, or Thebes. It is actual and 'nameable' and in this sense it is 'the perfection *that is assumed in its definition*'. He redefines perfection II as an intermediate terminus, the end of an intermediate motion; for example, a certain shade of grey or the 13768th step on the way from Athens to Thebes. This is not a stop and is not actual. Motion is named after its type I perfection (i.e. the walk to Thebes, or the change to black), but consists of a sequence of intermediate type II perfections. This way Aristotle's claim that motion is determined by its endpoint is maintained, but this 'determination' is not deterministic: the resumption of motion after another motion cannot be essential. The accidental factor intervenes at any intermediate terminus, even if no actual stop occurs.[120] The man who walks from Athens to Thebes can either arrive at his goal or not.

Conclusion

Averroes' method of interpretation is shrewd. By distinguishing between complete and intermediate motion he can maintain the basic structure of motion as Aristotle conceived it, but superimpose on it a fine structure. The complete motion is from rest to rest and the *terminus ad quem* defines its orientation and telos, but the fine structure guarantees indeterminism. Furthermore, by 'redefining' the familiar notions of first and second perfection Averroes can maintain Aristotle's definition of motion but significantly change the meaning of motion. The complete motion is defined by its telos, which is perfection in the first sense; the intermediate *termini*, which are perfections in the second sense, and 'measure'

[117] חדוש התנועה appears three times in this sentence only in the Hebrew. The second is apparently superfluous.

[118] Latin *formae*, Hebrew תכונות.

[119] *LC Phys*. V.12, Latin 217B16–C8, C13–D4; Hebrew 15a 19–22, 24–6. See also *LC Phys*. V.13 Hebrew only 16^{b}13–14; VI.32, Latin 266F14–G4, Hebrew 63^{a}1–4.

[120] p. 78 above.

the progress of the flowing form. On the face of it the Aristotelian conceptualization is maintained but both the geometrical representation and the ontological conception of motion are radically revised.

Averroes does not refer to Avicenna in his discussion of motion and there is no decisive evidence that he was acquainted with Avicenna's notion of intermediate terminus. Still, there is a good chance that he was.[121] McGinnis has shown that Albertus Magnus' ascribing to Avicenna the conception of motion as *fluxus formae* is misleading. It was not the case that Averroes introduced the conception of *forma fluens* against Avicenna's conception of motion as *fluxus formae.* A more likely presentation is that Averroes was triggered by Avicenna's insights and tried to incorporate the notion of intermediate terminus into his own account of motion. His presentation is more systematic and consistent than Avicenna's.

7.6. WHEN DID THE TURNING POINT OCCUR?

In book VI the turning point structure is the most notable: from the confusion that Averroes blames on the commentators to the solution that he claims to find in the text of Aristotle, from the polemical to the exegetical context. In the commentaries on VI.4 the two contexts are clearly distinguished. The turning point is reported in the middle and long commentaries in the polemical part. It was obviously initiated by Theophrastus' question and was the first step towards the new conception of motion as *forma fluens*. The breakthrough occurred in the polemical context and then Averroes further develops the new concept in the exegetical context, using a running commentary on Arisotle's text. Let me start with an outline of the three commentaries on Physics VI.4 and then proceed to the question when the turning point actually occurred.

7.6.1. Outline of the three presentations and preliminary conclusions

The Short Commentary

[S1] *The exegetical context*: A presentation (pre-turning point) of Aristotle's divisibility argument.[122]

[121] See also p. 163 below.
[122] *SC Phys*. Arabic 96.11–97.9, Hebrew 29b12–30a1.

[S2]–[S5] *The polemical context*

[S2] An explanation of Ibn Bājja's concepts of divisibility in boundaries and divisibility in contrary attributes.[123]

[S3] The presentation of the controversy among the commentators from the perspective of Ibn Bājja's answer. Alexander is not mentioned, Themistius is mentioned briefly.[124]

[S4] An interpolation: Averroes' answer to Theophrastus.[125]

[S5] Returning to Ibn Bājja's answer (only in the Hebrew translation).

The Middle Commentary (Chapter VI.7)

[M1] *The exegetical context*: A pre-turning point presentation of Aristotle's divisibility argument.[126]

[M2]–[M9] *The polemical context*

[M2] The background: the presentation of the debate among the commentators.[127]

[M3]–[M9] *The description of the turning point*

[M3] The abandoning of Ibn Bājja's view.[128]

[M4] Aristotle's argument is sound.[129]

[M5] The turning point: premise V/VI′. [130]

[M6] The answer to Theophrastus.[131]

[M7] Praise of Alexander.[132]

[M8] Accusing the commentators (en bloc, המפרשים) of misunderstanding Aristotle's intention (Kalonimus' translation only; differences between manuscripts).[133]

[M9] Praise of Aristotle (differences between the two translations).[134]

The Long Commentary (Comment VI.32)

[L1]–[L7] *The polemical context*

123 *SC Phys.* Arabic 97.10–99.1, Hebrew 30a1–29. Compare Lettinck 1994*a* 486–8.
124 *SC Phys.* Arabic 99.2–100.11, Hebrew 30a29–b26.
125 *SC Phys.* Arabic 100.12–101.9, Hebrew 30b26–31a14.
126 *MC Phys.* VI.7 72^a5–19.
127 Ibid. 72^a19–b9.
128 Ibid. 72^b9–73^a2.
129 Ibid. 73^a2–4.
130 Ibid. 73^a4–a20.
131 Ibid. 73^a20–74^a23
132 Ibid. 74^a23–b7.
133 Ibid. 74^b7–11.
134 Ibid. 74^b11–23.

[L1] Introduction: the doubt raised by the commentators.[135]
[L2] (compare M2) Presentation of the debate among the commentators (differences between the Latin and Hebrew translations).[136]

[L3]–[L7] *The description of the turning point*

[L3] (compare M3) The abandoning of Ibn Bājja's view.[137]
[L4] (compare M4) Aristotle's argument is sound (only in Hebrew).[138]
[L5] (compare M6) The answer to Theophrastus.[139]
[L6] (compare M8) The commentators (המפרשים) misunderstand Aristotle's intention.[140]
[L7] (compare M9) Praise of Aristotle (only in the Hebrew).[141]

[L8]–[L9] *The exegetical context*

[L8] A post-turning point presentation of Aristotle's divisibility argument.[142]
[L9] Discussion of the meaning of first *terminus ad quem* in each of the four types of change.

7.6.2. The dating of the turning point: discussion

Before the turning point Averroes accepted Ibn Bājja's answer; the turning point was the working out of his own new answer to Theophrastus' question. In the short commentary (paragraphs S2, S3, S5) Averroes explains Ibn Bajja's answer and concludes: 'Ibn Bājja has already provided the utmost explanation'.[143] Paragraph S4 of the short commentary is obviously a late interpolation,[144] in which Averroes

135 *LC Phys.* VI.32 Latin 265I12–L12, Hebrew 61^{b}26–62^{a}7.
136 Ibid. Latin 265L13–266C4; Hebrew 62^{a}7–30.
137 Ibid. Latin 266C4–C8; Hebrew 62^{a}30–b2.
138 Ibid. Hebrew only 62^{b}2–5.
139 Ibid. Latin 266C8–F11, Hebrew 62^{b}5–22.
140 Ibid. Latin 266F11–12, Hebrew 62^{b}22–3.
141 Ibid. Hebrew only 62^{b}23–31.
142 Ibid. Latin 266F12–K11, Hebrew 63^{a}1–26.
143 *SC Phys.* Hebrew only 31a19.
144 Paragraph S4 opens with the word 'I say', interrupts the presentation of Ibn Bājja's view in S3 and S5, and conflicts with the rest of the text of the short commentary. Already Gersonides noticed that S4 is an interpolation: 'It seems to us that this statement of Averroes is a revision (*hagaha*) which he made after having made this short commentary,

summarizes his own answer to Theophrastus that he developed later in the middle commentary.[145] The turning point is announced in the middle and long commentaries and started, as Averroes testifies, with the abandoning of Ibn Bājja's answer:

> We, as well as others, were thinking for a long time on what Ibn Bājja argued and approved of what he said, considering it to be the most satisfactory. But a certain objection occurred to me concerning this issue of divisibility which Ibn Bājja discussed.[146]

Our question, thus, is whether the turning point occurred when Averroes was writing the middle commentary (account I) or the long commentary (account II). I shall summarize the arguments for and against account II.[147]

Arguments for account II

- The first differencc thai meets the eye in the outline above is the order of presentation. In the middle commentary Averroes proceeds from a faithful pre-turning point presentation of Aristotle's text to the debate on this question. At this point he announces the turning point. In the long commentary the order is reversed: Averroes starts with the polemical part, announces the turning point, and then

and it is a second view of Averroes. And this second view he follows in his middle commentary on this book'. And in the middle commentary on the *Physics* Averroes did not follow Ibn Bājja's view, as we mentioned, and not his earlier statement in this book (Gersonides, commentary on *SC Phys*. Berlin MS 31b col. b 10–13, Vatican MS 61a11–14; See also Berlin MS 31b col. b 24–7, Vatican MS 61a 20–3). Another Hebrew commentator on the short commentary, Yeda 'aya ha-Penini testifies that he found most of the books that he studied corrupted at this point (Ha-Penini, commentary on *SC Phys*. Parma MS De Rossi 1399 141b24–5).

145 'And I say that all this is a departure from the understanding of Aristotle's demonstration. The doubts of the commentators would have indeed applied to what he says if those things which change in no time were in a subject other than those which change in time, i.e. if those things which change instantaneously were separate from those which change temporally. But since the a-temporal are the end of the temporal they are in one and the same subject; and if one then everything that changes instantaneously changes also in time. And when it is established that everything that changes in time is divisible, it has also been established that everything that changes instantaneously is divisble' (*SC Phys*.100.12–101).

146 *Mc Phys*. VI.7 72b14–17. In the long commentary he explains the objection: 'divisibility in attribute is accidental to the continuous body and Aristotle considers the essential divisibility of the continuous, namely its divisibility in boundaries.' *LC Phys*. VI.32 Latin 266C3–6, Hebrew 62a29–31. This criticism is sound. Aristotle apparently thought of division in boundaries.

147 The argument for account I, in this case, is the argument against account II.

applies the new understanding to the presentation of Aristotle's text where he further develops his new theory of motion. The latter order, from the polemical to the exegetical seems to account better for the order in which the events occurred.

- The turning point is reported in chapter VI.7 of the middle commentary and in comment VI.32 of the long commentary. The long commentary after VI.32 is indeed a post-turning point text.[148] In the middle commentary of VI.7 it is an isolated episode with no effect on the rest of the book. This makes sense if the turning point passage in chapter VI.7 is a late addition.
- In the long commentary Averroes explains why he started to doubt Ibn Bājja's solution: 'After I started *to comment on Aristotle's words* it seems to me that his words work out naturally in all respects'. He is probably alluding to his work on the long commentary. Several times he refers to the long commentaries as commentaries 'by word'.[149]
- There are two issues that are essential parts of the new interpretation about which Averroes still hesitates in the long commentary. In comment VI.32 he testifies 'but I always considered Ibn Bājja's answer to be better <<but no longer>>.'[150] The important words "but no longer" appear only in the Latin.[151] The difference between the two redactions indicates that Averroes had not yet settled this point when he started to work on the long commentary. Similarly he had not yet finally made up his mind on the major question whether generation and corruption are changes. The opening paragraph L1 of comment VI.32 has been edited.[152] It

[148] The core of the turning point is the substitution of premise V/VI′ for premise V/VI. Premise V/VI′ is used later in the long commentary, but not in the middle commentary. A most notable instance is the interpretation of *Physics* VI.5. Comment VI.40 of the long commentary start by citing the revised premise V/VI' and is a post-turning point text that relies on comment VI.32. Chapter VI.8 of the middle commentary, however, begins by citing the outdated premise V/VI is apparently a pre–turning point text that was written before chapter VI.7.

[149] See pp. 20, 53.

[150] *LC Phys*. VI.32 Latin 266C7–9, Hebrew $62^{b}1$–2.

[151] The parallel sentence in the Hebrew redaction is 'and he has already separated in the resolution of this doubt as he himself mentioned'. The meaning of 'separated' here is not so clear, but the same sentence appears also in the short commentary (SC Phys. Hebrew only 31a20).

[152] There are several modifications and minor additions in Hebrew version; e.g. Hebrew 62a22–4.

seems that the Latin is a pre-turning point text while the Hebrew was a post-turning point revision.[153] These examples indicate that the turning point was still 'in progress' when Averroes started to write the long commentary.

Objection to account II

The main objection to account II, as in the case of book VIII, is that it obliges us to assume that the middle commentary was revised.

Answer to the objection

The middle commentary consists of a pre-turning point presentation of Aristotle's text (M1), a presentation of the debate (M2), and a description of the turning point (M3–M9). If it were possible to show that the whole turning point part M3–M9 is later than M1–M2 it would have been a decisive argument for account II, but there is no such evidence. There is, however, good evidence that paragraph M7 is later than paragraph M2. In Appendix 5 I shall argue that paragraph M7 is late.

Conclusion

The arguments, for and against, as set out in the previous chapter, as well as in this one, support account II: the turning point 'occurred' late. The development of Averroes' new physics was a process that started in the 1180s and was worked out in the long commentary. Account II, however, obliges us to assume that the turning point passages in the middle commentary (chapter VIII.2.2 paragraphs MA4–MA5,

[153] I quote the Hebrew passage. 'Concerning this question the commentators have already raised a doubt about Aristotle, a doubt that cannot be resolved: they say that if by "change" he meant [change of] that which is truly moved, only in the three categories—quantity, place and quality—his argument would not pertain to change in substance. And it is manifest that any change in substance are divisible, like whatever undergoes change in the other <three> motions. Also, his text indicates that change in substance is <<not>> included in this account, which he intended to make here, and therefore "change" is said of the <four> <<three>> [types of] changed things, <those which he postulated to be the types of motion in the third [book]>.' *LC Phys*. VI.32 Latin 265I12–K14, Hebrew $61^{b}26$–$62^{a}2$. There are several less important differences among the Latin and two Hebrew manuscripts Paris MSS 883 and 884, which I have not noted. According to the Latin translation, Aristotle's argument does not pertain to change in substance; according to the Hebrew it does. Perhaps in the earlier Latin redaction Averroes was thinking of generation as an instantaneous change, in the latter as the conclusion of temporal change.

chapter VI.7 paragraphs M3–M9) are late revisions. In the present case we have no direct evidence that the whole turning point passage M3–M9 is late, but we have evidence that M7 is late: that the middle commentary was revised and consists of at least two strata.

APPENDIX 5: THE REVISION OF THE MIDDLE COMMENTARY AND THE ROLE OF ALEXANDER

The preliminary presentations of the debate on Theophrastus' question in the middle and long commentaries (paragraphs M2 and L2) are close in spirit to the short commentary: Averroes is still interested in Ibn Bājja's view more than in those of the Greek commentators. In the short commentary (S2–S3) he does not mention Alexander at all; in the middle and long commentaries (M2 and L2) he briefly summarizes Alexander's view,[154] probably relying on second-hand acquaintance.[155] In L2 he dismisses Alexander's answer as erroneous.[156] In paragraph M8 and L6, too, Averroes accuses 'the commentators' (*en bloc*) of misunderstanding Aristotle.

A drastic change of attitude towards Alexander occurs in paragraph M7 of the middle commentary. Here Averroes praises Alexander and tries to reconcile his own interpretation with that of his second-century predecessor.

We should not get further involved in the argument with Aristotle to the point of saying that these changes are temporal, as Alexander did. By God![157] Had not Alexander meant, when he said that every change is in time, that these are not changes but ends of changes? But Themistius did not understand his [Alexander's] statement the way we did, and

[154] Alexander denied the possibility of instantaneous change and held that all changes are temporal, even if in some cases it [the change] escapes perception (*MC Phys.* VI.7, 72ᵃ23–5). Simplicius offers a much longer and more detailed account of Alexander's answer (*On Phys.* 966.15–968.31, English: Konstan 1989, 62–5). The main points are: 'There would be motion also in the case of things that change all at once by virtue of the fact that for these too there is invariably something between, along which the change occurs' (968.5–7); 'for a part of the freezing milk changes all at once, but not the whole thing' (968.23).

[155] In the long commentary passage L2 the commentators referred to what Alexander had written 'and Alexander's answer is well known.' In M2, 'indeed Alexander replied, according to what they mention'. It is not specified who mentioned Alexander's view, but Gersonides' quotation of this sentence of the middle commentary reads: 'But Alexander replied, according to what Themistius understood from him . . .' (Gersonides *On MC Phys.* 112ᵃ14–15).

[156] 'But in Alexander's answer there is a well known error, as Aristotle and all the Peripatetics concede that there are atemporal changes.' *LC Phys.* VI.32 Latin 265M9–13, Hebrew 62a 11–12. The two extant Hebrew manuscripts of book VI differ.

[157] האלהים, in all Hebrew manuscripts (including Zeraḥya's translation) except Vatican 268, which reads אלא אם.

[did not recognize] that this [Alexander's] is the obvious interpretation of the words of the philosopher.[158] But[159] this is [indeed] what Alexander meant, since *this man is of a too high a stature and degree* (גדול השיעור והמעלה) to miss this obvious meaning of Aristotle's[160] words and to try to defend a false view, namely that the ends of changes are temporal.[161]

Paragraph M7 thus seems to be a late addition.

- It interrupts the order of the presentation of the middle commentary.[162]
- It is highly unlikely that M2 and M7 were written 'in one session'. The two paragraphs reflect significantly different attitudes to Alexander, typical of different periods in Averroes' career.
- Paragraph M7 is closer in spirit to the long rather than the middle commentary. Averroes was particularly interested in Alexander while he was writing and especially revising the long commentary, but not when he wrote the middle commentary. Attempts to reconcile Averroes' own solution with Alexander's are typical of the long commentary, particularly at the editing stage.

[158] Kalonimus: the philosopher; Zeraḥya: Aristotle.

[159] Kalonimus: but; Zeraḥya, perhaps.

[160] Kalonimus: the sage; Zeraḥya, Aristotle.

[161] *MC Phys.* VI.7 MS Hamburg 74^{a}23–b4, MS Paris 100^{b}9–18, Zeraḥya 90^{b}2–10.

[162] In the long commentary, the short paragraph L6, accusing the commentators of misunderstanding Aristotle's intention, leads logically from L5 (the answer to Theophrastus) to L7 (the praise for Aristotle). The parallel short passage M8 should have similarly linked M6 (the answer to Theophrastus) to M9 (the praise for Aristotle). The linking sentence M8 (lines 74^{b}8–11 in Kalonimus' translation) is missing in Zeraḥya's translation. There are several other textual problems in Kalonimus' translation (74^{b}14–15, 17). These might be due to the insertion of the added passage M7 before M8.

8

The Turning Point of *Physics* VII: The Breakdown of Physical Body[1]

GEOMETRY is the science that studies continuous magnitudes.[2] Aristotle defines magnitude as a continuous entity: 'that which is divisible into continuous parts.'[3] The essence of magnitude is its divisibility. The examples are geometrical: the one-, two-, and three-dimensional spatial magnitudes.[4] In analogy 'homoeomer' is a physical body whose parts are similar both to one another and to the totality.[5] It is a body that can be repeatedly divided without losing its identity. The mathematical notion of continuity and the physical notion of homoeomerity define the same structure—that of infinite divisibility. The structure of the part is identical to that of the whole. A line is divisible into lines, a chunk of earth into chunks of earth. Aristotle bases his anti-atomistic philosophy on the notion of homoeomerity.

1 This chapter is a revised and extended version of Glasner 2001*a*.

2 The concept of magnitude is introduced (without being defined) in the fifth book of Euclid's *Elements*. Concerning the different interpretations of Euclid's concept of magnitude, see Mueller 1981, 136–8. It should be recalled that the *Elements* is a compilation of mathematical knowledge, a substantial part of which was already current at the time of Aristotle.

3 *Metaphysics* Δ.13 1020^{b}12.

4 Ibid., 1020^{a}8–12. Aristotle explicitly says that 'beyond these there are no other magnitudes, because the three dimensions are all that there are.' *De caelo* I.1 268a 9–11. According to Speusippus, points too are magnitudes. See Taran 1981, 37; Mueller 1986, 118. Waschkies (1991, 152, 154) argues that, before Aristotle, only spatial magnitudes were considered to be continua and that the application of the notion of continuum to time and motion was a new idea in the middle of the fourth century. This is Aristotle's main task in *Physics* VI.

5 On Aristotle's notion of homoeomerity see Freudenthal 1995, 11. On Galen's see Strohmaier 1970, Arabic 44, German 45.

8.1. CAN PHYSICAL BODY BE A TRUE HOMOEOMER?

Is perfect homeoeomerity possible? Is an amount of water infinitely divisible into smaller amounts of water in the same sense that a geometrical solid is infinitely divisible? Aristotle offers two incompatible answers to this question.

In the geometrically oriented *Physics* VI he answers in the affirmative: physical and geometrical magnitudes are equally continuous. The kernel of *Physics* VI lies in the thesis of isomorphism, which is introduced in chapters VI.1 and VI.4. The thesis states a full structural parallelism between several entities, some of them mathematical and others physical. The preliminary statement of the thesis is found in chapter VI.1. In VI.4 Aristotle adds several more entities to the list, the most important being the moved body:

- The Thesis of Isomorphism (*Physics* VI.1): 'The same reasoning applies equally to magnitude [i.e. the distance traversed], to time, and to motion;[6] either all of them are composed of indivisibles and are divisible into indivisibles, or none [of them is].'[7]
- The Thesis of Isomorphism (*Physics* VI.4): 'Time, motion, the being in motion, the thing that is in motion and the respect must all be susceptible to the same divisions.'[8]

The crux of the thesis is the full parallelism between geometrical magnitudes and physical entities. The moved body is the most conspicuously 'physical' of the isomorphic entities listed by Aristotle.[9] Aristotle

[6] As we have seen in the previous chapter, Aristotle's notion of motion is by no means reducible to that of the distance traversed. Distance and motion are two distinct but similarly structured entities, described by two line segments (ABC and DEF respectively). *Physics* VI.1 231^{b}22–4.

[7] *Physics* VI.1, 231^{b}18–19. The argument of VI.1 confirms that the latter is the case: distance, time, and motion are all infinitely divisible, i.e., *continua*. After listing these three Aristotle adds a fourth, 'being in motion': 'Therefore, since where there is motion there must be something that is in motion, and where there is something in motion there must be motion, therefore the being-moved will also be composed of indivisibles' (231^{b}25). The argument is recapitulated in *Physics* IV.11 219^{a}10–14 and IV.12, 220^{b}25–6.

[8] Ibid. VI.4 235^{a}15–17; cf. *De caelo* III.1 299^{a}9–22; III.5 304^{b}1–2.

[9] The isomorphism applies to one-dimensional and three-dimensional entities alike. Such 'mixed' relations are not allowed in Greek geometry. See for instance Euclid,

nowhere clearly distinguishes between mathematical and physical bodies,[10] and in *Physics* VI he studies physical body qua three-dimensional magnitude.

Several statements in other books of the *Physics* point to a negative answer to our question. Aristotle conceived the world as a plenum, but not as a continuum as the Stoics were to conceive it a few decades later.[11] For Aristotle a heterogeneous body cannot be infinitely divisible. Thus he rejects Anaxagora's view that there is something of everything in everything:

> It is necessary that if a part of a thing can be as large or as small as you please, then so can the whole, and if it is not possible for any animal or plant to be as large or as small as you please, it is not possible that any part should be either for, if it could, so could the whole. Now flesh and bone are parts of animals, and fruits are parts of plants. Clearly then neither flesh nor bone nor anything of the sort can proceed far, indefinitely, either in enlargement or in diminution.[12]

This passage from *Physics* I, as well as of few other passges,[13] clearly conflicts with the theory of isomorphism of *Physics* VI. Murdoch identifies it as 'the ultimate source for the theory of *minima naturalia*'.[14] A theory of *minima naturalia* denies infinite divisibility to a physical body: there is a lower limit to the size of a physical body, beyond which it cannot be further subdivided and still retain its identity as this specific physical body.

A theory of *minima naturalia* should be clearly distinguished from a corpuscular theory. Holden distinguishes between a 'potential parts doctrine' and an 'actual parts doctrine'. According to the former, 'the

Elements V definitions 3 and 4. Aristotle solves this problem by ascribing to motion a dual nature: it is divisible in one dimension with respect to time, in three dimensions with respect to its distribution in the moving body. Having a dual nature, motion 'mediates' between the three-dimensional body and the other one-dimensional entities.

10 Aristotle's definitions of body are geometrical: The first definition is: 'A body is a magnitude which extends in (or is divisible in) three dimensions,' *De caelo* I.1 268^{a}8–9, I.7 274^{b}20; *Physics* III.5 204^{b}20; *Metaphysics* Δ.6 1016^{b}28, K.10 1066^{b}31–2; *Topics* IV.5 142^{b}24. The second definition is: 'That which is bounded by a surface.' *Physics* III.5, 204^{b}5; *Metaphysics* K.2, 1060^{b}15, K.10, 1066^{b}23. Compare Euclid, *Elements*, definitions XI.1 and XI.2.

11 On the Stoic strong theory of continuity see pp. 66–7 above.

12 *Physics* I.4 187^{b}14–20 (trans. Charlton). Aristotle is arguing with Anaxagoras. A similar but somewhat vague statement appears in *Physics* VI.10 241^{a}32–b2.

13 For example, *De gen. et corr.* I.10 328^{a}26–8; *De sensu* 6, 446^{a}8–9; *Physics* III.7 207^{a}33–6. See also Van Melsen 1960, 41–4; Murdoch 2001, 96–8.

14 Murdoch 2001, 91, 96.

parts into which a body can be divided are not distinct existents prior to their being actualized by a positive operation of division. Division *creates* these parts.... It does not simply separate pre-existing parts.'[15] According to the latter, the parts 'are each a distinct existent. They each exist independently of the whole... The parts are all *already* embedded in the architecture of the whole. Division merely separates them, it does not create them.'[16] A theory of *minima naturalia* is a theory of potential parts. It denies the homoeomerity of physical bodies without commitment to a corpuscular natural philosophy.

The theory of *minima naturalia*, as Van Melsen says, is found in Aristotle in an 'embryonic state'.[17] The term 'minimum' (*elachiston*) goes back to Epicurus,[18] and is used by Alexander.[19] Atoms are elementary indivisible particles. Minima need not necessarily be distinct particles but are, in some theoretical sense, the smallest things possible.[20] Several of Aristotle's Greek and Latin commentators elaborated on Aristotle's passage quoted above.[21] According to the prevalent

[15] Holden 2004, 18 (Holden's emphasis).

[16] Ibid. (Holden's emphasis). In both quotations Holden refers to what he calls 'metaphysical division'. An extended entity is metaphysically divisible if and only if it is logically possible that its spatially distinct parts could exist separately from one another (ibid., 12). It is physically divisible if its parts can be broken apart by a natural process (ibid., 11). Lennon (1993, 138–9) distinguishes between physical and metaphysical atomism: the former is the thesis 'that the infinite divisibility of matter is a physical impossibility,' while the latter denies internal relations and emphasizes the independence of things.

[17] Van Melsen 1960, 44.

[18] Epicurus, 'Letter to Herodotus'; see Long and Sedley 1987 # 9a, Greek: II, 32; English: I, 40; commentary I, 42. Furley (1967, ch. 8) suggests that Epicurus introduced the *minima* as a response to Aristotle's criticism of early atomism in *Physics* VI. According to the analysis of motion of *Physics* VI, 'everything that changes must be divisible'; 'that which is without parts cannot be in motion except accidentally' (*Physics* VI.4 234^b10–20; VI.10 240^b8). According to the analysis of contact, a continuum cannot be composed of indivisibles (VI.1 231^a21–b17). These arguments apparently threaten the atomistic theory, which was based on the notion of the atom as indivisible. The concept of boundary and the analysis of contact play an important part in the development of Epicurus' interpretation (Furley 1967, 115; Konstan 1979, 403). Compare also Vlastos (1965, 122).

[19] Commenting on the famous passage from *Physics* I.4, Simplicius quotes Alexander: 'In every separation a certain number of *elachista* is separated.' Van Melsen suggests that *elachiston* was Alexander's term for minimal part (Van Melsen 1960, 47; Wallace 1966, 1021 col. b).

[20] Scholars agree that Leucippus and Democritus conceived of atoms both as unsplittable atoms and as theoretical *minima* (Furley 1967, 111; Konstan 1982, 62–3; 1988, 5).

[21] e.g., 'the division of the form often comes to an end because it has a certain limit, with regard to the smaller as to the greater (for it has been said that forms are not

presentation, the theory of *minima naturalia* was developed by the Scholastics from the statements by Aristotle mentioned above. The role of Arabic atomism[22] and of Arabic Aristotelianism has not been seriously studied. The two pioneer students of Scholastic science, Pierre Duhem and Anneliese Maier, did not assign to Averroes any role in the development of this theory.[23] Van Melsen is the only scholar I know of who did justice to Averroes and his role in the development of the theory.[24] Still, he could not pursue this investigation because he did not have access to the short and the middle commentaries. We shall see that Averroes not only 'anticipated' the Scholastic theory of *minima naturalia*, but actually developed a complete and coherent theory of his own. In fact, his theory is much more than a theory of *minima naturalia*: it is a theory of actual parts, that is, a corpuscular theory, which goes far beyond the hints that Averroes found in Aristotle.

There are two principal reasons why scholars have not been aware of Averroes' theory. First, the exposition in the long commentary is rather vague. The middle commentary, where it is easier to follow the argument, was not translated into Latin and is extant only in Hebrew

naturally able to remain in every magnitude), but because of matter the cutting does not come to an end' (Philoponus *On Phys.* 481. 3–6; English: Edwards 1994, 143). 'It must be pointed out that a body, considered mathematically, is divisible to infinity. For in a mathematical body nothing but quantity is considered. . . . But in a natural body form also is considered' (Aquinas, *On Physics* (1963), book I, lecture 9, 34).

22 The historical connection between Epicurean and Kalām atomism is not yet fully understood. In 1936, Pines asked whether there was a resemblance between the *minima* (not the atoms!) of Epicurus and the *ajzā'* of the mutakallimūn (1936/1997, 112–13). He was not yet acquainted with Luria's 1933 paper, 'Die Infinitisimaltheorie der antiken Atomisten,' which had made some progress in the study of Epicurus' atomism. A few years ago, Dhanani re-examined the question in the light of recent research on both ancient and Kalām atomism. He did not find an explicit statement of a theory of minimal parts analogous to that of Epicurus, but concluded that there was sufficient evidence for arguing that many of the mutakallimūn entertained the notion of such minimal parts (Dhanani 1994, 106).

23 Duhem (1954, 42) quotes *Physics* I.4, and remarks, 'Ce texte ne semble guère avoir retenu l'attention d'Averroès . . . Mais très vite la Scolastique latine s'est emparée de cette courte phrase et a développé l'idée qu'elle contenait en germe.' Maier (1949, 180), who usually studies the views of Avicenna and Averroes carefully before coming to those of the Latin scholars, quotes only the relevant passage of Aristotle and remarks that the Scholastics developed their thesis from these statements. In his book on seventeenth-century atomism, Clericuzio (2000, 10) writes that 'the transformation of *minima naturalia* into physical units marked a significant step towards the establishment of corpuscular philosophy'. He ascribes the first step towards the concept of the minimum in physical terms to Buridan and Albert of Saxony.

24 Van Melsen 1960, 58–60; see also Pyle 1995, 217–19.

manuscripts. Second, Averroes does not present his theory in the 'expected context' of *Physics* I.4 as do Thomas and other Scholastics,[25] but rather in his commentaries on *Physics* VII.1. This context, we shall see, is very relevant to the understanding of Averroes' theory of *minima naturalia* in its relation to his theory of motion.

8.2. ARISTOTLE'S MOVING-AGENT ARGUMENT (*PHYSICS* VII.1)[26]

In book VI Aristotle deals with the simple situation of one body in motion, studying it qua homoeomer. This approach is no longer possible in book VII, where Aristotle proceeds to the more complex situation of several bodies in interaction. Book VII opens with the *moving-agent argument*: 'everything that is moved (*kinoumenon*) must be moved by something'.[27] Let me first summarize Aristotle's rather awkward argument:

- *Premise VII.A*: 'If anything ceases from moving as a consequence of another thing having stopped—it is moved by something other than itself'.[28]
- *Premise VII.B*: 'Everything that is moved is divisible.'[29]

25 Only a brief allusion to the theory appears in this context: 'flesh has a limited size with regard to smallness, below which it cannot go, i.e. there cannot be a smaller piece of flesh' (*LC Phys*. I.37 Latin 24M13–25A4, Hebrew 25a3–4).

26 Chapter VII.1–VII.3 of Aristotle's *Physics* are extant in two Greek versions, generally referred to as α and β. Ibn Ḥunayn's Arabic translation is based on version β, and this is the version that was known to Averroes. See Lettinck 1994*a*, 510. There is no indication that he knew about the existence of another version.

27 *Physics* VII.1 241^{b}34–242^{a}49 (version α), 241^{b}24–242^{a}15 (version β). The argument appears also in VIII.4, 256^{a}2: 'All things that are in motion must be moved by something.' The approaches and aims of the two arguments, however, are different. See Lang 1992, 35–6.

28 *Physics* VII.1 242^{a}2 version β. The α-version texts are somewhat different: 'It is not necessary for what is not moved by something to stop moving because of something else being at rest' (242^{a}34–6). 'If anything comes to rest because something else has stopped moving, it is necessarily moved by something' (242^{a}37), Wardy's translation with modifications. Aristotle derives this premise from a previous one: 'Something moved by itself will never cease from moving as a consequence of another thing having stopped moving' (VII.1 242^{a}1–2 version β). The derivation is by the conversion of the obverse.

29 *Physics* VII.1 242^{a}40 (version α), 242^{a}7 (version β). Aristotle relies here on *Physics* VI.4 234^{b}10.

- Hypothesis I: 'Assume an object AB that is moved essentially (*kath' hauto*)[30] and not by one of its parts being moved.'[31]
- Construction (relying on premise VII.B): 'Let it be divided at C.'
- Intermediate argument: 'If CB is at rest, then AB too is at rest.'[32]

The intermediate argument is proved *per impossibile*:

- Hypothesis II (to be refuted): 'While CB is at rest CA moves.'[33]
- Refutation of hypothesis II: Then AB does not move essentially. But it was assumed (hypothesis I) that it moves *essentially and primarily* (*kath' hauto kai prōton*).[34] Therefore, if CB is at rest then AB must be at rest.
- Conclusion: therefore, according to premise VII.A, AB is moved by something other than itself.

Aristotle argues that for any body AB assumed to be moved *essentially* there is something distinguishable from it, its part CB, which is responsible for its movement.[35] In the case of a homoeomer, which has no distinguishable parts, the argument is very difficult.

8.3. ALEXANDER VS. GALEN ON THE MEANING OF ESSENTIALITY

Once again we shall see that a problematic argument by Aristotle, which was open to criticism and different interpretations, provided fertile ground for Averroes' new ideas. Since antiquity, using Wardy's words, '*Physics* VII has suffered from neglect and bad press'.[36] This was partly due to the argument summarized above that has been subject to much criticism. In the second century Galen criticized it and Alexander tried to defend him. Our two extant sources on this controversy are

[30] The *per se* is missing in the Leiden manuscript of Isḥaq Ibn Ḥunayn translation (*Physics* Arabic: 733.12–734.1), as well as in the quotation by Averroes in text VII.1 of the long commentary (Latin 306A5, Hebrew 105^b3).

[31] *Physics* VII.1 241^b37–8 (version α), 241^b27 (version β) (trans. Wardy, modified).

[32] Ibid. 242^a7 (version β), 242^a41 (version α).

[33] Ibid. 242^a8 (version β), 242^a42–3 (version α).

[34] Ibid. 242^a5–9 (version β), 242^a38–44 (version α) (trans. Wardy, modified).

[35] Wardy 1990, 96. [36] Ibid. 85.

Simplicius' monumental commentary on Aristotle's *Physics* and Alexander's *Refutation of Galen's Treatise on the Theory of Motion.*[37] The latter was translated into Arabic,[38] and was, most likely, Averroes' source on this controversy.[39] The controversy is over the meaning of 'essentiality'. Galen and Alexander, we shall see, pull in opposite directions.

Essential motion, for Aristotle, is a manifestation of an inner unity of the moved body.[40] In the *Physics* VII.1 he posits three more or less equal conditions:[41] [I] that AB is moved essentially (*kath' hauto*, بالذات, בעצמות, *per se* or *essentialiter)*,[42] [II] that it is not moved by a part,[43] and [III] that it is moved primarily,[44] or 'according to the first intention' (على القصد الاول).[45] Wardy suggests two possible interpretations of *kath' hauto* here: the 'weak and reasonable' interpretation is intended to distinguish accidental unities (e.g., the assemblage man-with-faggots) from the authentic ***kath' hauta kinoumena*** [moved essentially things], for example, a man;[46] the 'stronger and less reasonable' interpretation denies that a man can move essentially because a man moves with his legs.[47]

In the parallel argument in *Physics* VIII.4 Aristotle endorses the *strong definition of essential motion:* a body is moved essentially if it is neither (1) moved as a part nor (2) by a part.[48]

[37] The question of the authenticity of Alexander's *Refutations* is highly interesting (see Fazzo 1997; Fazzo 2002), but needs not concern us in the present context as it did not concern Averroes.

[38] The *Refutation* has been edited (on the basis of the two extant manuscripts, Carullah and Escurial) and translated into English by Rescher and Marmura (1965). Pines (1961/1986) had studied this text earlier, but was acquainted only with Carullah manuscript, which is incomplete.

[39] This point will be substantiated in what follows.

[40] *Physics* VII.1 241^b39–40 (version α), 241^b28–9 (version β).

[41] He remarks, however, that being moved essentially is a stronger notion than being moved 'as a whole'. It is erroneous to think that DEF moves itself when in fact DE moves EF or the other way round (241^b30–33 version β). On the difference between the two versions of this passage see Wardy 1990, 95.

[42] In Isḥaq Ibn Ḥunayn's translation the word 'essentially' in this sentence is missing.

[43] *Physics* VII.1 241^b27 (version β), 241^b37–8 (version α). In the Arabic translation of Alexander's *Refutation* it is rendered 'according to first intention'.

[44] Ibid. 242^a9 (version β), 242^a44 (version α). The meaning of 'primarily' will be discussed in what follows.

[45] Following the Arabic translator of Alexander.

[46] Wardy 1990, 93. [47] Ibid. 94.

[48] *Physics* VIII.4 254^b10–11. In *Physics* VIII.4 too Aristotle lists several comparable categorizations of motion: (i) essentially (***kath' hauto***) vs. accidentally (***kata sumbebēkos***); (ii) by nature vs. by force; (iii) by itself vs. by another. The three pairs are close but, according to VIII.4, irreducible to one another. See Graham 1999, 74–5; Waterlow 1982, 205–7.

Is essential motion possible in the case of the simple bodies and the homoeomers which do not possess a sufficient degree of unity? Aristotle's answer is not clear-cut. Mary Louise Gill contends that Aristotle denies 'an internal active cause' to the simple bodies and the homoeomers because they are heaps and not substances: 'If the elements have such a principle, they deserve to be substances; and if they deserve to be substances at all, they threaten to be substances par excellence in the sublunary sphere, since their simple unity is unproblematic.'[49] Unlike Aristotle, Galen was not threatened by the idea of ascribing essential motion to the homoeomers. Rather, he contends that because of their natural unity and continuity they are the bodies par excellence, which are moved essentially:

When some magnitude, in the event that its parts are continuous, moves essentially and according to the first intention, *it must be one of the simple bodies*. These are the bodies whose parts are similar, since *these alone are the things that move essentially and according to the first intention*. Since the things whose natural principle of motion is in them are the first simple bodies, and since these consist of similar parts, *the part in these things is no other than the whole*. Hence Aristotle was not definitely right with respect to continuous things [when he held] that when one part of them stops, the whole then stops. For *the part in these things is no other than the whole*.[50] Under no circumstances is there any difference in these things between the part and the whole.[51]

The simple bodies are those whose parts are not only similar but identical.[52] From this strong 'qualitative' notion of unity, the whole and the part are indistinguishable; from a 'quantitative' or geometrical perspective, however, 'the part is greater than the whole'.[53] From this standpoint Alexander answers Galen:

He [Aristotle] also made use of that the part is not the whole and that the whole has parts that are similar. For the part in things whose parts are similar [i.e.

[49] Gill 1989, 238.

[50] Alexander, *Refutation*, Esc. 63^{a}9–15, English 33–4, Arabic 107. In his book, also preserved in an Arabic translation, he defines a homoeomer as 'that whose substance has a single form all throughout'. See Strohmaier 1970, Arabic 50, German 51, # 2. I am grateful to Gad Freudenthal for referring me to this text.

[51] Alexander, *Refutation*, Esc. 63^{b}18, English 35, Arabic 111.

[52] Galen distinguishes between identical parts and similar parts, accusing Aristotle and his followers of not observing this distinction. 'What is similar is composed of the essence [māhiyya] and the being-different [ghīriyyah], but the essence-parts predominate: the being-different-parts are few, for if they predominated it would no longer be similar, and what has this composition is named anhomoiomer.' (Ibid., Arabic 46, German 47, # 7).

[53] Euclid, *Elements* I, common notion 9 according to Heiberg.

homoeomers] *is other than the whole*, since the latter is *a whole of parts* while the former is not the whole but *only a part*.[54]

Galen subscribes to a strong notion of homoeomerity and a *weak notion of essentiality*:[55] being moved essentially means no more than being moved by a mover from within.[56] Alexander rejects Galen's simplification,[57] and defends the strong notion of essentiality. I shall quote several passages because here lies the basis of Averroes' theory of minima naturalia:

The things that move essentially are those that move in reality. For the things that are said to move essentially (بذاتها) are [I] things that are moving in themselves (بانفسها) and are not merely existing in a thing that moves; and [II] those that move *as a whole* and not through the movement of a part.[58] The things that move according to the first intention are all those things which are not characterized as moving when only one part of them moves.[59]

As for his expression [condition III] 'according to first intention' he does not mean by it the thing which is said to move because only some part of it moves. Rather, he means by it the thing that moves *in its entirety*.[60] The reason for the false doubts to which he [Galen] adheres and with which he

54 Alexander, *Refutation*, Car. 67^b6–7, English 19, Arabic 81. Similarly, 'the whole is other than the parts proper to it' (Car. 67^b26–7, English 21, Arabic 84).

55 He disregards the subtle differences between Aristotle's three conditions and simplifies matters greatly. Tieleman (1996, p. xxi) remarks that in a sense Galen's approach reflects the syncretism of his age, whose hallmark is 'an impatience with terminological niceties and fine conceptual distinctions.'

56 Galen does away with condition II—'It is not moved by a part'—and introduces instead the almost opposite Condition II_G: Its motion is induced by a mover from within. Then he reduces conditions I and III to II_G: It is clear that when we say that a thing [I] moves [essentially], we have indicated no more than that [III] it moves according to the first intention. This is because both these expressions merely refer to the things [II_G] whose source of motion exists in them and whose motion is not basically due to anything from the outside (Alexander *Refutation*. Esc. 62^b24–63^a1 English 33, Arabic 105; Rescher and Marmura's brackets).

57 'The things that move essentially are not only those which suit his [Galen's] purpose.' Ibid., Esc. 62^a24–5 English 31, Arabic 102. Perhaps Alexander alludes to Galen's conception of animal motion. He testifies that 'it is known that according to his [Galen's] opinion only the bodies that have souls move in reality and essentially' (Esc. 63^b15, English 35, Arabic 110). Indeed, according to Galen's definition the movement of an animal by its soul is essential; according to Alexander's it is not.

58 Ibid., Car. 67^b8–10, English 19, Arabic 81–2. Also, 'If it is only the thing that moves essentially that is said to move in reality, then it would have been shown as a whole that everything that moves in reality is moved by something' (English 21).

59 Ibid., Esc. 64^b24–6, English 38, Arabic 117.

60 Ibid., Esc. 63^b1–2, English 34, Arabic 109. Alexander suggests a thought experiment: 'In order for him [Galen] to see that he did not show anything, let him replace

continues thereafter is that he did not understand what is meant by [condition III] the thing that moves *according to the first intention*. Had he understood what Aristotle maintained about the thing that moves [so], namely that *all of it moves*—if it is indeed a thing that moves [according to condition I] essentially and [to IV] in reality[61]—he would not have denied any of the statements set down.[62]

For as we have repeatedly said [things that move accidentally][63] include [1] the things that move and are moved inasmuch as they exist in things that move and are moved, and [2] things that are moved through the movement of the part. Things that are moved essentially are the totality of [1] those that are not moving or moved only because they exist in the mover or the moved, and [2] not because a part of them moves or is moved.[64]

The thing that moves essentially is not that thing which is [composed] of parts that move.[65]

Alexander holds to a *strong definition of essential motion*: A body is moved essentially when it is moved 'as a whole' or 'in its entirety' or such that 'all of it moves'. Galen conceives unity in terms of homoeomerity, Alexander in terms of essentiality. The argument between them is between Stoic continuism and Aristotelian essentialism and reveals the incompatibility between the two views.

Which physical entity is a true whole to which essential motion can be attributed? In the *Refutation* Alexander does not offer a definite answer.[66] One millennium later, Averroes does. He pursues Alexander's interpretation and takes up where Alexander left: he defines the essential unit that moves as a whole and calls it a 'First-Moved part'. This way thus Averroes saves Aristotle's notion of essentiality in physics.

our expression "according to the first intention" with our expression "the whole"' (Esc. 64^b6–7, English 37, Arabic 115).

61 'In reality' بالحقيقة is an emphasis of Alexander not found in Aristotle.

62 Ibid., Esc. 64^a28–b4, English 37, Arabic 115. Condition I implies the other conditions: 'Things that do not move in an accidental way [i.e. move in an essential way]—these being things that move [III] according to first intention and [IV] in reality and [II] not because their motion consists in the motion of one of their parts' (ibid., Car. 67^a10–11, English 16–17, Arabic 76). Conditions I and III mean that AB is moved qua one whole, not qua a whole of parts whose motion depends on the motions of its parts. Condition II is included in I and the added condition IV—'in reality'—emphasizes that the argument is indeed about an actual motion of AB.

63 I have corrected the error in Rescher and Marmura's English translation.

64 Ibid., Esc. 67^a11–15, English 45, Arabic 131–2 (translation modified).

65 Ibid., Esc. 62^a27–b1, English 31, Arabic 103.

66 We cannot know if he was more explicit in his commentary on the *Physics*, but we know that Averroes did not read book VII of the commentary.

8.4. AVERROES' NOTION OF FIRST-MOVED PART

Alexander, as we saw in the previous section, coined the notion 'whole of parts' and distinguished between a 'whole of parts' and 'only a part'. He did not, however, pursue this distinction. Averroes did. There are two types of entities, those which are 'only parts' and those which are 'wholes of parts', that is, composed of entities of the first type. Averroes calls an entity of the first type a *mutaḥararriq al-awwal* (*mitno^{c}e^{c}a ri'shon*, *primum motum*, *res mota primo*). I shall render this as 'First-Moved'[67] or 'First-Moved part'.[68] The concept of a First-Moved part is the core of Averroes' theory of *minima naturalia.* Averroes introduces the new notion in his three commentaries on *Physics* VII.1. Let us start with the middle commentary:

The demonstration of this [of Aristotle's moving-agent argument] is: That which is moved essentially[69] is either [1] First, or [2] not-First. [1] The First-Moved is that which is not moved due to a part of it that is moved essentially or can be moved essentially, e.g. a part of earth or water[70] [so small] that no smaller part can assume the form of water,[71] for such a magnitude is bounded[72] in natural bodies. [2] The not-First [-Moved] is that which is moved as a whole because a part of it moves essentially, e.g. the motion of any magnitude of earth greater than the smallest part, or the local motion of an animal due to the vital heat that is in it. It is thus clear that the not-First-Moved is moved by something else, which is the First-Moved. It is therefore established that if a self-mover exists, in which the mover and the moved are one and the same thing, it must necessarily be first.[73]

A First-Moved is that which is moved, but not due to a part of it that moves *or can move* by itself. *A not-First-Moved* is that which moves as

[67] The simple morphology of the English language is very convenient for students, less so for translators. The translators of Aristotle's *Physics* have always had trouble with the Greek participle 'kinoumenon' and with distinguishing between the active and middle-passive uses of the verb 'kineō'.

[68] Hassing and Macierowsky (1992, 136–7) refer to this notion that appears in the long commentary on *Physics* VII.1 as the 'first moved part'. Their analysis is focused mainly on Averroes' contention that the first moved part is moved by its form.

[69] Averroes starts, following Aristotle, with a body that is moved essentially. Later he will argue that only the first is moved essentially.

[70] Zeraḥya: 'like a lesser motion of earth or water.'

[71] Zeraḥya: 'fire'.

[72] Zeraḥya: מוגדר Kalonimus MS Paris: מוגבל. In MS Hamburg we find the נמנה, which is, apparently a copyist error.

[73] *MC Phys.* VII.1 Kalonimus 83^a2–13. Zeraḥya 99^b21–100^a9. Kalonimus translated the last word correctly as an adjective (ראשון), Zeraḥya erroneously as an adverb (תחלה).

a whole because a part of it moves essentially. The not-First-Moved is moved by something else, namely the First-Moved.

The main point to note is that Averroes' notion of 'First-Moved' is very significantly stronger than Aristotle's notion of 'being moved primarily'.[74] Aristotle uses the word *prōton*, which is both an adjective and an adverb in Greek, and is commonly translated in this context as an adverb: 'primarily'. Averroes understands it as an adjective: 'first'. This is important: the conditions do not pertain to the motion of AB but to AB itself. AB is innately a First-Moved entity.

The First-Moved is thus the candidate for being an essentially moved entity. In *Physics* VIII.4 Aristotle ascribes essential motion to a body if it is moved (1) neither as a part (2) nor by a part. Averroes defines 'First-Moved' as that which satisfies (2).[75] The crucial point is now to show that such an entity really exists and that it also satisfies (1). He accomplishes these two tasks by identifying the First-Moved as the minimal part.[76] This solution is alluded to in the passage quoted above and also in the long and short commentaries:

There must be things that are First-Moved (*Prima mota*, מתנועעים ראשונים) since natural bodies are not infinitely divisible *in actu* qua natural bodies. For

[74] Condition III, see p. 148 above.

[75] Following Alexander, who turned (2) into a criterion of essentiality: 'That which comes to rest in its entirety when a part of it comes to rest does not move essentially' (*Refutation*, Car. 67^{b}16–18. Arabic 83 English 20).

[76] Averroes was familiar with the Aristotelian notion of the minimal part, e.g. in his middle commentary on *Physics* III.7: 'And to someone who would argue that the line is infinitely divisible qua pure line, but that qua a line of fire or a line of water it is not infinitely divisible, but is divisible into an *indivisible magnitude* that is the smallest magnitude that can assume the form of fire, as this magnitude is naturally limited . . . —we say that the master of this science [i.e. the mathematician] indeed studies magnitudes qua boundaries of natural enmattered bodies and that infinite divisibility indeed pertains to magnitude qua matter, not qua form. Qua form its divisibility is limited. This is why a magnitude of fire cannot be infinitely divisible qua a magnitude of fire; it can be infinitely divisible qua pure magnitude, not qua being a natural body' (*MC Phys.* III.3.5, 31^{a}22–5, ^{b}4–10). In the long commentary on the *Physics*: 'When we remove a part of fire from a given quantity of the element fire and repeat this action again and again we finally reach a quantity which is such that by a further division the fire would perish, because there is a certain minimal quantity of fire' (*LC Phys.* VIII. 44, Latin 384K). 'A line as a line can be divided infinitely. But such a division is impossible if the line is taken as made of earth' (IV.72, Latin 163H). 'It is impossible for something to increase or decrease infinitely, because if the quantity determined by nature is passed, whether by increase or decrease, the being perishes' (VI.32, Latin 267D). The last three passages are quoted from Van Melsen 1960, 58–60. See also *MC De cael.* Arabic 289.3–6; Hebrew 61^{b}22–4.

instance, in the case of fire the First-Moved is a part such that a part smaller than it would not be fire *in actu*.[77]

The First-Moved—i.e., that which is moved not due to a part of it that is moved—is that which is moved essentially. In these simple bodies—which are the cause of doubt—it is the minimal possible magnitude of fire that moves upwards or the minimal possible magnitude of earth that moves downwards, because the moved [part] of earth and of fire that is so described is a First-Moved because this movement cannot occur to a part of it, for a smaller part of fire cannot exist, because the magnitudes of existing things are limited.[78]

Averroes' First-Moved is, thus, moved essentially in the strong sense: neither by a part, nor as a part, but 'as a whole'. Averroes can, thus, complete the defence of Aristotle's argument against Galen, in the direction indicated by Alexander. The premises are valid and the argument *per impossibile* is sound:[79]

- Everything moved is either First-Moved or not-First-Moved.
- The statement to be proved is trivially true of the not-First-Moved that is moved by the First-Moved. The argument can, therefore, be restricted to a First-Moved AB.[80]
- Qua First-Moved, AB is moved essentially. Aristotle's conditions I-III are satisfied and the argument is valid.[81]
- The conclusion that the moved body is moved by something else is true in both cases and thus proved.[82]

With the new notion of the First-Moved part Averroes introduces a profound change into Aristotelian physics: he breaks down Aristotle's

[77] *LC Phys*. VII.2 Latin 307I3–9; Hebrew 107ᵃ25–7.

[78] *SC Phys*. Arabic 114.1–9, Hebrew 35ᵃ13–21.

[79] Hypothesis I is not invalid because there are First-Moved entities that are moved essentially and AB is assumed to be such an entity. 'When this is not stipulated, the demonstration is invalid' (*MC Phys*. VII.1 84ᵃ2–3). Similarly, according to the long commentary the refutation is valid because AB 'was assumed to be a First-Moved and this is impossible' (*LC Phys*. VII.1 Latin 307G3–9; Hebrew 107ᵃ14–16).

[80] 'This being so, let us inquire whether it is possible for there to be a First-Moved that will be moved by itself and rest by itself.' *MC Phys*. VII.1 83ᵃ13–15.

[81] 'It necessarily follows from its [AB's] being first, when we assume that a part of it, CB, is at rest (and this is possible in every moved-body qua a moved-body) that AB rests *as a whole*, because if the remaining part AC were moved or could be moved, then ACB would not have been First-Moved, and we assumed that it is; and this is impossible.' *MC Phys*. VII.1 83ᵃ26–b4.

[82] 'It follows necessarily that the First-Moved ACB, qua first, is moved by something else. As this was established for the First-Moved, it is true that everything moved is moved by something else (for the doubt concerned the First-Moved in the case of local motion).' Ibid., 83ᵇ8–12.

notion of homoeomerity and denies continuity in the physical world. Can his theory be viewed as a corpuscular theory or a theory of actual parts?

8.5. AVERROES' 'ARISTOTELIAN ATOMISM'

Van Melsen suggests that 'for Averroes natural *minima* mean much more than a theoretical limit of divisibility. They are for him *like physical realities*.'[83] This suggestion was not accepted by most scholars. Meinel remarks that 'the *minima* were not mechanical particles and could not simply be translated into corpuscular terms.'[84] Pabst complains that Van Melsen attributes 'corpuscular trains of thought' to Averroes but that the evidence he adduces is insufficient.[85] Murdoch criticizes him for assigning 'a great stride in the advancement of the notion of *minima naturalia* to Alexander of Aphrodisias'.[86] Let me re-address the question.

The terms of the discussion, were homoeomerity vs. essentiality: Galen conceived unity in terms of continuity or homoeomerity, Alexander in terms of essentiality.[87] These two conceptions of unity were not yet differentiated in Aristotle: body is one qua being continuous (i.e. in one piece), and qua having one motion.[88] Aristotle strongly associates one body and one motion.[89] The body's motion is a manifestation of its essence: 'the primary movement in each natural object is present in it by virtue of its own essence.'[90] Aristotle cannot explain, however, what is the unit with which the motion of water, for instance, is associated.[91] A simple body has its specific natural motion but, as Aristotle himself admits, cannot count as one entity: 'none of them [the four simple

[83] Van Melsen 1960, 60. [84] Meinel 1988, 70–71.

[85] Pabst 1994, 274. I would like to thank Heidrun Eichner for drawing my attention to Pabst's book (to which I had no easy access) and for sending me the relevant passages.

[86] Murdoch 2001, 94. [87] pp. 150–151 above.

[88] In his philosophical dictionary a thing is essentially one if it is continuous, and 'a thing is called continuous which has by its own nature one movement and cannot have any other.' *Metaphysics* Δ.6. 1015b35–1016a7.

[89] e.g. 'A single thing has a single movement' (*De caelo* II.14 $296^{b}30$); 'a single motion must be a motion of a magnitude . . . and the magnitude must be a single magnitude' (*Physics* VIII.10 $267^{a}23$–4).

[90] *Physics* V.4; See also VII.1 $241^{b}39$–40 (version α), $241^{b}28$–9 (version β).

[91] This problem reflects a very deep difficulty in Aristotle's philosophy that stems from his attempt to apply the same conceptual frame and terms of reference to the animate and to the non-animate world.

bodies and their parts] is a unity, but as it were a heap, until they are concocted and some unity is formed from them.'[92]

Lennox explains Aristotle's notion of oneness: 'An individual is numerically one in virtue of being either naturally (e.g. a cat), artificially (e.g. a table) or accidentally (e.g. a pool of water) physically continuous.'[93] For Averroes, the pool of water is no longer an 'accidental one' but rather an aggregate of 'natural ones':

> The motion of the body as a whole is the aggregate (קיבוץ) of the movements of the parts and the sum of the movements of the parts is *nothing but* the motion of the whole.[94]

> By God,[95] you should know the difference between ascribing it [the motion] to the whole and ascribing it to the parts. I mean that when it is ascribed to the whole it is one and when ascribed to the parts it is many.[96]

Averroes' great innovation lies in defining essential parts or units which are the 'carriers' of the essential motion of a body. It was Alexander who first advanced a more 'essentialistic' understanding of the elements. Kupreeva argues that the hylomorphic analysis of the elements was instrumental in Alexander's debate with the Stoics: Alexander emphasizes that the elements are not the bundles of elemental qualities but substances.[97] Alexander has to turn to the theory of *minima naturalia* to support his anti-Stoic position. The elements are not perfect homoeomers, because a certain amount of matter must remain in order for the form to persist.[98]

[92] *Metaphysics* Z.16 $1040^{b}5$–16, Ross' translation. Freudenthal analyses Aristotle's notion of concoction: 'All processes of concoction, natural or artificial, have in common that they bring together "things of the same kind," thereby producing homogeneous bodies.... It [concoction] leads up to a homoeomerous substance whose texture is uniform throughout and which has a characteristic logos of its components' (Freudenthal 1995, 22–3). In the early *Metaphysics* Δ the requirement is weaker: 'a bundle is made one by a band, and pieces of wood are made one by glue; and a line, even if it is bent, is called one if it is continuous, as each part of the body is, e.g. the leg or the arm.' *Metaphysics* Δ.6, $1016^{a}1$–3. See also *Physics* I.2, $185^{b}7$–8.

[93] Lennox 2001, 161.

[94] In *Physics* VI.4 $234^{b}22$–33 Aristotle contends that the motion of the whole is the sum of the motions of the parts. Aristotle apparently thought of the divisibility of motion with respect to the moved body, not with respect to time.

[95] Following Cambridge manuscript האלהים דע, MS Paris reads יודע'. Such exclamations are common in Arabic scholarly texts.

[96] *LC Phys.* VI.38 Hebrew $68^{a}23$–5.

[97] Kupreeva 2003, 313.

[98] Alexander, *On Mixture* XVI 235.29–34, English 167. Ascribing to Aristotle a weak notion of homoeomerity Alexander can reject the Stoic theory of total blending or 'coexistence'. Kupreeva shows that Alexander offers instead a theory of 'mutual replacement' that does not assume perfect homoeomerity. Kupreeva 2004, 301–4, 322.

Averroes pursues Alexander's understanding and carries out the hylomorphic analysis of the elements within the First-Moved unit. Gradually and carefully he leads up to the conclusion that the First-Moved unit is a complex entity having matter and form. In the middle commentary he distinguishes two faculties within the First-Moved unit, but does not yet refer to them as matter and form:

> The reason that a First-Moved [i.e. a minimal part] exists is merely the *distinction in reality between the mover and the moved*, for if the mover of the thing were the moved thing itself then there would have been no First-Moved, as it has been established that everything that is moved is divisible into that which is always divisible.[99]

A simple entity (e.g. a geometrical magnitude) can be infinitely divisible. Qua being moved, the physical body is infinitely divisible. It is the moving faculty that defines the First-Moved part as a 'unit'. In the short commentary Averroes continues the argument and eventually identifies [1] the being moved faculty as matter and [2] the moving faculty as form. The style is somewhat cumbersome, but the import of the passage is significant:

> Because it rests when a part of it rests[100]—it means that [2] the moving-part in it is deactivated (بطل) while [1] the moved-part remains, and that it [the moved part] is not the moving-part, because if the moving-part were the moved-part—the remaining part of the First-Moved would not have rested. This is because it [the moved part] [1] has not lost the faculty (معنى)[101] by which it is moved, because that which remains is a body and divisible, and indeed it is moved qua a body and divisible. And since the remainder rests when the part rests, it is understood that the First-Moved[102] has lost a faculty, other than the faculty [1] by which it is moved, and this is [2] the faculty by which the First-Moved becomes indivisible. Because if it were divided in this [faculty] it would not have rested when a part of it rested, and would not have been a First-Moved. Thus, in the moved thing there are necessarily two faculties: [1] one of them by which it is divided, and this is the faculty by which it is moved; and [2] the second, which is indivisible, and is the faculty that, when absent the movement is absent—and this is necessarily the moving-part. Therefore in such simple bodies the first-moved is divided qua moved-part[1], and indivisible

99 *MC Phys*. VII.1 83^{b}16–20.

100 The word is missing in the Riva da Trento edition.

101 'Faculty' is not one of the common translations of *ma*^{c}*na*. However, none of the common translations fits here. Since *ma*^{c}*na* is used in so many senses I took the liberty to translate it here according to the context.

102 Following C and H: المتحرك الاول. M and S read المتحرك الباقي..

qua moving-part [2]. Therefore the moving-part (محرك) in them is necessarily other than the moved-part (متحرك). And divisibility pertains to them qua their matter [1], and indivisibility qua form [2], and the form is the mover and is other than the moved.[103]

Averroes explains at length the roles of the two faculties within the First-Moved unit and in the last sentence identifies them as matter and form: matter [1] is the faculty for being moved and also for being a quantity and divisible;[104] form [2] is the faculty for moving and is indivisible.[105] Averroes can now easily explain the indivisibility of the form, which Aristotle found hard to explain.[106] The form of earth is associated with each minimal part of earth, which is indivisible and an ontologically stable entity.[107] The First-Moved part is thus a hylomorphic unit: it 'carries' the specific form of the body and dictates its specific motion.

From the long commentary we learn that the First-Moved unit is also a first-generated unit and thus as an actual entity:

The First in generation and corruption is the minimal part of the generated [body], for the minimum of all that is generated is of a limited quantity. For example, the minimal part of fire is limited, being the minimal part that can become fire.[108]

[103] *SC Phys.*, Arabic 114.16–115.12, Hebrew 35ª31–b18. Compare the last sentence: 'and division indeed applies to a thing *qua* body, not *qua* being composed of matter and form, since division applies to form only accidentally' (Falaquera, *De*ᶜ*ot ha-Filosofim*, 256ᵇ18–19).

[104] According to *Physics* VI.4, everything that is moved must be divisible.

[105] Gersonides comments: 'Therefore it is established that the form is the mover. Aristotle explained this when he suggested that in the homoeomers, e.g. the simple bodies, there is a minimal part that can move, and this he calls first-moved. This is so because movements are of natural bodies, and natural bodies, qua natural, are not infinitely divisible, but division naturally terminates with the smallest magnitude which can still assume this form, and *this is the first-moved (* about which it is doubted whether the mover is itself moved)' (Gersonides, *On MC Phys.* 118ª18–b4). Gersonides mistakenly ascribes Averroes' idea to Aristotle.

[106] Aristotle does not explain how, when a mass of water is divided, the form is retained in each part. Philoponus admits the divisibility of form: '*The division of the form* often comes to an end because it has a certain limit' (*On Phys.* 481, 3–6, English 143). '[When a body is generated] with each part of it *a part of the form* has come to exist, so that when the generation is finished and has come to an end, the form is completed' (*On Phys.* V 517.23, English 35).

[107] 'It is self evident that the division of magnitude is in the matter, not in the form, because the form remains what it is and the end and the perfection and wholeness of the thing are determined by the form' (*MC Phys.* III.3.7, Kalonimus 32ᵇ12–14, Zeraḥya 40ª13–16).

[108] *LC Phys.* VI.32, Latin 267D6–12, Hebrew 64ª1–4. The Latin text here is better than the Hebrew.

In the process of generation new small parts of flesh are generated in minimal pores in the tissue.[109] Averroes could have found these notions in Alexander.[110] The important point is that the minimal part is not produced by division but by generation. It is an actual particle.

In conclusion, Averroes' theory of *minima naturalia* is a theory of actual and essential parts and, as such, it bridges the gap between the two opposing systems, the Aristotelian and the atomistic. It is atomistic in the sense that a physical body is made of actual minimal building stones, and that no physical magnitude is infinitely divisible. It is deeply Aristotelian as the minima are essential parts, that is, units having matter, form and specific natural motion.

8.6. THE 'DIVORCE' BETWEEN MATHEMATICS AND PHYSICS

In *Physics* VI geometrical and physical objects are isomorphic, that is, equally continuous. In *Metaphysics* M and *Physics* II geometrical and physical objects are closely tied: the former are derived from the latter. In *Metaphysics* M the derivation is described simply in terms of 'regarding as': the mathematician regards physical things

109 'We say that the magnitude [the limb] has a natural capability of being extended in all directions. This lends it a certain diffuseness, so that the nutritive fluid is absorbed in all its parts, i.e. in all *the minute pores that are the smallest than can exist in flesh.* When these pores expand and become filled with that fluid, that fluid is transformed into parts of flesh, which become united with the parts of flesh that are between these pores, and these are the [small] parts such that smaller parts cannot exist.' *MC De gen. et corr.*, Hebrew 31.87–32.96, English 38, trans. Kurland with modifications.

110 e.g., according to *On Mixture*, moist bodies 'divide one another before being unified *and are juxtaposed together as corpuscles* (*kata mikra*).' 'Entrance through pores is not blending... but juxtaposition'(*On Mixture* XV, 231.12 (Todd, 154), 233.2 (Todd 159)). In his commentary on *Meteorology* IV, he wrote that things, when solidifying, 'bond together and contract in such a way that *they do not admit water through their pores because the pores are narrower than the bulk of water*' (*On Mete.* 214.22–3, trans. Lewis, 109). In question 2.23, reporting Democritus' explanation of the action of a magnet on iron, Alexander writes that the magnet is composed of finer atoms which penetrate the pores of the iron and 'move the bodies within it, spreading out through them because of their fineness' (*Quaestiones* 23, 72.28–73.18, English, Sharples 1994, 29). Averroes could, perhaps, have found a similar account of magnetism in the commentary on the *Physics*. Eichner, who studied the possible sources of Averroes' commentaries on *De Generatione et Corruptione*, concludes with fair certainty that Averroes was directly acquainted with Alexander's commentary. See Eichner 2002, 292; Eichner 2005; Kupreeva 2004, nn. 56 and 59. I am very grateful to Heidrun Eichner for sending me her dissertation and her book.

'not *as* moving, but merely *as* bodies and again merely *as* planes and merely *as* lengths'.[111] In *Physics* II the derivation is described in terms of abstraction (*aphairesis*) or separation: the mathematician separates (*chōrizei*) the objects of mathematics '*for in thought they are separable (chōrista*) from motion'.[112] The notion of abstraction was subject to a wide range of interpretations. According to the strong interpretation abstraction is 'a postulated object'. Lear describes it as the separation of a predicate, for example quantity, and 'the *postulation of an object* that satisfies that predicate alone'.[113] Barnes dismisses 'postulated objects' as heuristic devices and understands abstraction like 'regarding as', that is, a method of studying an object by mentally eliminating qualitative aspects and focusing on the formal quantitative ones.[114]

Averroes adopts a strong interpretation: the mathematical intelligibles do not exist in separation from matter (as Plato contended), but the intellect regards them as such.[115] He thinks of the mathematical objects in terms of 'abstraction',[116] and conceives abstraction as an active constructive process: the mind separates the components, notes the similarities and dissimilarities until the natures of the components become intelligible.[117] Working with abstractions the geometer can

[111] *Metaphysics* M.3, 1077^{b}28–30. On the 'as' or 'qua' locution, see Lear 1982, 168–75; Barnes 1985, 102–5. Ross 1924, ii. 416.

[112] *Physics* II.2, 193^{b}23–5, 33–4. Aristotle emphasizes 'in thought' in order to distinguish his own notion of separation from Plato's. See also Lear 1982, 162–3.

[113] Lear 1982, 186. Another strong Platonic interpretation was suggested by Mueller (1970, 159–61) and Anderson (1969): abstraction results in 'substance-like individuals with a special matter—intelligible matter.' See also Annas' criticism 1976, 29–31.

[114] Barnes 1985, 111–12. Cleary (1995, pp. xxxiv, 313) argues that abstraction is a logical procedure, not an ontological or epistemological one.

[115] *MC De an.* 121 # 312. Averroes explains that 'that which is separable in reality is also separable in thought but not vice versa' (*LC Phys.* II.19 Latin 55C; Hebrew: 57^{b}28–58^{a}2). On the two notions of separation in Averroes see Taylor 2007, 125.

[116] He uses the term more frequently and freely than Aristotle does. Aristotle mentions it in *Physics* II.2, but not in *Metaphysics* M.3 (Ross' translation is misleading in this case; Annas' translation is more accurate). Averroes uses it often in his commentaries on both chapters. 'The mathematician studies them by abstracting them in word from matter and separating them in thought from their subjects.' 'The mathematicians thus abstract the mathematical forms in word only, not in reality' (*MC Phys.* II.2.1, 14^{b}6–7; II.2.2, fo. 14^{b}23–4; see also III.3.5, 31^{b}17–19). 'Thought abstracts things and studies them as separate.' 'The mathematician abstracts the line and the surface.' 'The science of mathematics abstracts these things and studies them without any subject' (*MC Meta.* 136^{b}26–7, 137^{a}4, 137^{a}15–16; see also 137^{a}22–3).

[117] *SC Meta.* Arabic 60–61, Hebrew 128a col. b19–128b col. a5. *LC Phys.* II.18, Latin 54M, Hebrew 57^{b}17–19.

always extend or divide his objects;[118] the natural scientist is not granted such freedom.[119] *Continua*, for Averroes, belong to the domain of geometry, not of physics.

Averroes' interpretation, thus, openly conflicts with many statements of Aristotle, who often refers to physical entities as *continua*. Averroes' strategy, when dealing with such statements, was to translate 'continuous' to 'continuous qua continuous' or 'continuous qua quantity', namely to translate the physical term into a mathematical one. I shall list several examples from the commentaries on *Physics* VI.1 and III.6.

In *Physics* VI.1 Aristotle argues that 'nothing that is continuous is composed of indivisibles.'[120] In both the middle and short commentaries Averroes interprets 'anything continuous' as 'anything qua continuous'. The title of chapter VI.1 of the middle commentary is 'the continuous qua *continuous* is infinitely divisible.'[121] Its first sentence reads: 'Our intention in this book is to study the nature of the continuous and its attributes qua *continuous*.'[122] Its conclusion is: 'We assume that the continuous qua *continuous* is divisible.'[123] In the short commentary he opens with 'the continuous qua *continuous*'.[124] and concludes:

> It has thus been established that the continuous *qua continuous* <is not composed of indivisibles and is not divisible into indivisibles. But the continuous[125] *qua continuous*>[126] is necessarily divisible. Assuming these two statements, it follows that the continuous *qua continuous* is divisible into that which is always divisible, and that division occurs to it *qua continuous* and according to its nature,[127] *not qua a sensible body* that exists in actuality. The sensible

[118] 'According to the geometrical definition (ההגדרה המחשבית ההנדסית) it is always possible to substract from any line a smaller line; according to the natural proposition infinite subtraction is impossible' (*LC Phys.* III.60 Latin 114D–E, Hebrew $128^{a}21$–3). The mathematician regards the touching extremes of two magnitudes as one; not so the natural scientist, who conceives the boundaries as always discernible (*LC Phys.* V.22 Latin 223C–D, Hebrew $20^{b}19$-25). 'The geometrical proposition which states that it is possible, given a straight line, *to imagine* a greater line, is right, but the natural proposition which states that it is possible, given a line, to produce it indefinitely, is false' (*LC Phys.* III.60 Latin 114E, Hebrew $128^{a}23$ 25). See also *MC Phys.* III.3.5 31b4–32a6; *MC Meta* $137^{a}15$–23.

[119] Murdoch (1964, 423–5) shows how Averroes uses the notion of superposition of the boundaries (in his discussions of the definition of continuity of *Physics* V.3) 'to separate the conditions of mathematical continuity from those of natural continua'.

[120] *Physics* VI.1 $231^{a}24$.

[121] *MC Phys.* VI contents $66^{a}18$–19.

[122] Ibid. VI.1, $66^{a}19$.

[123] Ibid. $67^{b}18$.

[124] *SC Phys.* Arabic 85.3–4, Hebrew $25^{b}17$.

[125] In the text במתדבק; should be המתדבק.

[126] Missing in the Arabic.

[127] I have 'corrected' the text, which reads (both Arabic and Hebrew), 'and the soul is its nature'.

generated body is subject to such a division *not qua generated and enmattered, but qua being continuous*. Therefore there are no essential first parts (اجزاء أول) *qua quantity* into which the natural body is dissolved or of which it is composed.[128]

Let me return to *Physics* VI and to the thesis of isomorphism. For Aristotle time, motion, magnitude (the distance traversed), and the moved body are all equally divisible.[129] For Averroes they are not. The concrete physical entity, the moved body, is composed of minimal units, while time and distance are mental constructs and as such infinitely divisible. Commenting on the *Metaphysics,* Averroes inquires into the mode of existence of the objects of mathematics: 'Is it the existence [1] of the substance or [2] of the accidents or [3] of the things that *the soul makes out of that which exists in reality*,[130] like many of the relations and combinations?'[131] The answer is the third: 'Unless there was soul, there would be no number, as *there would be no time; so too for magnitudes*.'[132]

While time is an entity that has only mental existence,[133] motion has two modes of existence. Aristotle distinguished two kinds of divisibility of motion: 'In the first it is divisible in virtue of the time that it occupies. In the second it is divisible according to the motions of the several parts of that which is in motion.'[134] I shall refer to the first as divisibility 'in length' and to the second as divisibility 'in mass'. In the long commentary Averroes claims that the division in mass is prior to the division in length, because the former is 'outside the soul', whereas the latter 'does not have a [natural] cause' and is 'in the soul'.[135] Averroes

[128] *SC Phys.* Arabic 88.1–8, Hebrew $26^{b}8$–20. Averroes accepts Aristotle's statement that quantity is divisible essentially, quality only accidentally. *MC Phys.* VI.7, $75^{a}23$–$^{b}1$, *LC Phys.* VI.37 Latin 270F11–G4, Hebrew $67^{a}16$–22; the last sentence appears only in the Hebrew.

[129] p. 142 above. [130] אשר תפעלם הנפש בנמצאות

[131] *MC Meta.* $138^{a}1$–6. [132] *MC Meta.* $138^{a}9$–11.

[133] Averroes could have found this idea in several of his predecessors. Alexander emphasizes several times that time exists in the soul, 'For times only exist in potentiality and thoughtand not by being in actuality . . . The instant is in thought and not in actuality and what is between two instants is time' Alexander, *On Time* 62–3.

[134] *Physics* VI.4 $234^{b}20$–22; see also $235^{a}11$–13.

[135] *LC Phys.* VI.33, Hebrew only $64^{a}23$–7. It should be noted that Avicenna also distinguished between motion in the sense of a flow between the two endpoints and an intermediary motion-state. Only the second has an actual reality. Avicenna emphasizes that the former exists only in the mind. See Hasnawi 2001*b*, translation of Avicenna's text 244–6, analysis 228–37. Averroes does not mention Avicenna in this context. The question to what extent he was acquainted with the *Physics* of the *Shifā'* requires a detailed study. I have not studied this question.

may have been acquainted with Avicenna's admirable observation that motion 'leaves an impression on the imagination only because its form subsists in the mind by reason of the relation between that which is moved and the two places: the place that it leaves and the place that it reaches.'[136] For both Avicanna and Averroes motion qua continuous entity exists only in the mind.

Of the isomorphic continuous entities that Aristotle lists in *Physics* VI.4—time, motion, magnitude, and body—Averroes regards time, distance, and motion 'in length' as entities that exist only in the soul. All continuous entities are 'expelled' from the real world and become 'explanatory devices'. What exists in reality is the moved body which is composed of particles and in them parts of motion 'in mass'. *Real* motion is an entity that resides *in* a body. This is Averroes' axiom of inherence—motion is *in* a body. It is the last step in the development of his interpretation of premise VIII.[137] Let me conclude the discussion on Averroes' nominalism with a quotation from the *Tahāfut*:

> Motion has existence only in the intellect, since outside the soul there exists only the thing moved and *in it a part of the motion* (جزء من الحركة) *without any lasting existence.*[138]

In summary, for Averroes the *continuum* is a mathematical structure, not a physical one. I shall not deal here with the roots of this concept in Averroes' psychology and epistemology,[139] but proceed to show how he developed his new physics, which is not based on continuous structures.

8.7. WHEN DID THE TURNING-POINT OCCUR?

So far I have described Averroes' systematic construction of the notion of First-Moved part, which is the basis of his new physics. This construction draws heavily, as I have shown, on Alexander's *Refutation of Galen.*[140] We know for certain that Averroes shaped this concept while or after he had read Alexander's *Refutation*. When did this happen? The answer is found in the middle commentary.

The first part of chapter VII.1 is the interpretation of Aristotle's moving argument, in which Averroes presents the basis of his theory of

[136] Avicenna *Phys.* II.1 84; McGinnis's translation (2006, 198).
[137] See p. 88 above.
[138] *Tahāfut al-Tahāfut* 480.11–13, English 292.
[139] On this subject see Taylor 1998. [140] p. 154 above.

minima naturalia; the second part includes important bibliographical information. The two translations differ significantly; and the differences provide the key to the answer. The suffixes K and Z mark passages that appear only in Kalonimus' or only in Zeraḥya's translations, respectively. I offer here an outline of the first part and a full translation of the two versions of the second.

[M1–M4] Outline

[M1] The definition of the two new concepts: First-Moved and not-First-Moved.[141]
[M2] The presentation of Aristotle's argument that everything that is moved is moved by something.[142]
[M3-K] An addition that appears only in Kalonimus' translation.[143]
[M4] The distinction between moving and moved parts.[144]

[M5–M8] Zeraḥya's translation (complete text)

[M5] It so happened that people had an argument about this demonstration, so that we were also perplexed about it for a certain time.[145]

[M6-Z] And we were forced to understand Aristotle's intention here, and the reason for this was that Ibn Bājja took a different way from Aristotle on this issue.[146]

[M7] This will become clear to you from what he says at the beginning of this book. Furthermore, we did not have an interpretation of this demonstration by the commentators, because Themistius omitted it from his book and it is also missing from Alexander's book, in the copy that we found.[147]

[M5–M8] Kalonimus' translation (complete text)

[M5] It so happened that people were much perplexed about this demonstration, so that we were also confused about it for a certain time.[148]

[M6-K] And it was difficult for us to understand the depth of Aristotle's [thought] on this. The reason for this was that we did

141 *MC Phys.* VII.1 82^{b}14–83^{a}15.
142 Ibid. 83^{a}15–b12. 143 Ibid. 83^{b}12–16.
144 Ibid. VII.1, Kalonimus 83^{b}16–25, Zeraḥya 100^{b}11–19.
145 Ibid., Zeraḥya 100^{b}19–21. 146 Ibid., Zeraḥya 100^{b}21–2.
147 Ibid., Zeraḥya 100^{b}22–101^{a}3. 148 Ibid., Kalonimus 83^{b}25–6.

> not perceive that Aristotle stipulated that the assumed moved body is first [i.e. a First-Moved]. When this is not stipulated, the demonstration is invalid. It happened that many people had not understood this demonstration and found fault with Aristotle. Thus Galen wrote his famous treatise and Ibn Bājja, who had also not understood this assumption, tried to state this demonstration without this assumption and this led him to take a way different from Aristotle's, thinking [erroneously] that this was Aristotle's.[149]
>
> [M7] And this will become clear to you from what he says at the beginning of this book. Furthermore, the interpretation of this demonstration by the commentators *has not come into our hands*, for Themistius omitted it from his book and it is also missing from Alexander's in the copy that we found.[150]
>
> [M8-K] We further found [another text with] Alexander's interpretation on this passage and found that it agrees with what we wrote. It was an even longer commentary,[151] perhaps deeper.[152]

We can distinguish three strata in the middle commentary on VII.1: (1) the main body of the chapter, notably paragraphs M1, M2, and M4, which appear in both translations and present Averroes' theory of *minima naturalia*; (2) the Z-passages that appear only in Zeraḥya's translation; and (3) the K-passages that appear only in Kalonimus' translation. We have seen that Kalonimus' translation of the middle commentary on Book VIII is based on a more updated manuscript than is Zeraḥya's. I shall argue that this is the case in Book VII too: the Z-passages belong to an early and presumably original redaction of the chapter (probably written about 1170), the K-passages to a later redaction.

In M8-K Averroes attempts to harmonize his own view with that of Alexander. This trend is typical of the long commentary and of the late edition of the middle commentary.[153] In M3-K Averroes seeks to excuse himself for ascribing his own ideas to Aristotle: 'If there indeed is a First-Moved [entity] its comprehension will follow from what was said before, *and this is why Aristotle was silent*.'[154] Such excuses are not

149 Ibid., Kalonimus $83^{b}26-84^{a}8$. 150 Ibid., Kalonimus $84^{a}8-11$.

151 Literally 'It was even in a longer commentary'.

152 Ibid., Kalonimus $84^{a}11-13$.

153 Chapter VI.7, paragraph M7. See above Appendix 5, p. 139–140.

154 *MC Phys*. VII.1 $83^{b}12-13$.

found in the middle commentary but are common in the long one, and especially in stratum B of the long commentary.[155] The rest of M3-K seems to refer to stratum B of Book VIII of the long commentary:

> And in the eighth [book] we[156] have already noted, concerning this very issue, that if there were no First-Moved [parts] in the body that moves essentially, there would be infinitely many parts *in actu* in the moved body, because all of them would necessarily have to move and be moved simultaneously.[157]

The idea, alluded to in this passage, that a body is an aggregate of *actual* parts, is introduced in stratum B of the long commentary on Book VIII:[158]

> He said that it was established in the beginning of the seventh [book] that it is impossible for a body to move a body *in infinitum* and therefore the world must have a first motion or first motions. Otherwise there would be an infinite magnitude *in actu*.[159]

These examples suggest that the K-passages are from the late period, that of stratum B of the long commentary. This means that the middle commentary was revised when the long commentary was revised or later. As already mentioned, we know for certain that Averroes developed his theory after he had read Alexander's *Refutation of Galen*.[160] In paragaph M7 that appears in both translations Averroes confirms that he was not yet acquainted with Alexander's interpretation of *Physics* VII.1.[161] He probably never had access to Book VII of Alexander's commentary. In paragraph M8-K he testifies that he found *another* text by Alexander which was 'longer and deeper'. This text is most probably Alexander's *Refutation of Galen's 'Treatise on the Theory of Motion'*.[162] The *Refutation* is definitely a 'longer and deeper' treatment of chapter VII.1 than one can expect to find in a commentary on the whole *Physics*. I have shown above how Averroes draws on this text when he interprets *Physics* VII.1. We can safely conclude that Averroes discovered Alexander's *Refutation* after the original writing of the middle commentary and before the K-passages.

155 See p. 46 above.
156 Variant reading: others.
157 *MC Phys.* VII.1 83^b13–16.
158 In the Hebrew redaction of comments VI.33 and VI.38.
159 *LC Phys.* VIII.5, Latin only 342A6–B2.
160 See Section 8.4 above.
161 He testifies that his copy of Alexander's commentary did not include chapter VII.1. It seems that his copy of the long commentary did not include book VII at all. See p. 53 above.
162 See also Kukkonen 2002*c*, 162.

A further comparison of the Z-passages and K-passages supports this conclusion. In the former Averroes mentions no source except Ibn Bājja. In M6-K he faults Galen for not understanding Aristotle's assumption—something he could not learn from Ibn Bājja,[163] but could from Alexander's *Refutation.* Galen is not mentioned in the middle commentary, except in the late paragraph M6-K, while in the long commentary, he is mentioned several times.

The presentation of the long commentary seems to be the 'real time' response to the reading of Alexander's treatise. Averroes studied Alexander's text closely while he was writing the long commentary; he sometimes quotes him almost verbatim[164] and even perpetuates errors that originated with Alexander.[165] The exposition of the middle commentary (paragraphs M1, M2, and M4) looks like a formal *post factum* presentation of the ideas that were gradually developed in the long commentary.[166]

I conclude that in the case of *Physics* VII.1 we can state with some certainty that the turning point is reflected in the long commentary and was associated with Averroes' 'late discovery' of a text by Alexander of Aphrodisias, most probably his *Refutation of Galen.* Chapter VII.1 of the middle commentary as it has come down to us is revised. The major part of it—the main part and the K-passages—is a 'version B' text. Of the original version of this chapter we have only fragments: the Z-passages and perhaps paragraph M7. What can we say about paragraphs M1, M2, M4, and M7 that appear in both translations? On this hinges

[163] Who says only that 'Galen has written a treatise on the differences of opinions about this book' (Ziyada 106.15–107.1; Lettinck 1994*a*, 527–8).

[164] For example, Averroes: 'That which moves as a whole because a part of it moves the whole is moved as a whole accidentally, like the motion of the living body as a whole due to the vital heat or the limbs' (*LC Phys.* VII.1, Latin 306F1–12). Alexander: The motion of the thing 'that is spoken of as moving as a whole because some part of it is found to move' is accidental (Refutation English 16, Arabic 76, MS Car. 67^a7–9.); 'these things that move essentially . . . move as a whole and not through the movement of a part' (English 19, Arabic 81–2, MS Car. 67^b9–10). Both Alexander and Averroes fault Galen for misunderstanding Aristotle's hypothesis. What misled Galen was his weak understanding of the notion of essential motion. See Averroes, *LC Phys.* VII.1 Latin 306F12–G5; Hebrew 106^a3–8; Alexander's *Refutation* quoted above pp. 150–151.

[165] Alexander quotes two passages from Aristotle, *Physics* VIII.4 254^b7–14 and V.1 224^a21–26, of which the second is explicitly referred to as 'the beginning of book V' (*Refutation*, English 32). Averroes writes 'It is said at <<the beginning of>> the fifth book . . .' (*LC Phys.* VII.1 Latin 306–G1–5; Hebrew 106^a6–8). In fact the text is from Alexander's quotation of book VIII, not of book V.

[166] The notion of First-Moved, which develops gradually in the long commentary, is formally introduced right at the beginning in the middle commentary.

the main question, namely: when was the theory of *minima naturalia* developed? I shall come back to this question in Chapter 9 below.

APPENDIX 6: AVERROES' CONCEPT OF A NATURAL POINT

To my knowledge, there is no mention of the notion of First-Moved part from the period between the writing of the middle commentary and that of the long one.[167] The passages collected here were written in the 1170s and early 1180s and reflect an intermediate stage in the evolution of Averroes' thought on the structure of a physical body. At this period Averroes faced the challenge of Islamic atomism but, as it seems, has not yet read Alexander's *Refutation of Galen*.

In the middle commentary on *De caelo*,[168] Averroes introduces a new concept: a natural point (نقطة طبيعية, נקודה טבעית). What is true or false of mathematical points is not necessarily true or false when it concerns natural points.[169] 'We have already posited that that which has more parts (اجزاء) is heavier. This necessarily implies that it is heavier by virtue of something that is itself heavy: *the natural point*.'[170]

In the middle commentary on *Physics* IV.4 Averroes advances an argument in which he assumes a notion of a natural point: the centre-point of a rotating radius. The context is Aristotle's remark that the centre of a rotating body is at rest:[171]

> When a radius of a circle rotates about the centre, every point on the radius describes a circle and this is true also of the centre point itself. The circle generated by the centre point must be either in a void or in a spherical body. The first alternative is ruled out. The circle is therefore in a spherical body [i.e. corporeal]. This spherical body must be either in motion or at rest. In the first case the argument can be repeated. We can thus assume that it is at rest. Furthermore, the centre cannot be a point because a point can be in motion or at rest only accidentally.[172]

[167] The notion of First-Moved part is not mentioned in the middle commentaries on *De caelo* and *De anima* and *De gen. et corr.* I have not found the notion of a First-Moved in the *Tahāfut al-Tahāfut*. The treatise *De substantia orbis* (dated 1178) does not add any significant evidence.

[168] The context is Aristotle's argument that a body cannot be composed of points. If a body were composed of points a body of four points would be heavier than a body of three points, yielding the impossible conclusion that a point has weight (*De caelo* III.1, 299^{b}18–20). Aristotle offers three arguments that a point is neither heavy nor light: (1) being susceptible to intension and remission, the heavy and the light must be divisible (*De cael.* III.1 299^{a}30–b3); (2) qua dense and rare, they must be divisible (299^{b}3–10); (3) qua soft and hard, they must be divisible (299^{b}10–14). The point, however, is indivisible and therefore the point cannot be heavy or light.

[169] *MC De cael.* III.3.1. introduction, Arabic 285.10–13, Hebrew 60^{b}20–22.

[170] Ibid., Arabic 291.17–21, Hebrew 62^{b}5–8 (on *De caelo* III.1, 299^{b}15–23).

[171] *Physics* IV.4 212^{a}23.

[172] *MC Phys.* IV.1.9, 39^{b}14–25.

It seems that Averroes thought of the rotating radius of a corporeal sphere as composed of natural points. The centre point generates a little sphere that is at rest and round which the whole sphere rotates. This spherical shell generated by the 'next' natural point on the radius is rotating.

In the middle commentary on *De anima*, probably the latest among the middle commentaries, it becomes clear that the 'natural point' or 'natural unit' is itself a quantity or a *continuum*. The context is Aristotle refutation of the Pythagorean notion of the soul as a self-moving number.[173] In this context Averroes further pursues the idea of a 'natural point':

Since the units [of soul] are indivisible and have a position,[174] like points, their proponent [must admit that] they and the atoms are essentially the same. As these units, *though considered indivisible, cannot avoid the nature of quantity and continuity*—continuity being regarded as of this nature[175]—and as it is clear from the nature of continuous bodies that movement occurs to them, it is therefore necessary that the points have an agent and a recipient of motion. It is not because of their small or large size that bodies are either agents or recipients of motion, but rather because of their having quantity [as such], it being regarded as necessary that *motion is a concomitant feature of indivisible quantity*.[176]

A corporeal unit has position, is itself a continuous quantity, and is capable of motion. It is a small plenum and the association with motion brings Averroes close to his concept of First-Moved part.

APPENDIX 7: WAS AVERROES ACQUAINTED WITH ALEXANDER'S *REFUTATION OF GALEN ON TIME AND PLACE?*

In the long commentary on *Physics* IV, in the treatise on place and in the treatise on time (the first and third parts of Book IV respectively), two questions about Averroes' sources come up.

The first question concerns the 'densely logical' structure of the parts that deal with *Physics* IV.1, IV.10 and IV.11. Chapter IV.1 deals with six problems.

173 Aristotle dismisses two views of the soul: that it is a 'self-moving number' and that it consists of atoms (*De anima* I.4, 408^b32 ff). He considers the two views as more or less equivalent: 'it must be the same whether we speak of units or corpuscles' (*De anima* I.4, 409^a10–11).

174 Arithmetical units do not have position. See *Categories* 6 4b20–21, *An. Post.* I.27 87a35–37; *Meta.*Δ.6 1016b25–27, 30–31. Proclus ascribes the definition of the point as a unit with position to the Pythagoreans (*On Euclid*, 95). In the passage with which we are dealing Aristotle remarks that a point is a unit with position and adds that 'a number of the soul is somewhere and has position' (*De an.* I.4 409a6).

175 Ivry comments: 'Continuity, or extension, begins with *corporeal point* that occupies some space, however tiny, and it is therefore quantifiable' (Ivry 2002, 166 n. 20).

176 *MC De an.* English 32–3, ## 87–8.

Simplicius attests that Alexander uses two syllogisms in his treatment of the first problem.[177] Averroes does not use logical language in his discussion of the first problem, but his discussion of the second problem is 'professionally' logical.[178] Nothing similar appears in Philoponus, Themistius, or Simplicius, and no logical argument is ascribed by Simplicius to Alexander. The other logical remarks do not follow Greek sources either. Similarly, none of the Greek commentators can be the 'source' of the heavy formalization of Averroes' presentation of chapter IV.10.[179]

The second question concerns the discrepancy between what Averroes ascribes to Alexander, and what Simplicius ascribes to him.[180] Only the references to Alexander that were made at the editing stage of the long commentary (namely in the parts that appear only in Hebrew) agree with Simplicius.[181]

A possible explanation is that Averroes had another text of Alexander in addition, perhaps even before, his commentary on the *Physics*. Let us consider this possibility.

The majority of references to Galen in Averroes' long commentary on the *Physics* are in the parts that deal with *Physics* VII.1–2 and with *Physics* IV.11. I have argued in Chapter 8 that the references in book VII are to Alexander's *Refutation of Galen on Motion*. The references of book IV may well be to Alexander's *Refutation of Galen on Time and Place*. In his interpretation of chapter IV.11 Averroes mentions Galen several times. The issue is Galen's view that 'we cannot conceive time unless through change in our thought'. Themistius does not mention Galen's view but Simplicius does: 'The remarkable

[177] Simplicius, *On Phys*. 529.29–530.3.

[178] He lists four syllogisms, hypothetical and categorical, and an additional fifth argument about which Aristotle was 'silent'.

[179] The most 'heavily logical' are comments IV.95–6, while none of the commentators known to us offers a logical argument in this context. In comment IV.94 he follows Philoponus on one issue: the syllogism used by those who argued that time is the sphere is invalid. See Philoponus *On phys*. 713.9–12, Averroes *MC Phys*. IV.3.3 48a13–19, *LC Phys*. IV.94 (on *Physics* IV.10 218b5–9).

[180] e.g. Alexander is referred to in comment IV.30 Latin 133H1, H7, Hebrew 148b30, 149a3 (on *Physics* IV.4 211a1, third doubt). There is no 'confirmation' from Simplicius.

[181] In comment IV.11 Averroes ascribes the argument to Democritus mentioning Alexander as his source (*LC Phys*. IV.11 Hebrew only 140b19). Simplicius also ascribes the argument to Democritus. Simplicius does not ascribe this point to Alexander, but it is likely that Alexander was a source of both. In comment IV.90 Averroes mentions Alexander only in the edited part (*LC Phys*. IV.90 Hebrew only 191a29–30). In comments IV.101–2 he mentions Alexander five times (*LC Phys*. IV.101 Latin 181G6,13, Hebrew 197b10,11; IV.102 Hebrew only 197b20–30; IV.102 Latin 182A5, Hebrew 198a9; IV.102 Latin only 182E5), but only in the edited part does he refer to a logical argument of Alexander, and this is the only reference 'confirmed' by Simplicius. Averroes' remarks, that it is a third figure syllogism (*LC Phys*. IV.102 Hebrew 197b29). Cf. Simplicius *On Phys*. 713.27.

Galen, in the eighth book of his *On Demonstration*, suspects that Aristotle says that there is no time without change because we conceive it as changing'.[182] This treatise of Galen is lost and, as far as we know, was not translated into Arabic. Alexander's lost treatise *Refutation of Galen on Time and Place*, however, was translated into Arabic and is listed by al-Nadim.[183] It is thus possible that when Averroes wrote book IV of the long commentary he consulted Alexander's *Refutation of Galen on Time and Place*.[184] This account explains the poor agreement between Simplicius' and Averroes' testimonies in several passages: the former refers to the commentary on the *Physics*, the latter to the *Refutation of Galen*. It also suggests a possible source for the intensive logical character of Averroes' long commentary on *Physics* IV.1 and IV.10.[185] Perhaps Alexander's two *Refutations of Galen* were contained in a manuscript that was available to Averroes when he was writing the long commentary.

182 Simplicius *In phys*. 708.27–8; see also 718.13–719.21.

183 See Rescher and Marmura 1965, 2 and 12 n. 8.

184 The references to Alexander in comments IV.101–2 may well be to Alexander's short treatise *On Time*. Sharples who published this treatise discusses the question of its relation to the *Refutation of Galen on Time and Place* (1982, 72–8).

185 On Galen the logician see Barnes 1980, 176–7.

9

Summary and Conclusion

ARISTOTLE is known as the founder of a continuist physics. In *Physics* VI he contends that the underlying structure of physical reality is the *continuum*: body and motion are *continua*, just like time and distance. Therefore geometry, the science that studies continuous magnitudes, is applicable to the study of nature. In *Physics* VI Aristotle studies the situation of one body in motion, implicitly assuming that it is a homoeomer. In *Physics* VII he sees that he cannot extend his continuist thesis to complex non-homoeomerous bodies without committing himself to a stronger notion of continuity. He was acquainted with the strong concept of continuity that was put forward by Anaxagoras, who held that there is something of everything in everything. Aristotle did not pursue continuist physics as far as that and denied Anaxagoras' theory. It was through criticizing Anaxagoras that he laid the basis of the theory of *minima naturalia*: a physical body is not infinitely divisible but has a minimal possible size. His stance on the question of physical continuity was, therefore, inconsistent and proved to be untenable. It contained within itself the seeds of its own demise and harboured in potentia the physics that was to supplant it. When this is understood, it becomes less surprising that 'Aristotelian atomism' was developed by Aristotle's most faithful and thoughtful followers, Alexander and Averroes.

Like Aristotle's position on the continuity of physical reality, so his position on determinism was also equivocal. A strong connection between these two concepts was established not long after Aristotle's death. It was in the Hellenistic period that the notions of determinism and indeterminism were consolidated and anchored in opposing natural philosophies: the Epicureans based their indeterministic philosophy on an atomistic physics while their adversaries, the Stoics, based their strict determinism on a theory of strong continuity. Through a process of mutual criticism, these two positions were stated with greater precision, and it became gradually clear that Aristotle's position was vague and hard to maintain. This was the background to the controversy between Galen and Alexander over *Physics* VII.1. Alexander tried to defend Aristotle against Galen but, as far as we know, did not pursue his ideas to their logical conclusion. Averroes, who had attentively studied Alexander's defence of Aristotle, saw clearly that there was no way other than to give up continuist physics altogether. He boldly severed the ties between physics and geometry that Aristotle had posited in *Physics* VI, and maintained that the science of geometry was applicable to the study of mental constructs such as time or distance, but not to the study of body or of motion. To handle the concepts of body and motion, Averroes developed two non-continuist theories: a theory of matter based on the concept of *minimum naturale*, and a theory of motion based on the concept of motion as *forma fluens*. Together they produced the physical system that I have labelled 'Aristotelian atomism'. My conjecture is that the motive force behind Averroes' 'Aristotelian atomism' was his aspiration to find a sound scientific foundation for indeterminism. The three turning points described in Chapters 6–8 above are, thus, connected and can be viewed as three facets of one process.

When studying the turning point of *Physics* VIII in Chapter 6 above I raised the question of whether it occurred when Averroes was writing the middle commentary (account I) or when he was writing the long commentary (account II). The outcome of the long investigation was in favour of account II. After studying the three turning points I tend to think that the formation of Averroes' new physics was a process that started in the early 1180s, but consolidated only during the writing of the long commentary that was, presumably, completed in 1196.

We do not know when Averroes began to entertain indeterministic ideas but, at around 1180, at the time of his arguments with the mutakallimūn, he was already doing so. He was probably intrigued by the indeterministic implications of Kalām's discrete physics but, as a faithful Aristotelian, he was strongly opposed to what he viewed as their non-scientific approach, notably their denial of causality. Presumably when he found support in a reputable Aristotelian text, namely Alexander's *On the Principles of the Universe*, Averroes felt more self-assured and free to pursue his ideas. In Alexander he found a sound grounding for a physical theory that would be based on an Aristotelian conceptual basis, satisfy Aristotle's criteria for scientificity, and still be compatible with an indeterministic philosophy. Seeking a middle course between the strong determinism of the falāsifa's (most notably Avicenna's) and the denial of causality by the mutakallimūn, it was natural for him to turn to Alexander who, a millennium earlier, had confronted a similar situation and sought a middle 'Aristotelian' course between Stoic and Epicurean philosophies. Averroes embraced Alexander's anti-Stoic position, and found support in his strong notion of essentiality and his hylomorphic analysis of the elements.

The pattern of the turning point of book VII is similar to that of book VIII. Around 1180, at the time of his arguments with the mutakallimūnn, Averroes became interested in atomism, but could not accept Kalām's radical atomism.[1] Again he turned to a reputable Aristotelian text, Alexander's *Refutation of Galen*. Encouraged by Alexander, he developed the notion of First-Moved part that fits in an Aristotelian environment much better than the atoms of Muslim theologians. Averroes pursued the 'atomistic' reading of Aristotle farther than Alexander. His ideas are clearer and bolder and it seems that he was more prepared to introduce major revisions into Aristotelian natural philosophy. This was achieved in the long commentary. The particular interest in Alexander characterizes the late phase in Averroes' work, most notably the editing and rewriting of the long commentary. In this period Averroes made an effort to acquire Alexander's books and to study them. The writing of the introduction of the long commentary on the *Physics*, the revision of book I and, possibly, of other books as well, were made after Averroes had acquired parts of Alexander's commentary. The revision of book VIII was made after his reading of Alexander's *On the Principles of the Universe* and of book VII after the reading of his *Refutation of Galen on Motion*. It may be that book IV was revised after reading Alexander's *Refutation of Galen on Time and Place*.[2]

The pattern of the turning point of book VI is somewhat different. The analysis of motion in terms of *forma fluens* completes Averroes' agenda. In the long commentary on book VI he pursues and expands the 'contiguous model' of the sublunar world that he started to develop in book VIII. In the case of books VII and VIII Averroes did not have access to Alexander's commentary on the *Physics*,[3] and we saw that he used other treatises of Alexander. In the case of book VI, Alexander's

[1] In the *Kashf am Manāhij al-Adilla* (138–9, English 22) he adopts an Aristotelian position against Kalām's atomism, but dismisses the view that physical body is infinitely divisible.

[2] See Ch. 8, Appendix 7, p. 170 above.

[3] p. 53 above.

commentary was available to him but, unfortunately, not to us. We cannot therefore know if he found support in Alexander for his analysis of motion as *forma fluens*.[4] It is possible that his ideas on this issue were instigated by Avicenna's rejection of the interpretation of *entelekheia* as a process, and his conception of process as an entity that has no extramental existence. Averroes could have also borrowed from Avicenna the notion of intermediate terminus.

In the long commentary Averroes succeeded in elaborating an indeterministic interpretation of Aristotle's *Physics* without giving up Aristotle's strict notion of science. In his hands Muslim atomism was 'tamed': Kalām's atoms were reborn as Aristotelian units having matter and form; the cinematographic representation of motion was turned into a contiguous, causality-preserving one.

There has been much recent research on the different routes that led to the revival of atomism in the seventeenth century. In Part B of this book I considered the early stages of the 'Aristotelian route' and presented the major role, hitherto insufficiently examined, of Arabic philosophy in the evolution of this tradition. In medieval Arabic philosophy we find two versions of atomism: the 'hard' version of the theologians and the 'softer' version of Averroes. The former, to a certain degree, stimulated the latter and the latter, it seems, was of greater influence on the course of Western thought. The impact of Averroes' 'Aristotelian atomism' on Christian scholasticism, and especially upon the Latin Averroists, is a subject that calls for further study.

[4] Simplicius does not help much. In his commentary on book VI (*On Phys.* 986.13–14) he definitely states that a limit and that of which it is a limit are not the same thing. There is no mentioning that Alexander thought differently on this subject.

Bibliography

PRIMARY SOURCES (MANUSCRIPTS, EDITIONS, AND TRANSLATIONS)

Greek Authors (in chronological order)

Aristotle

The Complete Works of Aristotle, the revised Oxford translation. Ed. J. Barnes (Princeton, 1985), 2 vols.

Logic:

Categories and De Interpretatione, trans. J. L. Ackrill (Oxford, 1963).

Posterior Analytics, trans. J. Barnes (Oxford, 1975).

Physics:

Physics (Greek), ed. W. D. Ross (Oxford, 1936).

Physics (Arabic): *At-Ṭabī ʿa*, tarjamat Isḥāq Ibn Ḥunayn. Ed. A. Badawi (Cairo, 1964–5).

Physics Books I, II, trans. W. Charlton (Oxford, 1970).

Physics Books III and IV, trans. E. Hussey (Oxford, 1983).

The Chain of Change: A Study of Aristotle's Physics VII, trans. R. Wardy (Cambridge, 1990).

Physics Book VIII, trans. D. Graham (Oxford, 1999).

Physics, trans. R. Waterfield (Oxford, 1996).

Physique, trans. P. Pellegrin (Paris, 2002).

De generatione et corruptione

De generatione et corruptione, trans. C. J. F. Williams (Oxford, 1982).

Metaphysics:

Metaphysics (Greek), ed. W. D. Ross (Oxford, 1924).

Metaphysics Books Γ, Δ, and E, trans. Kirwan (Oxford, 1971).

Metaphysics Books Z and H, trans. D. Bostock (Oxford, 1994).

Metaphysics books M and N, trans. J. Annas (Oxford, 1976).

Euclid

Elements:

The Thirteen Books of Euclid's Elements, trans. T. L. Heath (Cambridge, 1925).

Galen

Über die Verschiedenheit der homoiomeren Körperteile. trans. G. Strohmaier (Berlin, 1970).

Alexander of Aphrodisias

On Phys.: *Commentaria in Aristotelem Graeca,* ii–iii (Berlin, 1883–9).

On Aristotle's Prior Analytics 1.1–7, trans. J. Barnes, S. Bobzein, K. Flannery, S. J. & K. Ierodiakonou (London, 1991).

On Meteorology 4, trans. E. Lewis (London, 1996).

On Time, trans. R. W. Sharples. *Phronesis* 27 (1982), 58–81.

On Fate, trans. R. W. Sharples (London, 1983).

La provvidenza, Questioni sulla Provvidenza, trans. S. Fazzo and M. Zonta (Milan, 1999).

On the Principles: On the Cosmos (Fī Mabādi' al-Kull), ed. & trans. C. Genequand (Leiden, 2001).

On Mixture: On Stoic Physics, A study of the *De mixtione.* Ed. & trans. R. B. Todd (Leiden, 1976).

The Refutation by Alexander of Aphrodisias of Galen's Treatise on the Theory of Motion, ed. & trans. N. Rescher and M. Marmura (Islamabad, 1965).

Quaestiones 1.1–2.15, trans. R. W. Sharples (London, 1992).

Quaestiones 2.16–3.15, trans. R. W. Sharples (London, 1994).

Themistius

On Phys.: *Commentaria in Aristotelem Graeca,* v (Berlin, 1899–1903).

Proclus

On Euclid: *In primum euclidis elementorum librum commentarii,* ed. G. Friedlein (Leipzig, 1873).

Philoponus

On Phys.: *Commentaria in Aristotelem Graeca,* xvi–xvii (Berlin, 1887–8).

On Aristotle's Physics 2 trans. A. R. Lacey (Ithaca, 1993).

On Aristotle's Physics 3, trans. M. J. Edwards (Ithaca, 1994).

Against Aristotle on the Eternity of the World, trans. C. Wildberg (Ithaca, 1987).

On Aristotle's Physics 5–8, trans. (from Arabic) P. Lettinck (Ithaca, 1994).

Simplicius

On Phys.: *Commentaria in Aristotelem Graeca,* ix–x (Berlin, 1882–95).

Commentaire sur les catégories, trans. I. Hadot (Leiden, 1990).

On Aristotle's Physics 6, trans. D. Konstan (Ithaca, 1989).

On Aristotle's Physics 7, trans. by C. Hagen (Ithaca, 1994).

On Aristotle's Physics 8.6–10, trans. by R. McKirahan (Ithaca, 2001).

Early Latin Authors

Lucretius

De rerum natura, trans C. Bailey (Oxford, 1947).

Arabic Authors (in chronological order)

Al-Fārābī

Commentary and Short Treatise on Aristotle's De interpretatione, trans. F. W. Zimmermann (London, 1981).

Al-Ghazālī

The Incoherence of the Philosophers, ed. & trans. M. E. Marmura (Provo, 1997).

Avicenna

Phys.: Al-Shīfā', *Al-samā*ᶜ *al-ṭabī*ᶜ*ī*, ed. S. Zayed, Preface and revision I. Madkour (Cairo, 1983).

Ibn Bājja

On Phys.: *Šurûḥāt al-samā*ᶜ *al-ṭabī*ᶜ*ī*, ed. M. Ziyada (Beirut, 1978).

Lettinck 1994*a* includes an English paraphrase of Ibn Bājja's commentary and in the appendix the complete Arabic text of the parts that were found in Berlin's manuscript and were not included in Ziyada's edition or in Fakhry's edition (Beirut, 1973).

Averroes

Logic:

Paraphrase de la logique d'Aristote, ed. G. Jéhamy (Beirut, 1982) 3 vols.

Middle Commentary on Aristotle's Prior Analytics, ed. M. M. Kassem, C. E. Butterworth, and A. A. Haridi (Cairo, 1983).

Long Commentary on Posterior Analytics:

Latin: *Aristotelis opera cum Averrois commentariis*, ii (Venice, 1562).

Hebrew: Parma Biblioteca Palatina, MS Ebreo De Rossi 3022.

Physics:

SC Phys.: Short Commentary on Aristotle's *Physics*:

Arabic: *Epitome in physicorum libros*, ed. J. Puig (Madrid, 1983).

Hebrew: trans. Moshe Ibn Tibbon (Riva di Trento, 1559); Vatican Urb. MS 39/1.

Spanish: *Epítome de física*, trans. J. Puig (Madrid, 1987).

MC Phys.: Middle Commentary on Aristotle's *Physics*:

Hebrew: *Averroes on the Principles of Nature: the Middle Commentary on Aristotle's Physics I–II*, ed. & trans. S. Harvey. Dissertation (Harvard, 1977).

Trans. Kalonimus ben Kalonimus, Hamburg Staats- und Universitaets-bibliothek, MS Cod. hebr. 264 (If not otherwise specified, references to the middle commentary are to this manuscript); Paris BN MS héb 941.

Trans. Zeraḥya ben Ishaq She'alti'el, Oxford Bodl. MS Neubauer 1386.

Trans. Anon. of chapters VIII.2.1–2 version A: New York JTS MS 2358/2; Oxford Bodl. MS Neubauer 1381/2.

Al-Masumi M. S. H 1956. 'Ibn Rushd's Synopsis of Aristotle's *Physics*', *Dacca University Studies*, 8: 65–98.

LC Phys.: Long Commentary on Aristotle's Physics:

Latin: *Aristotelis opera cum Averrois commentariis* vol. IV (Venice, 1562).

Book VII: *Commentarium Magnum In Aristotelis Physicorum Librum Septimum* (Vindobonensis [Vienna] lat. 2334). Ed. H. Schmieja (Paderborn, 2006).

Hebrew: books I–IV Paris BN héb MS 884; books V–VIII Cambridge, Mass. Houghton MS 40.

English: Prooemium: 'Hebrew Translation of Averroes' Prooemium to his Long Commentary on Aristotle's *Physics*', by S. Harvey. *Proceedings of the American Academy for Jewish Research*, 52 (1983), 55–84. Comment IV.71, trans. E. Grant in *A Sourcebook in Medieval Science* (Cambridge, Mass., 1974).

Questions in Physics:

Hebrew: *Sefer ha-Derushin ha-Tib*ᶜ*iyim*, ed. & trans. H. T. Goldstein (Dordrecht, 1991).

De caelo:

MC De cael.: *Middle Commentary on Aristotle's De caelo*:

Arabic: *Talkhīṣ al-Samā*ᶜ *wa-l-*ᶜ*ālam*, ed. G. al-ᶜAlawi (Fās, 1984).

LC De cael.: *Long Commentary on Aristotle's De caelo*:

Arabic (parts): *Šarḥ kitāb al-Samā*ᶜ *wa-l-*ᶜ*ālam*, ed. G. Endress. Reproduced from MS 11821, National Library, Tunis. (Frankfurt am Main, 1994).

Latin: *Averrois Cordubensis commentum magnum super libro De celo et mundo Aristotelis*, eds. F. J. Carmody, R. Arnzen, Praef. G. Endress, 2 vols. (Leuven, 2003).

De generatione et corruptione:

MC De gen. et conn.: *Middle Commentary on Aristotle's De generatione et corruptione*

Hebrew: *Commentarium medium et epitome in Aristotelis 'De generatione et corruptione' libros*, ed. S. Kurland. (Cambridge, Mass., 1958).

English: *Averroes on Aristotle's De generatione et corruptione: Middle Commentary and Epitome*, trans S. Kurland (Cambridge, Mass., 1958).

De anima:

MC De an.: *Middle Commentary on Aristotle's De anima*

Middle Commentary on Aristotle's De anima, ed. & trans. A. L. Ivry (Provo, 2002).

Hebrew: *Averroes' Middle Commentary on Aristotle's De anima* in the translation of Moses Ibn Tibbon. Ed. A.L. Ivry (Jerusalem, 2003).

LC De an.: *Long Commentary on Aristotle's De anima*
Latin: *Averrois cordubensis commentarium magnum in Aristotelis de anima libros*, ed. F. Stuart Crawford (Cambridge, Mass., 1953).
Hebrew: Moscow State Library, Ginsburg Collection MS 1421.

Metaphysics:
SC Meta.: *Short Commentary on Aristotle's Metaphysics*:
Arabic: Rasā'il Ibn Rushd (Hyderabad, 1946–7).
Hebrew: Paris BNF héb MS918, fos. 118b–149a, trans. Moshe Ibn Tibbon.
German: *Die Metaphysik der Averroes*, trans. M. Horten (Frankfurt am Main, 1912).
Die Epitome der metaphysik des Averroes, trans. S. van den Bergh (Leiden, 1924).

MC Meta.: *Middle Commentary on Aristotle's Metaphysics*:
Hebrew: Paris BNF MS héb 954.

LC Meta. Long Commentary on Aristotle's Metaphysics:
Arabic: *Tafsīr mā ba*ᶜ*d al-ṭabī* ᶜ*a*, ed. M. Bouyges, 3 vols. (Beirut, 1952).
Latin: *Aristotelis opera cum Averrois commentariis*, vol. VIII (Venice, 1562).
Hebrew: Paris BNF héb MS 887, trans. Moshe ben Shlomo Beaucaire of Salon.

Al-Kashf ᶜ*an Manāhij al-Adilla fi* ᶜ*Aqā'id al-Milla*: Faith and Reason in Islam, trans. I. Najjar (Oxford: Oneworld, 2001).

Tahāfut al-Tahāfut: The Incoherence of the Incoherence, trans. S. van den Bergh. (Cambridge, 1954/1987).

Hebrew Authors (in chronological order)

Shem-Tov ben Joseph Ibn Falaquera, *De*ᶜ*ot ha-Filosofim*, Parma, Biblioteca Palatina, MS Ebreo De Rossi 164.

Yedaᶜ**aya ha-Penini**, *A commentary on Ibn Rushd's short commentary on the Physics*, Parma, Biblioteca Palatina, MS Ebreo De Rossi 1399.

Levi ben Gershom (Gersonides), *Commentary on the Short Commentary on the Physics*, Berlin 110/1 (MS Or. fo. 1055); Vatican MS Ebr. 342/1.

—— *Commentary on the Middle Commentary on the Physics,* Paris BNF MS héb 964/1.

Medieval Latin Authors (in chronological order)

Thomas Aquinas, *Commentary on Aristotle's Physics*, trans. R. J. Blackwell, R. J. Spath, and W. E. Thirlkel (New Haven, 1963).

William of Ockham, *Expositio in librum praedicamentorum aristotelis*, ed. G. Gal, *Opera philosophica et theologica*, ii (New York, 1978).

—— *Quaestiones in libros physicorum Aristoteles*, ed. S. Brown, *Opera philosophica et theologica*, vi (New York, 1984).

SECONDARY SOURCES

Ackrill, J. L. 1963. See Aristotle, *Categories and De Interpretatione.*

Adamson P. 2006. 'The Arabic Sea Battle: al-Fārābī on the Problem of Future Contingents,' *Archiv für Geschichte der Philosophie*, 88: 163–88.

____ and Taylor R.C. 2005. *The Cambridge Companion to Arabic Philosophy.*

____, Baltussen H., and Stone M. W. F. (eds.) 2004. *Philosophy, Science and Exegesis in Greek, Latin and Arabic Commentaries* (2 vols.), Supplements to the *Bulletin of the Institute of Classical Studies*. London.

Al-ᶜAlawi J. D. 1986. *Al-Matn al-Rushdī: Madkhal li-qirā'a jadīda.* Casablanca.

Al-Masumi M. S. H. 1956. See Averroes, *Physics.*

Ancona C. de, and Serra, G. 2002. *Aristotele e Alessandro di Afrodisia nella tradizione Araba.* Padua.

Anderson, T. C. 1969. 'Intelligible Matter and the Objects of Mathematics in Aristotle'. *New Scholasticism*, 43: 1–28.

____ 1972. 'Aristotle and Aquinas on the Freedom of the Mathematician'. *The Thomist*, 36: 231–255.

Annas J. 1976/1988. See Aristotle, *Metaphysics books M and N.*

Arnzen, R., and Thielmann, J. (eds.) 2004. *Words, Texts and Concepts Cruising the Mediterranean Sea.* Leuven and Paris.

Asztalos, M., Murdoch, J. E., and Niniluoto I. (eds.) 1987. *Knowledge and the Sciences in Medieval Philosophy.* Proceedings of the Eighth International Congress of Medieval Philosophy (S.I.E.P.M) Helsinki.

Badawi A. 1964–5. See Aristotle, *Physics* (Arabic).

Baffioni, C. 2004. *Averroes and the Aristotelian Heritage.* Naples.

Bailey, C. 1947. See Lucretius, *De rerum natura.*

Balme D. M. 1939. 'Greek Science and Mechanism'. *Classical Quarterly*, 33: 129–38.

Barker, P., and Goldstein, B. R. 1984. 'Is Seventeenth Century Indebted to the Stoics?' *Centaurus*, 27: 148–64.

Barnes J. 1969. 'Aristotle's Theory of Demonstration.' *Phronesis*, 14: 123–52.

____ 1975. See Aristotle, *Posterior Analytics.*

____ 1980. 'Proof Destroyed', in Schofield, Burnyeat, and Barnes 1980, 161–81.

____ 1981. 'Proof and Syllogism', in Berti 1981, 17–59.

____ 1985. 'Aristotelian Arithmetic', *Revue de philosophie ancienne*, 3, 97–133.

____ et al. 1991. See Alexander of Aphrodisias, *On Aristotle's Prior Analytics 1.1–7.*

Bechler, Z. 1995. *Aristotle's Theory of Actuality.* New York.

Belo, C. 2004. 'Ibn Sīnā on Chance in the *Physics* of the *Ash-Shifā*'', in McGinnis 2004, 25–41.

____ 2007. *Chance and Determinism in Avicenna and Averroes.* Leiden.

Berti, E. (ed.) 1981. *Aristotle on Science: The Posterior Analytics*, Proceedings of the Eighth Symposium Aristotelicum 1978, Padua.

Bertolacci, A. 2005. 'On the Arabic Translations of Aristotle's *Metaphysics*', *Arabic Sciences and Philosophy*, 15: 241–75.

Blair, G. A. 1967. 'The Meaning of "Energia" and "Entelecheia" in Aristotle', *International Philosophical Quarterly*, 7: 101–17.

Bobzien, S. 1998. *Determinism and Freedom in Stoic Philosophy*, Oxford.

Bostock, D. 1991. 'Aristotle on Continuity in *Physics* VI', in Judson 1991, 179–212.

——1994. See Aristotle, *Metaphysics Books Z and H*.

Bouyges, M. 1952. See Averroès, Long Commentary on Aristotle's *Metaphysics*.

Brenet J. B. 2007. *Averroes et les Averroïsm Juif et Latin*. Turnhout, Belgium.

Brunschwig, J. 1980. 'Proof Defined', in Schofield, Burnyeat, and Barnes 1980, 125–60.

Burnett C. (ed.) 1993. *Glosses and Commentaries on Aristotelian Logical Texts*. London.

——1999. 'The "Sons of Averroes with the Emperor Frederique" and the transmission of the Philosophical Works by Ibn Rushd', in Endress and Aertsen 1999, 259–99.

——2005. 'Arabic into Latin: The Reception of Arabic Philosophy into Western Europe', in Adamson and Taylor 2005, 370–404.

Campanini, M. 2007. 'Averroes' Hermeneutics of the Qur'ān', in Brenet 2007, 215–29.

Canova B. 2007. 'Aristote et le coran dan *kitāb al-kashf ʿan manāhig al-adilla* d'Averroès', in Brenet 2007, 193–213.

Cleary J. J. 1988. *Aristotle on the Many Senses of Priority*. Carbondale and Edwardsville.

——1995. *Aristotle and Mathematics,* Aporetic Methods in Cosmology and Metaphysics. Leiden.

——1996. 'Mathematics and Cosmology in Aristotle's Philosophical Development', in Wians 1996, 193–228.

Clericuzio A. 2000. *Elements, Principles and Corpuscles: A Study of Atomism and Chemistry in the Seventeenth Century*. Dordrecht.

Couloubaritsis L. 1997. *La physique d'Aristote* (2nd edn). Brussels.

Davidson H. A. 1979. 'The Principle that a Finite Body can Contain only Finite Power', in Stein and Loewe 1979, 75–92.

——1987. *Proofs for Eternity, Creation and the Existence of God in Medieval Islamic and Jewish Philosophy*. Oxford.

——1997. 'The Relation between Averroes' Middle and Long Commentaries on the *De anima*', *Arabic Sciences and Philosophy*, 7: 139–51.

Dhanani A. 1994. *The Physical Theory of Kalām*. Leiden.

Dienstag J. I. (ed.) 1975. *Studies in Maimonides and St. Thomas Aquinas*. New York.

De Gandt, F., and Souffrin, P. (eds.) 1991. *La Physique d'Aristote*. Paris.

Druart T. A. 1994. 'Averroes: The Commentator and the Commentators', in Schrenck 1994, 184–202.

Edel, E. 1982. *Aristotle and his Philosophy*. London.

Duhem, P. 1956. *Le système du monde*, vii. Paris.

Edwards M. J. 1994. See Philoponus *On Aristotle's Physics 3*.

Eichner, H. 2002. 'Ibn Rushd's Middle Commentary and Alexander's Commentary in their relationship to the Arabic Commentary tradition on the *De generatione et corruptione*', in Ancona e Serra 2002, 281–97.

—— 2005. *Averroes' Mittlerer Kommentar zu Aristoteles' De generatione et corruptione*. Paderborn.

Endress G. 1995. 'Averroes' *De caelo*: Ibn Rushd's Cosmology in his Commentaries on Aristotle's *On the Heavens*', *Arabic Sciences and Philosophy*, 5: 9–49.

—— 2002. 'Alexander Arabus on the First Cause. Aristotle's First Mover in an Arabic treatise attributed to Alexander of Aphrodisias', in Ancona and Serra 2002, 19–74.

—— and Aertsen J. A. (eds.) 1999. *Averroes and the Aristotelian Tradition*. Leiden.

Englert, W. G. 1987. *Epicurus on the Swerve and Voluntary Action*. Atlanta, Ga.

Fakhry, M. 1953/1975. 'The "Antinomy" of the Eternity of the World in Averroes, Maimonides and Aquinas', *Le Museon*, 66: 139–55, reprinted in Dienstag 1975, 107–23.

Fazzo, S. 1997. 'L'Alexandre arabe et la génération à partir du néant', in A. Hasnawi et al., *Perspectives arabes et médiévales sur la tradition scientifique et philosophique grecque*, 1997.

—— 2002. 'Alexandre d'Aphrodise contre Galien: la naissance d'une légende', *Philosophie antique*, 2: 109–44.

—— and Zonta, M. 1999. See Alexander of Aphrodisias, *La Provvidenza*.

Fioravanti, G., Leonardi, C., and Perfetti, S. 2002. *Commento filosofico nell'occidente latino (secoli XIII–XV)*. Turnhout.

Flannery, K. L. 1995. *Ways into the Logic of Alexander of Aphrodisias*, Leiden.

Fontaine, R. 1998. 'Red and Yellow, Blue and Green: The Colours of the Rainbow according to Medieval Hebrew and Arabic Scientific texts', in Toby Y. (ed.) 1998. *'Ever and 'Arav: Contrasts between Arabic Literature and Jewish Literature in the Middle Ages and Modern Time*. Tel-Aviv, pp. vii–xxv.

Frank, R. M. 1964. 'Bodies and Atoms: The Ash'arite Analysis', in Marmura 1984*a*, 39–53.

Frede, D. 2003. 'Stoic Determinism', in Inwood 2003, 179–205.

Freudenthal, Gad. 1988. 'La philosophie de la géométrie d'al-Fārābī', *Jerusalem Studies in Arabic and Islam* II, 104–219.

—— 1993. 'Les sciences dans les communautés juives médiévales de Provence: leur appropriation, leur rôle', *Revue des études juives*, 152: 29–136.

Freudenthal, Gad. 1995. *Aristotle's Theory of Material Substance*. Oxford.
—— 1998. 'L'héritage de la physique stoïcienne dans la pensée juive médiévale', *Revue de Métaphysique et de Morale* 4: 453–77.
—— 2002. 'The Medieval Astrologization of Aristotle's Biology: Averroes on the Role of the Celestial Bodies in the Generation of Animate Beings,' *Arabic Sciences and Philosophy*, 12: 111–37.
—— 2006. 'The Medieval Astrologization of the Aristotelian Cosmos: from Alexander of Aphrodisias to Averroes', *Mélanges de l'Université Saint-Joseph*, 49: 29–68.
Freudenthal, Gideon 2003. 'A Philosopher between Two Cultures', in Freudenthal Gideon (ed.) 2003. *Salomon Maimon Rational Dogmatist, Empirical Skeptic*. Dordrecht, 1–17.
—— 2004, 'Shlomo Maimon: Parshanut ke-shiṭat hitpalsefut'. *Daat*, 53: 125–60 (Hebrew).
Furley D. J. 1967. *Two Studies in the Greek Atomists*. Princeton.
—— 1982. 'The Greek Commentators' Treatment of Aristotle's Theory of the Continuous', in Kretzman 1982, 17–36.
Gätje, H. 1966. 'Zur arabischen Überlieferung des Alexander von Aphrodisias', *ZDMG* 11: 225–78.
Genequand, C. 2001. See Alexander of Aphrodisias: *On the Principles*.
Gill, M. L. 1989. *Aristotle on Substance*. Princeton.
Glasner R. 2001*a*. 'Ibn Rushd's Theory of *minima naturalia*', *Arabic Sciences and Philosophy*, 11: 9–26.
—— 2001*b*. 'New Information on Zeno of Elea's Argument from Bisection', *Aleph*, 1: 285–93.
—— 2007. 'The Evolution of the Introduction in Averroes' Commentaries: A Preliminary Study', in Brenet 2007.
—— 2009. 'Two Notes on the Identification of Some Anonymous Hebrew Commentaries on the *Physics*', to appear in *Aleph*, 9.
—— forthcoming. '*Physics* VI Reconsidered'. In preparation.
Gohlke, P. 1924. 'Die Entstehungsgeschichte der naturwissenschaftlichen Schriften des Aristoteles', *Hermes*, 59: 274–94.
Goldstein, H. T. 1965. 'Averroes on the Structure and Function of *Physics* VII.1', in *Harry Austrin Wolfson Jubilee Volume*, i. 335–55.
—— 1991. See Averroes, *Questions in Physics*.
Gottchalk H. B. 1990. 'The Earliest Aristotelian Commentators', in Sorabji 1990, 55–82.
Graham, D. W. 1987. *Aristotle's Two Systems*. Oxford.
—— 1996. 'The Metaphysics of Motion: Natural Motion in *Physics* II and *Physics* VIII', in Wians 1996, 171–92.
—— 1999. See Aristotle, *Physics Book VIII*.
Granger, G. G. 1976. *Théorie aristotélicienne de la science*. Paris.
Grant E. 1974, *A Sourcebook in Medieval Science*, Cambridge, Mass.

——— 1978. 'The Principle of Impenetrability of Bodies in the History of Concepts of Separate Space from the Middle Ages to the Seventeenth Century', *Isis* 69: 551–71.

——— 1981. *Much Ado about Nothing*. Cambridge.

——— 1987. 'Ways to Interpret the terms "Aristotelian" and "Aristotelianism" in Medieval and Renaissance Natural Philosophy', in *History of Science*, 25: 335–58.

Griffel, F. 2002. 'The Relationship between Averroes and al-Ghazālī: as it Presents Itself in Averroes' Early Writings, Especially in his Commentary on al-Ghazālī's al-Mustaṣfā', in Inglis 2002, 51–63.

Gutas D. 1993. 'Aspects of Literary Form and Genre in Arabic Logical Works', in Burnett 1993, 29–76.

——— 1999. 'Averroes on Theophrastus, through Themistius', in Endress and Aertsen 1999, 125–44.

Guthrie W. K. C. 1978. *A History of Greek Philosophy*, v. Cambridge.

Hadot I. 1990. See Simplicius, *Commentaive surles Catégories.*

Hagen C. 1994. See Simplicius, *On Aristotle's Physics 7.*

Harvey S. 1977. See Averroes, *Middle Commentary on the Physics.*

——— 1980. 'Averroes' Three Short Commentaries on Aristotle's "Topics", "Rhetoric", and "Poetics"', *Review of Metaphysics*, 33: 616–18.

——— 1982. 'A Unique Averroes MS in the British Museum', *Bulletin of the School of Oriental and African Studies*, 45: 571–4.

——— 1983. See Averroes, *Long Commentary on Aristotle's Physics.*

——— 1997, 'Averroes' Use of Examples in his Middle Commentary on the *Prior Analytics*, and Some Remarks on his Role as Commentator', *Arabic Sciences and Philosophy*, 7: 91–113.

——— 2004*a*. 'The Impact of Philoponus' Commentary on the *Physics* on Averroes' Three Commentaries on the *Physics*', in Adamson et al. 2004, 89–104.

——— 2004*b*. 'The Author's Introduction as a Key to Understanding Trends in Islamic Philosophy', in Arnzen and Thielmann 2004, 15–32.

——— Forthcoming. 'Similarities and Differences among Averroes' Three Commentaries on Aristotle's *Physics*'.

Hasnawi A. 2001*a*. 'Topic and Analysis: The Arabic Tradition', in Sharples 2001, 28–62.

——— 2001*b*. 'La définition du mouvement dans la Physique du Šifā' d'Avicenne', *Arabic Sciences and Philosophy*, 11: 219–56.

——— Abdelali, E. J., and Aouad M. 1997. *Perspectives arabes et médiévales sur la tradition scientifique et philosophoque grecque*, Leuven and Paris.

Hasse, D. N. 2007. 'Latin Averroes Translations of the First Half of the Thirteenth Century.' Lecture given at the S.I.E.P.M. conference in Palermo.

Hassing, R. F., and Macierowsky, E. M. 1992. 'Latin Averroes on the Divisibility and Self Motion of the Elements', *Archiv für Geschichte der Philosophie*, 74: 127–57.

Heath, T. L. 1925. See Euclid, *Elements*.

——1949. *Mathematics in Aristotle*. Oxford.

Holden, T. 2004. *The Architecture of Matter: Galileo to Kant*. Oxford.

Hugonnard-Roche H. 1977. 'Remarques sur l'évolution doctrinale d'Averroès dans les commentaires au *De caelo*: le problème du mouvement de la terre', *Mélanges de la casa di Velasquez*, 13: 103–117.

——1984. 'L'épitomé du *De caelo* d'Aristote par Averroès: questions de méthode et de doctrine', *Archives d'histoire doctrinale et littéraire du moyen âge*, 51: 7–39.

——1985. 'Méthodes d'argumentation et philosophie naturelle chez Averroès', *Miscellanea mediaevalia*, 17: 240–53.

——1999. 'Averroès et la tradition de *Second Analitiques*', in Endress and Aertsen 1999, 172–87.

——2002. 'Logique et physique: la théorie aristotélicienne de la science interprétée par Averroès'. *Medioevo*, 27: 141–64.

——2004. 'Remarques sur les commentaires d'Averroès à la *Physique* et au *De caelo* d'Aristote', in Baffioni 2004, 103–19.

Hussey, E. 1983. See Aristotle, *Physics Books III and IV*.

——1991. 'Aristotle on Mathematical Objects', in Mueller 1991, 105–33.

Inglis, J. 2002. *Medieval Philosophy and the Classical Tradition in Islam, Judaism and Christianity*, Richmond, Surrey.

Inwood, B. (ed.) 2003. *The Cambridge Companion to the Stoics*. Cambridge.

Ivry, A. L. 1979. 'Averroes on Causation', in Stein and Loewe 1979, 143–56.

——1984. 'Destiny Revisited: Avicenna's Concept of Determinism', in Marmura 1984*a*, 160–71.

——(1995). 'Averroes' Middle and Long Commentaries on the *De anima*', *Arabic Sciences and Philosophy*, 5: 75–92.

——(1999). 'Averroes' Three Commentaries on *De anima*', in Endress and Aertsen 1999, 199–216.

——(2002). See Averroes, *Middle Commentary on De anima.*

——(2003). See Averroes, *Middle Commentary on De anima.*

Jadaane, F. 1968. *L'influence du stoïcisme sur la pensée musulmane*. Beirut.

Janssens, J., and De Smet, D. (eds.) 2002. *Avicenna and his Heritage*. Leuven.

Jéhamy, G. 1982, see Averroes, *Paraphrase de la logique d'Aristote*.

——2002. 'La méthodologie d'Averroès: le grand commentateur', in Khoury 2002, 107–16.

Judson, L. (ed.) 1991. *Aristotle's Physics*. Oxford.

Kenny, A. 1979. *Aristotle's Theory of the Will*, New Haven.

Khoury, R. G. 2002. *Averroes oder der Triumph des Rationalismus*. Heidelberg.

Kirwan, C. 1971, 1993. See Aristotle, *Metaphysics* Books Γ, Δ, and E.

Klein-Braslavy, S. 2003, 'Prologues et épilogues', in Sirat et al. 2003, 61–73.

——2005. 'The Alexandrian Prologue-Paradigm in Gersonides' Writings', *Jewish Quarterly Review*, 95: 257–89.

Kneale, W., and Kneale, M. 1962. *The Development of Logic*, Oxford.

Kogan, B. 1984. 'Eternity and Origination: Averroes' Discourse on the Manner of the World's Existence', in Marmura 1984*a*, 203–35.

—— 1985. *Averroes and the Metaphysics of Causation*. New York.

Konstan, D. 1979. 'Problems in Epicurean Physics', *Isis*, 70: 397–417.

—— 1982. 'Ancient Atomism and its Heritage: Minimal Parts', *Ancient Philosophy*, 2: 60–75.

—— 1988. 'Points, Lines and Infinity: Aristotle's *Physics* Zeta and Hellenistic Philosophy', *Proceedings of the Boston Area Colloquium in Ancient Philosophy*, 3, ed. J. Cleary, 1–32.

—— 1989. See Simplicius, *On Aristotle's Physics 6.*

Kosman L. A. 1969. 'Aristotle's Definition of Motion', *Phronesis*, 14: 40–62.

Kretzmann N. (ed.) 1982. *Infinity and Continuity in Ancient and Medieval Thought*. Ithaca, NY.

—— Kenney, A., and Pinborg, J. (eds.) 1982. *The Cambridge History of Later Medieval Philosophy*, Cambridge.

Kukkonen T. 2000*a*. 'Possible Worlds in the *Tahāfut al-Tahāfut*: Averroes on Plenitude and Possibility', *Journal of the History of Philosophy*, 38: 329–47.

—— 2000*b*. 'Possible Worlds in the *Tahāfut al-Falāsifa*: Al-Ghazālī on Creation and Contingency', *Journal of the History of Philosophy*, 38: 479–502.

—— 2001. 'Plenitude, Possibility, and the Limits of Reason: A Medieval Arabic Debate on the Metaphysics of Nature', *Journal of the History of Ideas*, 61: 539–60.

—— 2002*a*. 'Averroes and the Teleological Argument'. *Religious Studies* 38, 405–28.

—— 2002*b*. 'Infinite Power and Plenitude: Two Traditions on the Necessity of the Eternal', in Inglis 2002, 183–201.

—— 2002*c*. 'Alternatives to Alternatives: Approaches to Aristotle's *per impossibile* arguments', *Vivarium*, 40: 137–73.

Kupreeva, I. 2003. 'Qualities and Bodies: Alexander against the Stoics', *Oxford Studies in Ancient Philosophy*, 25: 297–344.

—— 2004. 'Alexander of Aphrodisias on Mixture and Growth', *Oxford Studies in Ancient Philosophy*, 27: 297–334.

Lacey, A. R. 1993. See Philoponus, *On Aristotle's Physics 2.*

Lang, H. S. 1992. 'Parts, Wholes, and Motion: *Physics* 7.1', in H. S. Lang, *Aristotle's Physics and its Medieval Varieties*, New York, 35–62.

Lapidge, M. 1978. 'Stoic Cosmology', in Rist 1978, 161–85.

Lay, J. 1996. 'L'abrégé de l'Almagest: un inédit d'Averroé en version hebraïque', *Arabic Sciences and Philosophy*, 6: 23–61.

Lear, J. 1982. 'Aristotle's Philosophy of Mathematics', *Philosophical Review*, 91: 161–92.

Lennon, T. M. 1993. *The Battle of the Gods and Giants*. Princeton.

Lennox, J. G. 1984. 'Aristotle on Chance', *Archiv für Geschichte der Philosophie*, 66: 52–60.

Lennox, J. G. 2001. *Aristotle's Philosophy of Biology*. Cambridge.

Lettinck, P. 1994*a*. *Aristotle's Physics and its Reception in the Arabic World*. Leiden.

—— 1994*b*. See Philoponus, *On Aristotle's Physics 5–8*.

—— 1997. 'Ibn Bājja as a Commentator of Aristotle', in Hasnawi et al. 1997.

Lewis, E. 1996. See Alexander, *On Aristotle's Meteorology 4*.

Lewis, F. A. 1996. 'Aristotle on the Unity of Substance', in Lewis and Bolton 1996, 39–81.

—— and Bolton R. (eds.) 1996. *Form, Matter and Mixture in Aristotle*. Oxford and Malden, Mass.

Long, A. A., and Sedley, D. N. 1987. *The Hellenistic Philosophers*, 2 vols. Cambridge.

Lüthy, C., Murdoch, J., and Newman W. R. 2001. *Late Medieval and Early Modern Corpuscular Matter Theories. Medieval and Early Modern Science*, New York.

McGinnis, J. (ed.) 2004. *Interpreting Avicenna: Science and Philosophy in Medieval Islam*—Proceedings of the Second Conference of the Avicenna Study Group. Leiden.

—— 2006. 'A Medieval Arabic Analysis of Motion at an Instant: the Avicennan Sources to the forma fluens/fluxus formae Debate', *British Journal for the History of Science*, 39: 189–205.

McKirahan, R. 2001. See Simplicius, *On Aristotle's Physics 8.6–10*.

Mahdi, M. 1967. 'Alfarabi against Philoponus', *Journal of Near Eastern Studies*, 26: 233–60.

Maier, A. 1949. 'Mathematisch-physicalische Fragestellungen', in *Die Vorläufer Galileis im 14. Jahrhundert*. Rome, 81–215.

—— 1958. '*Forma fluens* oder *Fluxus formae*?', in *Zwischen Philosophie und Mechanik*. Rome, 61–143.

Manekin, C. H., and Kellner, M. M. (eds.) 1997. *Freedom and Moral Responsibility*. Bethesda, Md.

Mansion, A. 1934. 'Note sur les traductions arabo-latines de la Physique d'Aristote dans la tradition manuscrite', *Revue néoscolastique de philosopie*, 37: 202–18.

—— 1946. *Introduction à la physique aristotélicienne*. Louvain and Paris.

Marmura, M. E. (ed.) 1984*a*. *Islamic Theology and Philosophy: Studies in Honor of George F. Hourani*, Albany, NY.

—— (ed.) 1984*b*. 'The Metaphysics of Efficient Causality in Avicenna', in Marmura 1984*a* 172–87.

—— 1991/2. 'Avicenna and Kalām', *Zeitschrift für Geschichte der arabischen-islamischen Wissenschaften*, 7: 172–206.

—— 1997. See Al-Ghazālī, *Incoherence*.

Mates, B. 1961. *Stoic Logic*, Berkeley.

Meinel, C. 1988, 'Early Seventeenth-Century Atomism: Theory, Epistemology, and the Insufficiency of Experiment', *Isis*, 79: 68–103.

Mendelsohn, E. (ed.) 1982. *Transformation and Tradition in the Sciences*. Cambridge.

Miller, F. D. 1982. 'Aristotle against the Atomists', in Kretzmann 1982, 87–111.

Moody, E. A. 1975*a*. *Studies in Medieval Philosophy, Science and Logic*. Berkeley.

—— 1975*b*. 'Galileo and Avempace', in Moody 1975*a*, 203–86.

Morrow, G. R. 1970. See Proclus, *A Commentary on the First Book of Euclid's Elements*.

Mueller, I. 1970. 'Aristotle on Geometrical Objects', *Archiv für Geschichte der Philosophie*, 52: 156–171.

—— 1981. *Philosophy of Mathematics and Deductive Structures in Euclid's Elements*. Cambridge.

—— 1986. 'On Some Academic Theories of Mathematical Objects', *Journal of Hellenic Studies*, 106: 111–120.

—— 1987. 'Mathematics and Philosopy in Proclus' Commentary on Book I of Euclid's Elements', in Pépin and Saffrey 1985.

—— 1990. 'Aristotle's Doctrine of Abstraction in the Commentators', in Sorabji 1990, 463–80.

—— (ed.) 1991. *Peri Tōn Mathēmatōn, Apeiron*, 24.

Murdoch, J. E. 1964. 'Superposition, Congruence and Continuity in the Middle Ages', in *Mélanges Alexander Koyré*, i. 416–44.

—— 1969. 'Mathesis in philosophiam scholasticam introducta. The Rise and Development of the Application of Mathematics in Fourteenth Century Philosophy and Theology', *Arts libéraux et philosophie au moyen âge*, Montreal and Paris.

—— 1972, 'Naissance et développement de l'atomisme au bas moyen âge latin', in *La science de la nature*, 1972. Montreal and Paris, 11–32.

—— 1982*a*. 'Infinity and Continuity', in N. Kretzmann, A. Kenney, and J. Pinborg (eds.), *The Cambridge History of Later Medieval Philosophy*. Cambridge, 564–591.

—— 1982*b*. 'Atomism and Motion in the Fourteenth Century', in Mendelsohn 1982, 45–66.

—— 2001. 'The Medieval and Renaissance Tradition of *Minima Naturalia*', in Lüthy et al. 2001, 91–131.

—— and Sylla, E. D. 1978. 'The Science of Motion', in Lindberg 1978, 206–64.

Newman, W. R. 2001. 'Experimental Corpuscular Theory in Aristotelian Alchemy: From Geber to Sennert', in Lüthy et al. 2001, 291–329.

Normore, C. G. 1982 'Walter Burley on Continuity', in Kretzmann 1982, 258–69.

Pabst, B. 1994. *Atomtheories des latinischen Mittelalters*. Darmstadt.

Pépin, J., and Saffrey, H. D. 1985. *Proclus, lecteur et interprète des anciens*, Actes du colloque international du CNRS. Paris.

Pines, S. 1936/1997. *Studies in Islamic Atomism*. Berlin/Jerusalem.

Pines, S. 1961/1986. 'Omne quod movertur necesse est ab alio moveri: A Refutation of Galen by Alexander of Aphrodisias and the Theory of Motion', *Isis*, 52: 21–54. Reprinted in *The Collected Works of Shlomo Pines*, ii. 218–51.

——1963, 'The Philosophical Sources of *The Guide of the Perplexed*', Translator's Introduction to Moses Maimonides, *The Guide of the Perplexed* (Chicago, 1963), pp. lvii–cxxxiv.

Puig Montada, J. 1983. See Averroes, *Epitome in physicorum libros*.

——1986. 'Maimonides and Averroes on the first Mover', in Pines and Yovel 1986, 213–23.

——1987. See Averroes, *Epítome de física*.

——1991. 'Tres manuscritos del epítome de la física de Averroes en El Cairo', *Anaquel de estudios árabes*, 2: 131–7.

——1992. 'Materials of Averroes' Circle', *Journal of Near Eastern Studies*, 4: 241–60.

——1993. 'Un aspecto de la influcncia de Avempace en Averroes', *Anaquel de Estudios Īrabes*, 4: 149–59.

——1996. 'Aristotle and Averroes on *Coming-to-be and Passing-away*', *Oriens*, 35: 1–34.

——1997. 'Les stades de la philosophie naturelle d'Averroès', *Arabic Sciences and Philosophy*, 7: 115–37.

——1998. *Averroes, juez médico y filósofo andalusí*. Andalucia.

——1999*a*. 'Zur bewegungsdefinition im VIII Buch der Physik', in Endress and Aertsen 1999, 145–59.

——1999*b*. 'Averroes y el problema de la eternidad del movimiento', *Ciudad de dios*, 212: 231–44.

——2001. 'Avempace y los problemas de los libros VII y VIII de la "Física"', *Ciudad de dios*, 214: 163–88.

——2002 'Averroes' Commentaries on Aristotle: To Explain and to Interpret', in Fioravanti et al. 2002, 327–58.

——2005*a*. 'Necesidad y posibilidad, Avicena y Averroes', in M. J. Soto Bruna (ed.), *Metafísica y antropología en el siglo XII*, Navarre.

——2005*b*. 'Necessity and Possibility in Averroes', a lecture given at Marquette University, Nov. 11, 2005.

——2009. 'Fragmentos del gran commentario de Averroes a la Física', in Al-Qantara: *Revista de estudios árabes*, 30.

Pyle, A. 1995. *Atomism and its Critics: From Democritus to Newton*, Bristol.

Rashed, M. 1997. 'A "New" Text of Alexander on the Soul's Motion', in Sorabji 1997, 181–95.

Rashed, R. 1999. 'Al-Kūhī vs. Aristotle on Motion', *Arabic Sciences and Philosophy*, 9: 7–24.

Renan, E. 1852/1997. *Averroès et l'averroisme*. Paris.

Rescher, N., and Marmura, M. 1965. See Alexander of Aphrodisias, *The Refutation.*

Rist, J. M. (ed.) 1978. *The Stoics*, Berkeley.

Ross, W. D. 1924, See Aristotle, *Metaphysics.*

____ 1936, See Aristotle, *Physics.*

Sambursky, S. 1959. *Physics of the Stoics,* London.

Schmieja, H. 1986. 'Drei Prologe im grossen Physikkommentar des Averroes?', *Miscellanea mediaevalia*, 18: 175–189.

____ 1999. 'Secundum aliam translationem—ein Beitrag zur arabisch–latinischen Übersetzung des grossen Physikkommentars von Averroes', in Endress and Aertsen 1999, 316–36.

____ 2000. 'Urbanus Averroista und die mittelalterlichen Handschriften des Physikkommentars von Averroes', *Bulletin de philosophie médiévale*, 42: 133–53.

____ 2001. 'Der Physikkommentar von Averroes in der Editio Iuntina: Die mittelalterlichen Quellen für Buch 6, Text 87', *Bulletin de philosophie médiévale*, 43: 75–93.

____ 2006. See Averroes, *Long Commentary on Aristotle's Physics.*

Schofield M., Burnyeat, M., and Barnes, J. (eds.) 1980. *Doubt and Dogmatism*. Oxford.

Schrenck, L. P. (ed.), *Aristotle in Late Antiquity*. Washington.

Sharples R. W. 1975. 'Aristotelian and Stoic Conceptions of Necessity in *De fato* of Alexander of Aphrodisias', *Phronesis*, 20: 247–74.

____ 1982. See Alexander of Aphrodisias, *On Time.*

____ 1983. See Alexander of Aphrodisias, *On Fate.*

____ 1992. See Alexander of Aphrodisias,*Quaestiones 1.1–2.15.*

____ 1994. See Alexander of Aphrodisias,*Quaestiones 2.16–3.15.*

____ 2001. *Whose Aristotle? Whose Aristotelianism?*, Aldershot.

Sirat, C., and Geoffroy, M. 2005. *L'original arabe du grand commentaire d'Averroès au De anima d'Aristote*, Paris.

____ Klein-Braslavy, S., and Weijers, O. 2003. *Les méthodes de travail de Gersonide et le maniement du savoir chez les scholastiques*. Paris.

Smith, R. 1982. 'The Relationship of Aristotle's Two Analytics', *Classical Quarterly*, NS 32: 327–35.

Snyder, H. G. 2000. *Teachers and Texts in the Ancient World*, London and New York.

Solmsen, F. 1960. *Aristotle's System of the Physical World*. Ithaca, NY.

Sorabji, R. 1980. *Necessity, Cause and Blame, Perspectives on Aristotle's Theory*, Ithaca, NY.

____ 1983. *Time, Creation and the Continuum*. London.

____ (ed.) 1987. *Philoponus and the Rejection of Aristotelian Science*. London.

____ 1988. *Matter, Space and Motion*. London.

Sorabji, R. (ed.) 1990. *Aristotle Transformed: The Ancient Commentators and their Influence*. London.

—— (ed.) 1997. *Aristotle and After*. Bulletin of the Institute of Classical Studies, Suppl. 68.

Stein, S., and Loewe, R. (eds.) 1979. *Studies in Jewish Religious and Intellectual History*. Tuscaloosa, Ala.

Stern, J. 1997. 'Maimonides' Conception of Freedom', in Manekin and Kellner 1997, 217–66.

Strohmaier, G. 1970. See Galen, *Über die Verschiedenheit der homoiomeren Körperteile*.

Stroumsa, S. 2005. 'Philosophes Almohades? Averroes, Maimonides, et l'idéologie almohade', in P. Cressier, M. Fierro, and L. Molina (eds.), *Los Almohades: Problemas y perspectivas*. Madrid: *CSIC* ii. 1137–62.

Stuart Crawford, F. 1953. See Averroes, *Long Commentary on De anima*.

Sylla, E. D. 1982. 'Infinite Divisibility and Continuity in Fourteenth-Century Theories of Alteration', in Kretzmann 1982, 231–57.

—— 1991. *The Oxford Calculators and the Mathematics of Motion 1320–1350*. New York and London.

—— 1993. 'Aristotelian Commentators and Scientific Change: The Parisian Nominalists on the Cause of Natural Motion of Inanimate Bodies', *Vivarium*, 31: 37–83.

—— and McVaugh, M. (eds.), *Texts and Contexts in Ancient and Medieval Science: Studies on the Occasion of John E. Murdoch's Seventieth Birthday*. Leiden.

Taran, L. 1981. *Speusippus of Athens*. Leiden.

Taylor, R. C. 1998. 'Averroes on Psychology and the Principles of Metaphysics', *Journal of the History of Philosophy*, 36: 507–23.

—— 2004. 'Improving on Nature's Exemplar: Averroes' Completion of Aristotle's Psychology of Intellect', in Adamson et al., 2004, ii. 107–30.

—— 2005. 'Averroes: Religious Dialectic and Aristotleian Philosophical Thought', in Adamson and Taylor 2005, 180–200.

—— 2007. 'Intelligibles in Act in Averroes', in Brenet 2007, 111–40.

Thijssen, J. M. 1991. 'Some Reflections on Continuity and Transformation of Aristotelianism in Medieval (and Renaissance) Natural Philosophy'. *Documenti e studi sulla tradizione filosofica medievale*, 2: 503–28.

Tieleman, T. 1996. *Galen and Chrysippus on the Soul*. Leiden.

Todd, R. B. 1972. 'Alexander of Aphrodisias and the Alexandrian *Quaestiones* II.12'. *Philologus*, 116: 291–305.

—— 1976. See Alexander of Aphrodisias *On Mixture*.

Twetten, D. B. 1995. 'Averroes on the Prime Mover Proved in the *Physics*', *Viator*, 26: 107–34.

—— 2007. 'Averroes' Prime Mover Argument', in Brenet 2007, 9–75.

Van Melsen, A. G. 1960. *From Atomos to Atom*. New York.

Vaux, R. de 1933. 'La première entrée d'Averroës chez les latines', *Revue des sciences philosophoiques et théologique*, 22: 193–245.

—— 1990. 'L'argument du livre VII de la *Physique*: une impasse philosophique', in Verbeke *D'Aristote à Thomas d'Aquine*. Leuven.

Vlastos, G. 1965. 'Minimal Parts in Epicurean Atomism', *Isis*, 56: 121–45.

Wallace, W. A. 1966. 'Atomism', in the *New Catholic Encyclopedia.*

Wardy, R. 1990. *The Chain of Change*, See Aristotle, *Physics* VII.

Waschkies, H. J. 1991. 'Mathematical Continuum and Continuity of Movement', in De Gandt and Souffrin, 1991, 151–79.

Waterfield, R. 1996. See Aristotle, *Physics.*

Waterlow, S. 1982. *Nature, Change, and Agency in Aristotle's Physics*. Oxford.

Wedin, M. V. 2000. *Aristotle's Theory of Substance*. Oxford.

Weisheipl, J. A. 1965. 'The Principle *Omne quod movetur ab alio movetur* in medieval Physics', *Isis*, 56: 26–45.

—— 1982. 'The Interpretation of Aristotle's *Physics* and the Science of Motion', in Kretzmann et al. 1982, 521–36.

Westernick, L. G. 1990. 'The Alexandrian Commentators and the Introductions to their Commentaries', in Sorabji 1990, 325–48.

White, M. J. 1992. *The Continuous and the Discrete: Ancient Physical Theories from a Contemporary Perspective*. Oxford.

—— 2003. 'Stoic Natural Philosophy (Physics and Cosmology)', in Inwood 2003, 124–52.

Wians, W. C. (ed.) 1996. *Aristotle's Philosophical Development: Problems and Prospects*. Lanham, Md.

Wieland, W. 1962. *Die aristotelische Physik,* Göttingen.

Wildberg, C. 1987*a*. See Philoponus, *Against Aristotle on the Eternity of the World.*

Wildberg, C. 1987*b*. 'Prolegomena to the Study of Philoponus' *contre Aristotelem*', in Sorabji 1987, 197–209.

Williams, C. J. F. 1982. See Aristotle, *De Generatione et Corruptione.*

Wingate, S. D. 1931. *The Medieval Latin Versions of the Aristotelian Scientific Corpus, with Special Reference to the Biological Works*, London.

Wisnovsky, R. 2003. *Avicenna's Metaphysics in Context*, Ithaca, NY.

Wohlman, A. 2004. 'Les deux facettes de l'unique vérité', *Revue Thomiste*, 104: 579–600.

Wolfson, H. A. 1929. *Crescas' Critique of Aristotle*. Cambridge, Mass.

—— 1973, *Studies in the History of Philosophy and Religion*, ed. I. Twersky and G. H. Williams. Cambridge Mass.

—— 1973*a*. 'Plan for the Publication of a *Corpus commentariorum averrois in aristotelem*', 430–54 [1963].

—— 1973*b*. 'The Twice-Revealed Averroes', 371–401.

—— 1976. *The Philosophy of Kalam*. Cambridge, Mass.

Zimmermann, F. 1987. 'Philoponus' Impetus Theory in the Arabic Tradition', in Sorabji 1987, 121–9.

Zonta, M. 1994. 'Osservazioni sulla traduzione ebraica del commento grande di Averroè al *De anima* di Aristotele', *Annali di ca' foscari*, 33: 15–28.

—— 1998. 'Al-Fārābī's Commentaries on Aristotle's Logic', in U. Vermeulen and D. de Smet, *Philosophy and Arts in the Islamic World*. Leuven.

—— 2001. 'Aristotle's *Physics* in Late-Medieval Jewish Philosophy (14th–15th Century) and a Newly-Identified Commentary by Yehudah Messer Leon', *Micrologos*, 9: 203–17.

Arabic Vocabulary

الاتصال في الجسم 84
اجزاء 145 n.22
اول اجزاء 162
ادكن 121 n.61
امر 120 n.55
الانقسام بالنهايات 116 n.40
إنما 94 n.175
بطل 157
تابع ال 72
تتالى 76 n.77
تفسير 1, 10, 52
تقسيم 11
تلخيص 1, 10–11, 52–3
توسط 121 n.60
جزء من الحركة 163
جملة 11
بالجنس 94
جوامع 1,10
الحادثة 82, 131
حدث 79 n.100
الحدوث الدائم ,الحدوث 107
بالحقيقة 151 n.61
بالذات 148
بذاتها 150
روحنيون 65
شرح 1, 10, 53
شرح على اللفظ 20
شرح على المعنى 20
الشافع 64
ضرورة 69
غيرية 149 n.52
فعل 112 n.16
الفعل 73 n.61
القدم 107
على القصد الاول 148
قوة ,بالقوة 73 n.61, 78 n.93
بالكمال ,الكمال 73 n.61
كمالات 130
ماهية 149 n.52
محرك ,متحرك 158
متحرك الاول 152, 157 n.102
متحرك الباقي 157 n.102
المتصل 64
مسائل 10
معنى 157
فلاسفة 174
مقالة ,مقالات 11, 52–3
مقدمة 70 n.39
ممكن 78 n.93
بانفسها 150
نقطة طبيعية 168
في النوع 94 n.171
يتلو 64

Hebrew Vocabulary

האלהים 139 n.157, 156 n.95
נסחת אלכסנדר; העתקת אלכסנדר 25 n.24
אם אלא 139 n.157
אמנם 94 n.175
אמצעי 49, 121 n.60
אמר 35 n.46
עוד אמר, אמרו, אחר אמר 15
אפיקורסים 26 n.33
אפשר 78 n.93
האפשרי 77 n.92
באור כפי העניין 20
באור מילה במילה 20
גדול השיעור והמעלה 140

גיליון 29
דבקות 76 n.79
דיבוק 76 n.79; 77 n.90, 77 n.92
הגדרה מחשבית הנדסית 161 n.118
הגהה 135 n.144
הזדוגות 76 n.78
הישרות 47 n.45
המצלתי (sic) 77 n.86
המשכה 31 n.20, 76 n.77
הנחה 48
הפך 117 n.45
הפעלות 125
הקדמה, הקדמות 48
השגה 55
התעכב 120 n.55
זר 46
חדוש התנועה 132 n.117
יחויב 69
יסבול 15
ירוץ מרוצת הטבע 60 n.11
ירצה 15
כח 49 n.54, 77 n.86
כלל 11
כפי שיבדאהו אריסטו 130 n.105
מאמר 11
מבלתי אמצעי 49
מתדבק, מדובק 77 n.92
מוגבל 152 n.72
מוגדר 152 n.72
מופת 77 n.86
מחויב 77 n.92
ממוצע 121 n.60
ממינה 76 n.81
מנגד 117 n.45
מנע 126 n.86
מניע לא יתנועע 84 n.124
מפרשים 134–5
מקבל 117 n.45
מקרה מהתנועות 82 n.119
משתווים 52 n.73
מתדבק 64, 161 n.125
מתחדשת 79 n.100
מתנועע ראשון ;מתנועעים ראשונים 152–3
מתנועע מאליו 84 n.124
נגלה מאמר 51 n.69
נגלה מבואר 51 n.69
נכרך 64
נלוה 64
נמנה 152 n.72
נמשך 64, 72
נפלא 46
נקודה טבעית 168
סותר 96 n.186, 117 n.45
ספר הדרושים הטבעיים 17
עצמותו 148
פינות השמונה ראשים 43 n.12
פרוש 35 n.46
צהוב 121 n.61
קיבוץ 156
קמלי 121 n.61
ראשון 152 n.73
שלמויות 130
שלמות 123 n.70
שתק 46
תחלה 152 n.72
תכונות 132 n.118
תכוף 64
תכיפה 31 n.20, 76 n.78
תכלה 83 n.123
תכלית 123 n.70
תנועה 77 n.92, 82 n.119
תנועה בדבר מה 88 n.153
תנועה בעצם 82 n.119
תנועה שחולקה חלקים 77 n.88
תנועות אשר תמנעום מנוחה 126 n.86
תעלה אל 83 n.123
תנועה היא בעצמה מדובקת 77 n.92
תפעלם הנפש בנמצאות 162 n.130

Greek and Latin Vocabulary

ad infinitum 77
anankaion 69
anankē 69 n.38
aphairesis 160
atelēs 112, 128 n.93
chorista 160
chorizei 160
continuum 109, 116 n.35, 117
declaratio diminuta 102
declaratione 102
deinde dixit 15
dico, dixit 101, 15
diminutum 96 n.186
dunamis 112, 128 n.96
ekhomenon 64
elachiston 144
energeia 112
entelekheia *see* English index
ephexēs 64
euthus sunepomenēn 89
expositio, hec exposition 101–2
fluxus formae/forma fluens *see* English index
idest, id est 15
igitur 15
kata sumbebēkos 72, 148 n.48
kath' hauto 147–8
kinēsis 88 n.153, 110, 112, 127
kinoumenon 146, 152 n.67
liber 11, libro Alex 25 n.24
manet 120 n.55
medio 49–50
metabolē 110, 115; tēn metabolēn 115
minima naturalia *see* English index
paraphrasis 11
perfectio 103
per impossibile 83, 87
per se 148
prooemium 32
prōton 115, 147
potentia 78 n.93
primum motum/prima mota 152–3
prin 70
motus/mota 126 n.86, 152
sermone 102
summa, summae 11, 15
sunekhes 64
ta pragmata ta dunamena kineisthai 70
tacuit 46
terminus a quo/ad quem *see* general index

Index of Names and Subjects

abstraction 160–1
Ackrill, J. L. 71 n.51
accidental relations; *see* essential vs. accidental
accidental succession; *see* succession
actuality (energia) 70, 73 n.61, 89, 112, 128–31
  vs. actualization 128
  vs. motion 128 n.93
  vs. perfection (entelekheia) 112 n.16
  vs. potentiality/capacity 84 n.128, 96 n.186, 130 n.108
Adamson, P. 71 n.51
Aegedius Romanus 37 n.52
Aertsen, J. A. 12 n.15, 35 n.43
aggregate 156, 166
al- ˁAlawi 19 n.3, 20 n.11, 106 n.234
Albertus Magnus 112, 114, 133
  on *forma fluens* vs. *fluxus formae*; 114 n.27
Albert of Saxony 145 n.23
Alexander of Aphrodisias 22, 24–5, 26–7, 43–4, 46–8, 65–7, 80–1, 88, 94, 100, 103, 105–6, 116, 124, 134, 139–40, 144, 147–57, 159, 162–73
  Arabic versions of his books 65
  authenticity of Arabic versions 53, 56, 148 n.37
  campaign against the Stoics 80, 156, 174
  vs. Galen 147–51, 173
  influence on Averroes' 52–6, 106, 167, 173–4
  Simplicius and Averroes as sources for 25, 170–1
  source for Averroes 22 n.5, 24 –5 nn.21 and 23–5, 43–4 n.16, 52–6, 151 n.66, 166, 170–1, 174
  See also elements, homoeomerity, vertical cosmology
al-Fārābī 4, 22–3, 26, 41–2, 60, 71 n.51, 74–6, 85–6, 90, 102–3,105
  Averroes' charges against 85–6, 102–3
  against Philoponus 75
  on possible and impossible successions 75 n.74, 87 n.145, 105–6
al-Ghazālī 23–4, 26, 108 n.246
  Averroes' debate with 44, 93
al-Masumi, M. S. H 11 n.7, 100 n.203
al-Nadim 171
Alonso, M. 20 n.11
Anaxagoras 101 n.214, 143, 172
Anderson, T. C. 160 n.113
Annas, J. 160 n.113, n.116
Aquinas 145 n.21
Archimedes 26
argument *per impossibile* 46, 147, 154
Aristotle
  against Anaxagoras 143
  against atomism 2, 141, 144 n.18, 159
  "Aristotelian atomism" 2, 172–5
  corpus 3, 41 n.3; translations of 1, 146 n.26
  difficulties in 3–5
  essentialism 148–51
  praise of 5, 61, 134, 135, 140 n.162.
  silence of 46, 165–6
  standards of scientific thinking; *see* science
Aristotelianism 1, 2–3, 5; Arabic 145; flexibility of 2–3
Arnzen, R. 44 n.21
Athens 115, 132
atomism 174
  Aristotle against 2, 141, 144 n.18, 159
  Averroes' acquaintance with Greek and Muslim atomism 67
  Averroes' "Aristotelian atomism" 2, 172–5
  Epicurean 144 n.18
  Epicurean vs. Kalām's 67–8, 145 n.22
  Kalām's 63, 67–8, 145, 168, 175
  seventeenth-century's 145 n.23, 175

atomism (*cont.*)
physical vs. metaphysical 144 n.16
atoms
in Alexander 159 n.110
vs. First-Moved parts 174–5
vs. minima 144, 144 n.20, 145 n.22
time atoms in Islam 68 n.32
units of soul and 169
Averroes
corpus 10–18, 19, 32, 42, 62
faithful/devout Aristotelian 73, 173
hesitating 4, 59–60, 99, 108
intellectual biography 30, 93,
strategies as commentator 3–6, 83, 85–6, 120, 132, 161
new physics of 1–3, 5, 27, 63, 93, 138, 163, 173
order of writing 19–21, 98, 105
sons of 37 n.52
Avicenna 22–3, 26, 71 n.50 , 75 n.74, 84 n.127, 85, 102, 112, 113 n.19, 114 n.27, 124, 127, 128 n.95, 129, 133, 145 n.23, 162 n.135, 163, 174–5
deterministic philosophy 62, 174
possible source for Averroes 162 n.135, 175
axiom of Inherence *see* premise VIII weak version

Badawi, A. 14
Balme, D. M. 69 n.36
Barker, P. 65 n.19
Barnes J. 45, 46 n.37, 47 nn.38 and n.43, 160, 171 n.185
Belo, C. 71 n.50, 84 n.127, 106 n.240, 125 n.81
Blair, G. A. 112 n.16
Bobzien, S. 63 n.5, 65 n.17, 69 n.36
body
aggregate of actual parts 166
cannot be infinite 12 n.12, 50–2
geometrical definitions of 143 n.10
geometrical vs. natural/physical143, 145 n.21, 160–1
divisibility of 153, 158 n.105, 160–162
oneness of 155, 155 n.89
see also celestial body
Bostock, D. 72, 73 n.58,115, 116 n.35
boundary
boundary entity 91, 127–8, 131
Epicurus on 144 n.18
fuzzy 67
mathematician vs. natural 161 n.118
of motion interval 89, 91
states between 111, 116 n.35, 121, 132
see also endpoint, terminus, divisibility in boundaries
Bouyges, M. 14 n.30, 25 n.24, 35 n.45, 36 nn.47 and 49
Boyle 2 n.5
Brunschwig, J. 46 n.38
Buridan 145 n.23
Burnett, C. 37 n.52
Butterworth, C. E. 43
Campanini, M. 107 n.242
capacity (*dunamis*)
in definition of motion 73 n.61, 112–3, 127
coexistent with vs. temporal prior to motion 86–7, 89–91, 103, 128 n.96
for motion in fire or wood/oil 90–1
Philoponus on 86 n.138, 128 n.96
for single vs. contrary motions 71 n.46
see also dunamis, potentiality
Carmody, F. J. 44 n.21
categories 112–3, 114 n.28, 125, 138 n.153
change in 113 n.20, 119
quantity/passion 113
causality 63 and n.4, 66–8
denial of 63, 173–4
see also necessity
celestial bodies 68, 80, 87, 95, 99 n.198
divine/eternal 80–1, 88
subsist through their movement 107
see also first moved body
celestial motions 25 n.26, 68, 78–9, 82, 87
continuous 68, 78, 124
essentially eternal 82, 97
guarantee contiguity in the sublunar world 78, 125
celestial realm/region 68, 76, 78, 81, 84
homogeneous 125
celestial movers 125
chain
causal 66–7

of changes/motions 73, 78–9
contiguous 78, 83, 84, 109, 120, 123, 126–7
successive 76, 78
chance 63; treatise on 16 n.35
change
change of change/motion of motion 69, 72–3 and n.59
complete/essential vs. intermediate 118, 122–3, 131
consequent upon accidentally 72, 82, 119 n.51, 122
between contraries or contradictories 111, 117
essential 118, 122
first 96 n.182, 103; in nature/time 97 n.189; impossibility of 69, 102
from rest to rest 117–18, 117 n.45, 122, 132
from something to something 110–11, 115, 117 nn.45–6, 119 n.53, 121–2
of genus at endpoint 118–19
homogeneous vs. heterogeneous entity 119
instantaneous 111–12, 116–18, 136 n.145, 138 n.153, 139 n.154
kinds of 39
Charlton, W. 143 n.12
Cleary, J. J. 160 n.114
Clericuzio, A. 2 n.5, 145 n.23
commentary
genre of 3
according to signification 20, 53
standards for writing 41
types of 1, 10
word-by-word 1, 20, 22, 53, 56, 120, 137
commentators 24–5, 26 n.29, 52–3, 59–60, 164–5
Averroes' attitudes to 4, 22, 24–7, 74–5, 80
Averroes' charges against 59, 133–5, 140 n.162
controversies among 114–17, 120, 133–6, 138–9
Greek 41, 120, 139, 144
Latin 144
contiguity 31, 63–9, 75–8, 83–4, 105 n.228
as approximation to continuity 85
Aristotle's definition of 64, 65 n.16
vs. continuity 68–9, 75, 81, 84, 106, 123–4
as 'corporeal continuity' 64 n.15, 84–5
and possibility 84
temporal 66
see also chains
continuity 63–5, 67, 75–80, 84–5, 97, 106–7
Aristotle's definition of 64
of celestial motions 79, 84
continuous motions 65, 68, 77–8, 83, 125; essentially continuous 97
of interval/magnitude 115, 120, 141
and necessity 84
mathematical vs. physical 63, 85 n.130
and oneness 155 n.88
'continuous qua continuous' 161
continuum 141 n.4, 143, 163, 169, 172
Stoics conceived the world as 84, 143
cannot be composed of indivisibles 144 n.18
exists only in the soul 163
controversies/debates
Alexander's with the Stoics 156
Averroes' with the theologians 43–4, 93, 107
among the commentators 59, 114, 116–7, 120, 134–40, 140 n.162
on determinism 63
see also polemical context
corpuscular natural philosophy/theory 144–5, 155
see also atomism, *minima naturalia*
cosmology 67, 80, 106–7
Crawford F. Stewart 12 n.15

Davidson, H. A. 75 n.74
De Chenes, D. 2 n.5
debates *see* controversies
Democritus 144 n.20, 159 n.110, 170 n.181
determinism 62–6, 69
in Aristotle 69, 172
Averroes' objection to 61

determinism (*cont.*)
cosmological implications of 67
future sea battle argument 71
in Muslim philosophy 86, 174
physical basis of 65–6
in Stoic philosophy 63, 65–6
Dhanani, A. 68 n.32, 145 n.22
dico passages 101, 103, 104
discrete physics 68, 173
distance 142, 162–3
divine body; *see* body
divine intervention 68
divisibility/division 64, 124 n.72, 136, 141, 143, 153 n.76, 155, 156 n.94, 158, 162
in boundaries vs. in attributes/contraries 116–7, 122–3 n.69, 134, 136 n.146
equal 39, 142, 162, *see also* isomorphism
of form 158 n.106
infinite 141–3, 144 n.16, 153 n.76
in length vs. in mass 162
metaphysical vs. physical division 144 n.16
divisibility argument (*Physics* VI.4) 114–15, 117, 133–4
'everything moved must be divisible' 59, 115, 118 n.50, 121, 144 n.18
difficulties in 115–17, 120
in the long commentary vs. middle commentary 120–2
premise V/VI 110–11, 115, 117, 119, 122 n.65, 134, 137 n.148
premise V/VI' 117, 134, 137 n.148
revisions in 59, 135, 137–8
Druart, T. A. 22
Duhem, P 1, 145
dunamis
term used for potentiality and possibility 78 n.93
two meanings of 128 n.96
see capacity, potentiality

Edwards, M. J. 128 n.95, 145 n.21
Eichner, H. 65 n.19, 155 n.85, 159 n.110
Eleatics 70 n.41
elements/simple bodies 125, 149, 155–8
hylomorphic analysis of 156–8, 174
theory of mutual replacement 156 n.98
Empedocles 101 n.214
endpoints 110, 115–24, 127–9, 132
change of genus at 118–19
true vs. intermediate 119–20, 127, 122–3, 132
see also boundary, *terminus*
Endress, G. 12 n.14, 15, 35 n.43, 44 n.21
Englert, W. G. 68 n.31
entelekheia 103, 112
vs. *energia* 112 n.16
two senses of 127, 128 n.96
see also perfection
Epicurus/Epicurean school 26
indeterminism 63
introduced the term 'minimum' 144
atomism 67, 145 n.22, 172
vs. stoic school 174
essential vs. accidental relations
terms of discussion of determinism vs. indeterminism 69, 78, 83
see also accidental succession
essential vs. accidental divisibility 136 n.146, 162 n.128
Aristotle's notion of essentiality in physics 151
essential motion 125, 147–54
Alexander vs. Galen on 150, 155, 174
definitions of 148–51, 167 n.164
of First-Moved parts 152–4, 156, 166
impossible in indivisibles 12 n.12
impossible in medium 125
in moving-agent argument 147–53
essential parts 156, 158–9, 162
eternity 62, 68, 71, 76–80, 82, 85, 90
accidental to sublunar motions 82–3, 97
essential to celectial motions 82, 97
vs. generation 107
in number vs. in species 80–1, 94 n.171
'broken eternity' 81
ether 80

Euclid 64 nn.8 and 13, 110 n.8, 141 n.2, 142 n.9, 143 n.10, 149 n.53
notion of continuity 63 n.8
notion of magnitude 141 n.2
Eudemus 25 n.26, 26
exegesis 3, 60, 117, 133–5, 137

Fakhry, M. 62 n.2
Fazzo, S. 53 n.85, 148 n.37
fire and wood/oil 89–91
first motion, motion of the outermost sphere 83–4, 87, 94, 102
essentially eternal 84, 88, 94, 97, 166
prior in time vs. in nature 83, 87–8
see also essential motion, succession argument interpretation B
first mover/moved body 84, 94, 102, 104
all motions terminate at 79–80
must be eternal 84, 88, 97, 104
see also celestial bodies
First-Moved part/unit 151–4, 157–8, 164
Flannery, K. L. 44 n.16
fluxus formae/forma fluens
Albertus Magnus on 112, 144, 133
Aristotle's view 114 n.28
Averroes' theory of *forma fluens* 112–17, 119, 133, 174
Aviceanna on 112, 133
Maier on 112–14
McGinnis on 133
Fontaine, R. 121 n.61
form
as moving faculty 157–8
associated with First-Moved part 158
divisible according to Philoponus 158 n.106
indivisible 158
Frede, D. 65 n.17
Freudenthal, Gad 11 n.8, 19 n.2, 65 n.19, 68 n.33, 79 nn.97 and 99, 80 n.106–7, 81, 141 n.5, 149 n.50, 156 n.92
Freudenthal, Gideon 3 n.8
Frederick II 37 n.52
Furley, D. J. 64 n.15, 68 n.31, 144 nn.18 and 20

Galen 4, 24, 26, 43 n.16, 60, 141 n.5, 147–51, 154–5, 163, 165–71
vs. Alexander on *Phys.* VII.1 147–51, 173
Arabic translations of 65
Averroes' defence of Aristotle against 154
Averroes' charges against 165, 167
Gassendi 2 n.5
Genequand, C. 106
generation
capacity for 89–90
coexistent vs. prior to motion 90
continuous vs. instantaneous 79 n.99, 111, 119 nn.52–3
and corruption 39, 111, 117 n.46, 125, 126 n.88, 137
eternal generation in Neoplatonism, Kalām and Averroes 106–7
first generated part 158
Gennagé, E. 80 n.104
geometry 63, 67 n.30, 128, 141, 142 n.9, 172–3
for Aristotle, applicable to the study of nature 172
for Averroes, applicable to the study of mental constructs 173
geometrical approach of *Physics* VI 110, 112, 115, 125, 142
geometrical vs. natural definitions 161 n.118
no notion of proximity in 64 n.13
science of continuous magnitudes 141, 161, 172
Gersonides 31–2, 158 n.105
Gill, M. L. 149
Glasner, R. 32 n.26, 35 n.44, 42 nn.6 and 8–9, 53 n.84, 55 n.93, 106 n.235, 110 nn.3 and 5, 141 n.1
God 65 n.20, 68 n.32, 106–7
Goldstein, B. R. 65 n.19
Goldstein, H. T. 17–18, 82 n.117, 83 n.123, 86 n.134, 89 n.155, 105 n.230
Graham, D. W. 71 n.50, 72 n.54, 111 n.11, 124 n.74
Grammarians 27, 43 n.16
Grant, E. 2, 63 n.3, 125 n.77, n.79, n.80
Griffel, F. 108 n.247
Gutas, D. 11, 22 n.4
Guthrie, W. K. C. 124 n.74

Hadot, I. 41 n.1
Harvey, S. 11, 13, 16 n.a, 17 n.38, 19, 20 n.9, 23, 37 n.52, 41 n.2, 42 nn.4, 5, 7 and 10, 47 n.43, 53 n.81, 54 n.89, 55 n.96, 93 n.169, 100 n.203
Hasnawi, A. 128 n.95, 162 n.135
Hasse, D. N. 12 n.16
Hassing, R. F. 152 n.68
Heath, T. L. 109 n.2
Heiberg, I. L. 149 n.52
Hellenistic period 63, 65, 172
Hermannus Alemannus 13
heterogeneity
 of change/motion 117–19 and n.53, 125, 129
 and divisibility in attributes 116 n.41
 of physical entities 123, 125–6, 143
Holden, T. 143, 144 nn.15–16
homoeomer/homoeomerity 141–2, 144, 146–7, 149–51, 155–6, 158 n.105, 172
 definitions of 141, 149 n.50
 vs. essentiality 155
 strong vs. weak notion of 149–50, 174
homogeneity
 in celestial region 125
 of change/motion 110, 113, 129
 and divisibility in boundaries 116
horizontal approach/cosmology 79–80, 82–3
Hugonnard-Roche, H. 44–5, 46 n.31, 47 n.39, 48 n.50
hylomorphic analysis *see* elements
Hussey, E. 51 n.65

Ibn Bājja 4, 26 nn.36–7, 45 n.30, 47 n.44, 53, 60, 69, 73, 85, 88 n.153, 90, 102, 106 n.231,112 n.15, 116, 121–2, 123 n.69, 139, 164–5, 167
 answer to Theophratus 116–7, 134–7
 Averroes' charges against 164–5
 criticism of Aristotle 4, 73
 source for Averroes 6 n.14, 22–3
 see also divisibility in boundaries vs. attributes
Ibn Rushd 1, *see* Averroes
Ibn Sinā *see* Avicenna
indeterminism 62–3, 69, 82, 107, 172
 Averroes' campaign 92
 Averroes' project to find scientific basis for 173, 175
 free will 68 n.31
indivisible parts/indivisibles 12 n.12, 67 n.30, 142, 144 n.18, 153 n.76, 161
indivisibility
 of atoms/minimal parts 144 and n.18, 153 n.76, 168 n.168
 of boundary entities 118, 124 n.72
 of First-Moved parts 157–8 and nn.102–3
 of form, 158 and n.107
 of natural points 169
infinity/infinite
 body cannot be 50–2
 first principles cannot be 48–9
 number cannot be 50
 infinite movements 82
 infinite past generations 73 n.60
 infinite successions of motions 73 n.59, 75 n.74, 77
in genus
 continuous in genus 96 n.186
 infinite in genus 82
 motion in genus 68, 93–4, 96 and n.186, 102
in species 80–1, 96
intention
 motion according to first intention/primarily 148, 150–1
interpenetration of bodies 67
interpretations A/B *see* succession argument
interval
 interval-like entity 115, 123, 127
 line/spatial 110
 model of motion 113–16, 120–2
 motion/change 65 n.16, 89, 91, 110–11
 open-ended 128
 time 64
 see also fluxus forma
introduction
 Alexandrian 41–2
 eight-points 42–3, 54
 in Averroes' commentaries 42–3, 52, 56
Is'âq Ibn Óunayn 14, 38 n.58, 78 n.93, 112 n.16, 120 n.55, 121

n.61, 146 n.26, 147 n.30, 148 n.42

Islam
- Averroes' attitude to 107 and n.242

isomorphism
- Averroes' thesis of 142–3, 162
- between mathematical and physical entities 142, 159
- between one-dimensional and three-dimensional entities 142 n.9

Ivry, A. L. 20 n.11, n.12, 21 n.13, 66 n.22, 84, 169 n.175

Jadaane, F. 65 n.19, n.20

Jéhamy, G. 20 nn.8 and 10, 43 n.16

Juntas edition 12, 13 n.24, 16, 17 and n.39, 42 n.10

Kalām 63, 106–8
- Averroes' criticism of 108
- atomism 145 n.22, 174
- concept of *ajzā'* 145 n.22
- indeterminism 63, 173
- influence on Averroes 107–8, 173
- nonscientific approach 172–4
- *see also* Mutakallimūn

Kalonimus ben Kalonimus 11, 13, 30–1, 100, 134, 164–5

Kenny, A. 63 n.4

Kirwan, C. 111 n.12

Klein-Braslavy, S. 41 nn.1 and 2

Kneale, W., and Kneale, M. 46 n.38, 47 n.43

Kogan, B. 44 n.17, 65 n.19, 68 n.32, 108 n.246, 124 n.73

Kolbrener, W. 59

Konstan, D. 116 n.36, 139 n.154, 144 n.18, n.20

Kosman, L. A. 112 n.16, 128

Kukkonen, T. 25 n.26, 44, 62 n.2, 84 n.128, 107 n.245, 166 n.162

Kurland, S. 107 n.245, 159 n.109

Kupreeva, I. 156, 159 n.110

Lapidge, M. 66

Lear, J. 160

Lennox, J. G. 63 n.4, 156

Lennon, T. M. 144 n.16

Lettinck, P. 22 n.5, 72 n.57, 73, 75 n.75, 88 n.153, 90 nn.159 and 161–2, 100 n.211, 105 n.226, 112 n.15, 116 n.40, n.41, 120 n.56, 134 n.123, 146 n.26, 167 n.163

Lewis, E. 159 n.110

Leucippus 144 n.20

linking question 74–6, 96, 98

logic/logical 20, 41
- Averroes' logical remarks/arguments 34, 44–52
- Averroes' logical sources: al-Fārābī 43 n.16; Aristotle 43; Philoponus 45 and n.29
- demonstrative vs. dialectical arguments 45–6
- in Alexander 169–71
- Sophistical arguments 55 n.98
- Stoic logic 43, 44 n.16
- *see also* syllogism

Long, A. 66 n.24, 67 n.28, 144 n.18

Long Commentary on Aristotle's *Physics* 12–17, 32–40
- editing and rewriting 32–4, 39–40, 92, 99
- enigmatic text 92, *see* riddles
- late stratum 41–56, 167
- logical orientation 43–52
- manuscript of 39
- two versions/redactions of 32, 36–7
- two strata of 39, 62, 92, 101–4, 107–8
- translations 12–14

Luria, S. 145 n.22

Lüthy 2 n.5

Macierowsky, E. M. 152 n.68

magnitude 63–5, 67, 141–3, 149, 152–5, 157–9, 161–3, 166
- in Aristotle, Euclid and Speusippus 141 and nn.2–4
- mathematical 64, 142
- physical 142, 159
- *see also* interval

Mahdi, M. 105 n.226

Maier, A. 1, 112–14, 145

Mantino Jacob 11, 42 n.10

Marcus Aurelius 66

Marmura, M. 66 n.22, 68 n.32, 148 n.38, 150 n.56, 151 n.63,171 n.83

Mates, B. 45 n.26

mathematics
- mathematical objects; in Aristotle 64, 153 n.76, 159–60; in Averroes 85 n.130, 160–2

mathematics (*cont.*)
mathematical vs. physical continuity/divisibility 141–3, 145 n.21, 153 n.76, 160–3
matter 91, 114, 125 n.81
divisibility of 144 n.16, 145, 153 n.76
and minimal part 156–8
McGinnis, J. 112 n.17, 114 n.29, 127 nn.89 and 90, 128 n.95, 129 n.98, n.100, 133, 163 n.136
McKirahan, R. 111 n.11
Meinel, C. 155
Melissus 45 n.29
Michael, E. 2 n.5
Michael Scotus 12, 24 n.23, 37
Middle Commentary on Aristotle's *Physics* 11–12, 19, 23–4, 74
Arabic outline 11 n.7, 100
not a paraphrase 93
revisions 30, 99, 101, 165
strata 139, 165
translations, relation between 11, 13, 30–1, 100, 134, 164–5
versions 30–1, 82, 92, 94–5, 97–101, 106
Milton John 59
Minima naturalia/minimal parts 143–6, 150, 155, 162, 168, 172
in Alexander 144, 155, 159
in Aristotle 144
in Averroes 145–6, 163–5
and First-Moved part 152
generation of 159
Moshe ben Shlomo of Sālon 13
Moshe Ibn Tibbon 10, 94 n.175
Motion
continuity of, Averroes vs. Aristotle 64, 109, 117, 129
continuous vs. contiguous 76–9, 82, 85, 95, 102–3
definition 47 n.45, 73 n.61, 103, 112–3
eternal 71, 79, 80, 82, 86–8, 102–3
generated 79, 82, 87, 89–91
as a kind of change 110–11
many successive vs. one continuous 78, 95–6
natural motion 89–91, 125, 155, 159
upward motion of fire 89–91
see also fluxus formae, forma fluens, first motion, essential motion
mover 62, 70–1, 79, 83–4, 87–8, 94, 96–7, 99, 103–5
unmoved mover 62, 83, 99 n.198, 125
moving-agent argument (*Physics* VII.1) 59, 146, 152, 163–4
difficulties 147
premise VII.A 146–7
premise VII.B 146–7
revisions 165–7, 174
Mueller, I. 141 nn.2 and 4, 160 n.113
Murdoch, J. E. 2, 85 n.130, 113, 114 nn.27 and 29, 143, 155, 161 n.19
Mutakallimūn/Muslim theologians 23–4, 26, 67 n.30, 75, 107, 145 n.22, 173–4
Averroes' public debates with 44, 93, 173–4
logical argumentation 44
nonscientific approach 172–4
referred to as 'our contemporaries', 'grammarians', 'our friends' 26–7, 23 n.7
see also Kalām

Narboni 32 n.26
Narwinio (or Garwinio), the sage 31
natural science 20, 42, 44–5
natural point, Averroes concept of 168–9
Neoplatonism 22, 86, 106; on capacity 86 n.138
necessity
necessitating vs. non-necessitating causes 66 n.22, 71 nn.46 and 51, 105 n.230
vs. possibility 84 n.127
Newman, W. R. 2
nominalism/nominalists 114, 163
number
cannot be infinite 49–51
exists in soul 162
infinite number of things impossible 66, 75, 87 n.145
in number vs. in species 81–2, 94 n.171, 119 n.53, 126, 156
self-moving number 169 and nn.173–4

oneness, one 81, 126, 156
essential one 155 n.88
occasionalism 67, 75, 107
ontology, narrow 72, 89
Osler, M. J. 2 n.5

Pabst, B. 155
parts
identical and similar parts 149 n.52
whole of parts vs. only a part 150–2
perfection I/II 128–32
Philoponus' definition 128
challenged by Avicenna 129
Averroes' new definition 130–2
Peripatetics 22 n.4, 24, 26
perpetuity 77–8, 82
Philoponus 4, 22–3, 25, 45, 60, 65, 69, 73–5, 76 n.75, 83 n.122, 85–6, 89–91, 100, 105, 106 n.231, 112 n.16, 120 n.56, 124, 128, 145 n.21, 158 n.106, 170
physical body/entity/object 159
cannot be infinite 50–1
divisibility 143, 157, 161, 172
Pines, S. 106 n.236, 145 n.22, 148 n.38
Plato 160
plenum 143
Plutarch 67
pneuma 80
Pneumatics *see* Stoics
pores/void spaces 66 n.20, 159 n.109
possibility/possible
Avicenna's and Averroes' understandings of 84 n.127
and contiguity 84
'the possible' 77–8, 84
possible/impossible successions 76–7, 87 n.145, 105 n.228
polemical context 60, 117, 120, 133–4, 136–7
leads to 'an intensive inquiry' 60
see also controversies
potential parts vs. actual parts 143–5
potentiality 84 n.128, 128–9, 130 n.105
distinguishes a dimensional from boundary entity 127–8
and possibility 78 n.93
see also dunamis, capacity
premise V/VI and V/VI' *see* divisibility argument
premise VII.A and VII.B *see* moving-agent argument
premise VIII *see* succession argument
principles, cannot be infinite 48–9
priority
natural 87 and n.143, 90 n.159
temporal 70, 86–7, 89, 95, 96 n.186
Proclus 169 n.174
proximity
degrees of 63, 75–6
no notion of in geometry 64 n.13
Puig Montada, J. 10, 11 n.6, 12 n.13, 19 n.3, 20 n.10, 12, 28–9, 36 n.50, 37 n.51, 44 n.22, 53 n.81, n.83, 68 n.33, 71, 72 n.52, 86 n.138, 87 n.140, 142, 89 n.157, 90 n.160, 94 n.175, 99, 108 n.246
Pyle, A. 145 n.24
Pythagoreans 169
Rashed, M. 124 n.75
Renan, E. 13
Rescher, N. 148 n.38, 150 n.56, 151 n.63, 171 n.183
revisions 28, 36, 41, 174
direct vs. indirect evidence 28
in introductions 42
editing vs. rewriting 32–4, 39–40, 92, 99
in the short commentary 28–9
in the middle commentary 100, 138–9, 165–7
in the long commentary 35, 41–3, 46, 52
in the long commentary on *Metaphyscis* 36
see also divisibility argument, moving-agent argument, succession argument
riddles in long commentary
first riddle 92–3, 97–8, 101
second riddle 92, 101–4, 108
Riva di Trento 10
Ross, W. D. 64 n.10, 71 n.46, n.51, 116 n.34, 156 n.92, 160 n.111, n.116
rotating radius argument 168–9
Ruland, H. J. 65 n.19

sage
  Averroes calls Alexander 80
  Averroes calls Aristotle 76–7
  Narwinio 31
Sambursky, S. 66 n.23, n.27
Schmieja, H. 12–13, 15 n.34, 26 n.35, 42 n.10, 101 n.213, 103 n.219
scholastics, scholasticism 1–3, 112, 145
science
  demonstrative vs. dialectical 45–6
  Aristotleian standards 63, 69, 173, 175
  Averroes' scientific approach 75
  scientific basis for indeterminism 62–3, 75, 107, 173
  exegetical 3
  freedom in 160–1
  Kalām nonscientific approach 172–4
  see also causality
school of Alexandria 41
Sedley, D. N. 66 n.24, 67 n.28, 144 n.18
Sennert 2 n.5
Sharples, R. W. 63 n.4, n.6, 65 n.19, 66 n.20, 67 n.28, 69 n.36, 159 n.110, 171 n.184
Shem Tov ben Yosef ben Shem Tov 32
Shem-Tov ben Yosef Ibn Falaquera 30 n.13, 130 nn.107–8, 131 n.111
Short Commentary on Aristotle's *Physics* 10–11, 19, 23–4, 74
  introduction 23 n.7, n.10
  late stratum of 23
  manuscripts and versions 29
  revisions 28–9, 35, 130
  textual difficulties of 28–9 and n.9, 130
  translation, Hebrew 10
  versions 28–9, 82, 94–5, 98–9
simple bodies *see* elements
Simplicius 25, 45 n.40, 59 n.2 111 n.10, n.11, 112 n.15, n.16, 116 n.36, 128 n.96, 139 n.154, 144 n.19, 148, 170–1, 175 n.4
Smith, R. 46 n.36
Snyder, H. G. 65 n.18
Socrates 73 n.60
Sorabji, R. 63 n.4, n.6, 66 n.22, 68 n.32
soul
  Pythagorean conception as a self-moving number 169
  and motion 125 n.75, 150 n.58
  entities that exist only in the soul 22 n.5, 162–3 and n.133, 162
Speusippus 141 n.4
sphere outermost/celestial
  motion of 83, 87, 94, 99 n.198, 127, *see also* first motion
  place of 26 n.37
  and time 170 n.179
  see also first moved body
stability of the world 76, 80–1
Stern, J. 66 n.22
Steinschneider, M. 13, 32 n.26
Stoics 63, 65–8, 75, 80, 84, 143, 151, 156, 172, 174
  absence of corpus of canonical texts 65
  Alexander vs. 156
  Arabs' acquaintance with 65
  Averroes' acquaintance with 65–6
  called 'the learned' by Averroes 65 n.20
  called 'the pneumatics' in Arabic 65
  determinism 63, 65, 66
  logic 43, 45, 48, 65
  notions of continuity and contiguity 63, 66–8, 84, 151
  theory of total blending 156 n.98
Strohmaier, G. 141 n.5, 149 n.50
Stroumsa, S. 108 n.247
sublunar world/region 68–9, 76, 78–81, 83–4, 89
  chains/changes/motions/processes 68–9, 73, 75–6, 78–9, 82–3, 93–4, 109
  contiguous model of 124–7, 174
  heterogeneity of 124–6
substance 72–3, 80, 89, 113, 119, 138 n.153, 149
succession 31, 65 n.16, 75–6
  accidental 67, 69, 72–3, 75 n.74, 78–9, 82, 85, 87 n.145, 113, 130–2
  Aristotle's definition 64
  infinite impossible according to Philoponus on 75 n.75
  infinite possible/impossible according to al-Fārābī 75–7, 87 n.145, 96, 105 n.228

interrupted succession in atomism 63
succession argument (*Physics* VIII.1) 28, 59, 62, 69, 70, 73–7, 79–80, 82–3, 86, 89, 92
deterministic implications of 62–3
interpretation A 74, 85–6, 91–2, 95–6, 101–2
interpretation B 74–5, 82, 84–6, 92, 95, 97, 102
in the short commentary 88, 104
in the middle commentary 87, 104
in the long commentary 101–4
Philoponus' criticism 73–4, 89, 91
Philoponus vs. Simplicius on 90 n.160
premise VIII 87 n.143, 95
weak 70, 86, 88–9, 103, 163
strong statement of 70, 74, 86–9, 94, 103, 163
intermediate statement 75, 87
Swerve 68
Sylla, E. D. 2, 113, 114 n.27, n.29
syllogisms 170
in Aristotle, Hellenistic commentators and Averroes 45–52
categorical 46–7, 49, 51
conjunctive/disjunctive 47
first/second-figure 49–51
hypothetical 45 n.30, 46–8, 51
per impossibile 51
see also logic

Taran, L. 141 n.4
Taylor, R. C. 3, 107 n.242, 160 n.115, 163 n.139
terminus
a quo/ad quem (departure/arrival) 111, 115–6, 120–1, 122 n.65, 127
first *terminus ad quem* 115–6, 120, 135
intermediate 119–21,127, 132–3
Thebes 115, 132
Themistius 20 n.9, 22 n.4, 25, 26 n.29, 43, 52–3, 86 n.138, 100, 104, 116 n.37, 128 n.95, 134, 139, 164, 170
Theodorus Antiochenus 42 n.10
Theologians *see* Mutakallimūn
Theophrastus 22 n.4, 24 n.20, 26, 43, 116–19, 133–6, 139, 140 n.162
Theophrastus' question 116–19, 133, 135, 139
answers to 117–19, 134–6, 140 n.162
Thomas Aquinas 146
Thomas-Institute 12 n.18
Tieleman, T. 150 n.55
time 141 n.4, 142, 143 n.9, 156 n.94, 162–3, 169–71
has only mental existence 162, 162 n.133
Todd, R. B. 66 n.20, 81 n.108, 159 n.110
translations
of Averroes 1
Latin insufficient 3
abbreviations in Latin 37
see also short commentary, middle commentary, long commentary
turning point
al-Fārābī's role 105
Alexander's role 167
dating 92–3, 133–5, 163
in *Physics* VI 89, 108–9, 117, 119, 133–9
in *Physics* VII 141, 167
in *Physics* VIII 84, 89, 92–3, 95–6, 99, 105
'turning-point passage' 74–6, 83, 92, 94, 96–9, 102, 105
two accounts 93, 97,108, 136–8, 173
turning-point pattern 4, 59, 114
Averroes charges the commentators 59, 133, 140 n.162, 164–7
Averroes ascribed his solution to Aristotle 60
Averroes hesitates 4, 59–60, 99, 108
Averroes praises Aristotle 61, 134–5, 140 n.162
Twetten, D. B. 87 n.142

unity 151, 155
accidental 148
unification 80
see also oneness/one
unmoved mover 62, 83–4, 125

van den Bergh, S. 44 n.16, 66 n.20
van Melsen, A. G. 143 n.13, 144–5, 153 n.76, 155
Vaux R. de 12 n.16
versions 28, 59
  A versions 74, 86, 89, 91–2
  B versions 74–5, 79, 82, 85–6, 91–2, 94–5, 97–100, 105
  see also short commentary, middle commentary, long commentary
vertical arguments/cosmology 79–81, 83, 106
  Alexander on 80
Vlastos, G. 144 n.18
void 12 n.12, 26 n.37

Wallace, W. A. 144 n.19
Wardy, R. 38 n.58, 83 n.121, 146 n.28, 147–8
Waschkies, H. J. 141 n.4
Waterlow, S. 111 n.14, 128, 129 n.98
Weisheipl, J. A. 113 n.19
Westernick, L. G. 41 n.1
White, M. J. 64 n.12, n.15, 67 n.29, 113
Wildberg, C. 86 n.138, 89 n.157, 90 n.158, 112 n.16, 128 n.96
William of Moerbeke 14 n.26
William of Ockham 114
Williams, C. J. F. 79 n.98
Wingate, S. D. 12 n.17
Wisnovsky, R. 112 n.16, 127 n.92, 128 n.94–6
Wohlman, A. 107 n.242
Wolfson, H. A. 1, 3 n.9, 12 n.15, 42 n.10, 66 n.20, 68 n.32, 78 n.93
word-by-word *see* commentary

Yeda̠ʿaya ha-Penini 29 n.9
Yehuda Messer Leon 13 n.21
Yisʿaq ben Shem Tov 32

Zenodic 26 n.33
Zeraʿya ben Isʿaq ben She'alti'el 11, 100, 164–5
Zimmermann, F. W. 71 n.51, 41 n.2
Ziyada, M. 73 n.61, 88 n.153, 167 n.163
Zonta, M. 12 n.15, 13 n.21, 42 n.5

Index locorum

Greek Authors
Aristotle
Categories and De Interpretatione
6, 4b20–21 169 n.174
9, 113 n.19
De int.
9, 69 n.36
9, 19a31–3: **71 n.51,** 71 n.52
Prior Analytics
I.23, 40b22–6 46 n.36
I. 44, 50a18 **46 n.38**
II.20, 46 n.36
Posterior Analytics
I.2, 71b20–25 46 n.35
I.27, 87a35–37 169 n.174
Topics
I.1, 100a25–30 48 n.48
IV.5, 142b24 **143 n.10**
Sophistical Refutations
I.2 48 n.48
Physics
I.2, 185b7–8 156 n.92
I.3, 45 n.29
186a6–10 **48 n.49**
186b4–12 37 n.55
187a1–11 54 n.91
I.4, 48; 144 n.19; 145 n.23; 146
187b7–188a18 48 n.51
187b10–13 **48 n.52**
187b14–20 **143 n.12**
I.5, 188a30 45 n.30
I.7, 109 n.1
II 69 n.36
II.1, 89 n.157
193b18 110 n.4
II.2, 160 n.116
193b23–5, 33–4 **160 n.112**
II.5, 196b19–21 45 n.29
III 77 n.89
III.1, 73; 113; 131
200b16 **109 n.2**
200b19 63 n.8
200b33–5 **113 n.23**
201a10 **70 n.42**
III.2, 112
201b16–18 **47 n.45**
201b32–3 **112 n.16**
III.4, 100
204a1–7 100 n.204
III.5, 50
204b4–9 50 n.59
204b5–6 **50 n.61, 143 n.10**
204b8–9 **51 n.65**
204b10–205a8 50 n.60
204b12–18 51 n.71
204b13–14 **52 n.74**
204b20 **143 n.10**
205a8–24 50 n.60
205b24–31 50 n.60
205b31–206a8 50 n.60
III.6, 161
III.7, 153 n.76
207a33–6 143 n.13
III.8, 208a20 **77 n.89**
III.45, Arab. 229.8–12 13 n.24
Arab. 229.12–230.1 13 n.24
IV.1, 169; 171
IV.3, 210b18 55 n.97
IV.4, 168
211a1 170 n.180
211b5 45 n.30; 47 n.44
212a23 168 n.171
IV.5, 26 n.37
IV.8, 26 n.37
IV.10, 169–71
218b5–9 45 n.29; 170 n.179
IV.11, 169–70
219a10–14 110 n.4, 142 n.7
IV.12, 220b25–6 113 n.18; 142 n.7
V.1, 113 n.23
224a21–26 167 n.165
224b1, b35 110 n.4
225a4–19 113 n.20
225b7 113 n.20
V.2, 69; 72–3; 78; 89; 130; 132
225b14–16 72 n.53, **72 n.55**
225b21–33 **72 nn.55 and 56**
225b30 110 n.4

Aristotle (*cont.*)
226a14 110 n.4
226a19–22 72 n.55
V.3, 64; 65 n.16; 75; 161 n.119
226b33–227a1 64 n.11
227a9–11 **64 n.12**
227a14–16 **64 n.14**
V.4, 65 n.16; 155 n.90
228a3–5 126 n.83
228a20–b6 **65 n.16**
V.16, 226a12–23, Arab. 564.4–568.3 14 n.24
VI.1, 47 n.44; 115 n.33; 142; 161
231a21–b17 144 n.18
231a24 **161 n.120**
231b12 121 n.60
231b15–18 45 n.30
231b18–19 **142 n.7**
231b22–4 110 n.6; 142 n.6
231b25 **142 n.7**
232a18 **64 n.9**
VI.2, 25 n.26; 63
232b20 110 n.9
232b24–5 **63 n.8**
VI.4, 9; 26 n.37; 39 n.63; 59; 101; 114–15; 117; 120; 133; 142; 158; 163
234b10 110 n.4; 146 n.29
234b10–20 **115 n.32; 144 n.18**
234b11–12 **120 n.55**
234b18 121 n.61
234b20–22 **162 n.134**
234b22–33 156 n.94
234b27–33 88 n.153
235a11–13 162 n.134
235a15–17 **142 n.8**
VI.5, 131 n.115; 137 n.148
235b6 **122 n.65**
235b7 110 n.4
236b11–14 124 n.72
VI.6, 236b19 110 n.9
237a19 110 n.4
237a33 124 n.72
237b8 124 n.72
237b10–21 111 n.12
VI.7, 237b23 110–1 n.9
VI.8, 239a23 110 n.4; 111 n.9
VI.10, 240b8 **144 n.18**
241a28 110 n.4
241a32–b2 143 n.12
VII.1–VII.3 146 n.26
VII.1–2 170
VII.1, 9; 26 n.37; 38; 59; 70; 83; 87; 101; 104; 146; 148; 152; 166–7; 173
241b24–242a15 (ver. b) **146 n.27**
241b34–242a49 (ver. a) **146 n.27**
241b27 (ver. b) **147 n.31**; 148 n.43
Arab.: 733.12–734.1 147 n.30
241b28–9 (ver. b) 148 n.40; 155 n.90
241b30–33 (ver. b) 148 n.41
241b37–8 (ver. a) **147 n.31**; 148 n.43
241b39–40 (ver. a) 148 n.40; 155 n.90
242a1–2 (ver. b) **146 n.28**
242a2 (ver. b) **146 n.28**
242a5–9 (ver. b) 147 n.34
242a7 (ver. b) **146 n.29**; **147 n.32**
242a8 (ver. b) **147 n.33**
242a9 (ver. b) 148 n.44
242a30–b4 110 n.4
242a34–6 (ver. a) **146 n.28**
242a37 (ver. a) **146 n.28**
242a38–44 (ver. a) 147 n.34
242a40 (ver. a) **146 n.29**
242a41 (ver. a) **147 n.32**
242a42–3 (ver. a) **147 n.33**
242a44 (ver. a) 148 n.44
VII.1–2, 242b33–243a6 (ver. b) 38 n.58
VII.2 38
VII.37, 250a15–19, Arab. 792.13–793.5 13 n.24
250a19–25, Arab. 793.6–13 13 n.24
VIII 62; 69 n.36
VIII.1, 9; 35 n.41; 59; 62–3; 69; 72–4; 79; 83–6; 88–9; 91; 101
250b11 **94 n.177**
251a8–17 95
251a8–28 101
251a8–b10 10 n.4; **28**; 30, 69 n.38
251a8–10 **70 nn.40 and 42,** 112 n.16
251a15 **70 n.43**
251a17 **70 n.44**

251a17–20 **70 n.45**
251a20–b9 71 **n.46**
251a27–8 71 **n.**47
251b5–9 **96 n.182**
251b9–10 Arab. 806.8 71 **n.**47
251b28–31 71 n.48
251b29–252a4 29 n.8
252b5 **71 n.49**
VIII.2, 252b10 110 n.4
VIII.3, 253b25 111 n.14
VIII.4, 148; 153
254b7–14 167 n.165
254b10–11 148 n.48
255b29–31 113 n.19
256a2 **146 n.27**
VIII.7, 261a27–b16 124 n.71
261a32–b7 123 n.67
VIII.8, 262a22–4, 28–33, **111 n.11**
VIII.10, 267a12–14 **124 n.74**
267a23–4 **155 n.89**
De caelo
I.1, 268a8–9 **143 n.10**
268a 9–11 **141 n.4**
I.2, 89 n.157
I.7, 274b20 **143 n.10**
I.8, 277a15 110 n.4
II.14, 296b30 **155 n.89**
III.1, 299a9–22 142 n.8
299a30–b3 168 n.168
299b10–14 168 n.168
299b15–23 168 n.170
299b18–20 168 n.168
III.2, 89 n.157
301b 28–30 **124 n.74**
III.5, 304b1–2 142 n.8
De generatione et corruptione
I.10, 328a26–8 143 n.13
II.10, 83
336a14–18 **79 n.98**
II.11, 337b15 69 n.36
De anima
I.4, 408b32 ff. 169 n.173
409a4 109 n.2
409a6 **169 n.174**
409a10–11 **169 n.173**
II.1, 412a22 **127 n.92**
De sensu
6, 446a8–9 143 n.13
De Part. an. 640a4 69 n.36
De Gen. an. 734a25 69 n.36
Metaphysics
Γ.8, 1012b28 110 n.4
Δ.2, 69n.36
Δ.6, 1015b35–1016a7 **155 n.88**
1016a1–3 **156 n.92**
1016b25–27 169 n.174
1016b28 **143 n.10**
1016b30–31 169 n.174
Δ.12, 1019b31–2 78 n.93
Δ.13, 1020a8–12 141 n.4
1020a11 63 n.7
1020a29–32 113 n.18
1020b12 **141 n.3**
E.3, 69n.36
E.3, 1027a29–32 111 n.12
1027b1–5 71 n.51
1027b11–14 **71 n.51**
Z.16, 1040b5–16 **156 n.92**
Θ.3–4, 69 n.36
Θ.6, 1048b29–30 **128 n.93**
K.2, 1060b15 **143 n.10**
K.9, 1065b16 **112 n.16**
K.10, 1066b23 **143 n.10**
K.10, 1066b31–2 **143 n.10**
K.12, 110 n.4
M.3, 160 n.116
1077b28–30 **160 n.111**
Nic. Ethics
III.1–5 69 n.36

Euclid
Elements
I 149 n.53
I.2 110 n.8
I.3 110 n.8
I.10 64 n.8
II.1–11 64 n.8
III.2–3 64 n.13
V definitions 3 and 4 143 n.9
XI definitions 1 and 2 143 n.10

Galen
Über die Verschiedenheit der homoiomeren Körperteile
Arab. 44, German 45 141 n.5
Arab. 46, German 47 **149 n.52**
Arab. 50, German 51 149 n.50
Alexander of Aphrodisias
On Aristotle's Prior Analytics
Introduction, 47 n.43
1.3–5, **48 n.48**
11.18–21, 46 n.37
17. 9, **47 n.38**

Aristotle (*cont.*)
On Meteorology
IV
214.22–3 **159 n.110**
On Metaphysics
123.8–14 **56 n.100**
On Fate
XXII, 193.7–8 **66 n.26**
192.3–7 **67 n.28**
XXV, 195.23–5 **80 n.106**
On Mixture
X, 223.6–14 **81 n.108**
XV, 231.12, 233.2 **159 n.110**
XVI, 235.29–34 156 n.98
On the Principles
25–6, 106 n.238
67.47 **124 n.75**
70–71 # 52, **103 n.219**
73, # 57, **80 n.105; 81 n.109**
73, # 58, **81 n.111**; 94 n.171
85, # 80, **81 n.112**; 94 n.171
On Time
60 **88 n.154**
62–3 **162 n.133**
Quaestiones
2.23 72.28–73.18 **159 n.110**
Refutation of Galen on Motion
Eng. 16, Arab. 76, Car. 67a7–9 **167 n.164**
Eng. 16–17, Arab. 76 **151 n.62**
Eng. 19, Arab. 81, Car. 67b6–7 **150 n.54**
Eng. 19, Arab. 81–2, Car. 67b8–10 **150 n.58**
Eng. 19, Arab. 81–2, Car. 67b9–10 **167 n.164**
Eng. 20, Arab. 83, Car. 67b16–18 **153 n.75**
Eng. 21, Arab. 84, Car. 67b26–7 **150 n.54**
Eng. 21 **150 n.58**
Eng. 31, Arab. 102, Esc. 62a24–5 **150 n.57**
Eng. 31, Arab. 103, Esc. 62a27–b1 **151 n.65**
Eng. 32, **167 n.165**
Eng. 33, Arab. 105, Esc. 62b24–63a1 **150 n.56**
Eng. 33–4, Arab. 107, Esc. 63a9–15 **149 n.50**
Eng. 34, Arab. 109, Esc. 63b1–2 150 n.60
Eng. 35, Arab. 110, Esc. 63b15 **150 n.57**
Eng. 35, Arab. 111, Esc. 63b18 **149 n.51**
Eng. 37, Arab. 115, Esc. 64a28–b4 **151 n.62**
Eng. 37, Arab. 115, Esc. 64b6–7 **151 n.60**
Eng. 38, Arab. 117, Esc. 64b24–6 **150 n.59**
Engl. 45, Arab. 131–2, Esc. 67a11–5 **151 n.64**
Themistius
On Physics
82.32 100 n.211
83.4–5 100 n.211
210.4–5 86 n.138
Philoponus
On Physics
58–60 23 n.12
59.15–24 45 n.29
59.25–60.18 45 n.29
60.19–61.10 45 n.29
61.11–21 45 n.29
271.27–272.13 23 n.12; 45 n.29
341.10–342.9 23 n.12
342.17–28 23 n.12
342.17–20 **128 n.95**
351.10–14 128 n.95
409.21–4 100 n.211
409–13 100 n.205
410.6 100 n.211
417.1–4 **50 n.62**
481. 3–6, **145 n.21; 158 n.106**
517.23, **158 n.106**
520.5–10 **73 n.59**
523.12–15 **75 n.75**
548.15–20 76 n.75
549.11–15 76 n.75
649.2–22 120 n.56
709–10 23 n.12
713.9–12 45 n.29; 170 n.179
Simplicius
On Cataegories 41 n.3
On Physics
469.32–470.2 100 n.211
469–71 100 n.205
529.29–530.3 170 n.177
559.25–31 55 n.98
576.30–577.6 25 n.26
708.27–8 **171 n.182**
713.27 170 n.181
718.13–719.21 171 n.182

923.8–9 59 n.2
941.22–942.24 25 n.26
941.23–942.13 25 n.26
942.13–24 25 n.26
966.15–27 116 n.36
966.15–968.31 **139 n.154**
968.23 112 n.15
986.13–14 175 n.4
1127.3–4 86 n.138
1130.8 112 n.16
1130.12, 13 86 n.138
1130.30–1131.2 86 n.138, 128 n.96
1131.5–6 128 n.96
1133.23 86 n.138
1133.24–7 **89 n.157**
1133.31–1134.14 **90 n.158**
1281.7–10 111 n.10
1281.20 111 n.11
1282.13–1283.20 111 n.11
1283.9 111 n.11

Early Lat. Authors
Lucretius
De rerum natura
II.250–51 **66 n.25**

Arab. Authors
Al- Fārābī
On Categories 42 n.5
On De interpretatione 42 n.5
Avicenna
Al-Shīfā'
II.1, 83 129 n.100
II.1, 84 **127 n.89–90; 163 n.136**
Ibn Bājja
On Physics
99.14–20 **116 n.40**
99.20–100.4 116 n.41
154.5–6 68 n.35
160.13–14 90 n.159
172.10–13 90 n.161
Averroes
Middle Commentary on Prior Analytics 43 n.16
Long Commentary on Posterior Analytics 42; 43 n.16
Heb. 7b2–3 **53 n.82**
Middle commentary on Topics 42; 43 n.15–6
Middle Commentary on Sophistical Refutations
Jéhamy ii. 729.9–11 20 n.10
*Jéhamy*ii. 729.12–13 20 n.8
Physics
Short Commentary on Aristotle's Physics
Introduction
I. Arab. 8.5, Heb. 2a16 23 n.7
Arab. 8.7, Heb. 2a18 23 n.7
Arab. 8.9, Heb. 2a20 23 n.10
Only Heb. 3b5 23 n.6
II. Arab. 21.10, Heb. 5b26 23 n.4, n.6
Arab. 26.11, Heb. 7a32 23 n.6
Arab. 26.17, Heb. 7b8 22 n.4
III. Arab. 31.10–14, Heb. 9a4–10 **129 n.104**
Arab. 35.10–15, Heb. 10a23–7 100 n.206
Arab. 43.8, Heb. 13a2–3, Spanish 143 28 n.2
IV. Arab. 55.16–17, Heb. 16b1 22 n.3, 23 n.9
Arab. 56.4, Heb. 16b10 22 n.3
Arab. 56.11, Heb. 16b17 23 n.6
Arab. 62.16, Heb. 19a1–2 22 n.5
V. Arab. 76.7–15, Heb. 23a2–12, Spanish 177 **131 n.116**
VI. Arab. 85.3–4, Heb. 25b17 161 n.124
Arab. 88.1–8, Heb. 26b8–20 **162 n.128**
Arab. 96.11–97.9, Heb. 29b12–30a1 120 n.57; 133 n.122
Arab. 97.10–99.1, Heb. 30a1–29 134 n.123
Arab. 99.2–100.11, Heb. 30a29–b26 134 n.124
Arab. 99.8, Heb. 30b6 22 n.4
Arab. 99.13, Heb. 30b11 22 n.3
Arab. 100.3, Heb. 30b16 22 n.4
Arab. 100.7, Heb. 30b19 22 n.3
Arab. 100.12–101.9, Heb. 30b26–31a14 134 n.125, **136 n.145**
Heb. 31a19–20 22 n.3; **135 n.143, 137 n.151**
Arab. 103.2, Heb. 31b26 22 n.4
Arab. 105.16, Heb. 32b29 22 n.4
Arab. 106.2, Heb. 33a4 22 n.4
VII. Arab. 114.1–9, Heb. 35a13–21 **154 n.78**
Arab. 114.16–115.12, Heb. 35a31–b18 **158 n.103**

Averroes (*cont.*)
Arab. 116.13, Heb. 36a11 22 n.3
VIII. **Version B**[1]
Arab. 129.6 70 n.39
Heb. 39b–40b 29 n.3
Arab. 129.7, Heb. 39b8–9 **88 n.153**
Arab. 130.6–131.1, Heb. 39b15–23 88 n.149
Arab. 131.1–4, Heb. 39b23–8 88 n.150
Arab. 131.6–132.12, Heb. 39b30–40a16 88 n.151
Arab. 132.16–17, Heb. 40a16–18 **88 n.152**
Arab. 133.5–134.3; Heb. 40a24–31 **94 n.171, 94 n.176**
Arab. 133.8–134.3; Heb. 40a28–31 **82 n.118**
Arab. 134.4, Heb. 40b6 23 n.7
Arab. 134.7–135.2, Heb. 40b11–18 **85 n.131**
Arab. 134.10–1, Heb. 40b14–6 23 n.3 and n.6, n.10
Arab. 135.1, Heb. 40b16 23 n.8
Arab. 135.3–6, Heb. 40b19–22 23 n. 10, **105 n.230**
Arab. 135.7–8, Heb. 40b23–5 **85 n.132**
Version A
Arab. 129.8, 11–12 94 n.173
Arab. 130.12–3 94 n.173
Heb. 40b31 29 n.5
Heb. 41a1, 5, 7, 11, 12, 94 n.173
Arab. 131.10–11, Heb. 41a22–4 **87 n.140**
Arab. 131.11–132.15, Heb. 41a24–b1 90 n.159
Arab. 132.15–17 Heb. 41b1–6. **90 n.163**
Heb. 42a3 94 n.173
Arab. 133.19, 134.12–14, 135.17–19 29 n.8
Arab. 134.12–135.16 Heb. 41b20–42a2 29 n.8
Arab. 135.10; Heb. 40b27 28 n.2
Arab. 135.19–20, Heb. 42a3–4 94 n.173 and **174**
Arab. 141.4, Heb. 43b22 22 n.4
Middle Commentary on Aristotle's Physics
I.2.1.4, 5a16–b13 23 n.12
I.2.1.4 7a20–23 45 n.28; 48 n.53
I.2.2.2, 7a19–b15 48 n.51
7a19–b9 12 n.12
I.2.4, 5a17–19, 19–21, 21–b7 45 n.27; 45 n.29
5b7–13 45 n.29
I.3.1, 8a8–15 45 n.27–8, n.30
I.3.2, 8b15–26 12 n.12
II.2.1, 14b6–7 **160 n.116**
II.2.2, 14b23–4 **160 n.116**
II.3.2, 18b17–25 23 n.12, 45 n.27–9
III.2.1, 23a1–26 12 n.12, 23 n.12
III.2.2, 23b10–13 23 n. 12, **129 n.102**
23b19–20 **129 n.103**
23b20–22 129 n.101
III.3.3, 27a3–14 12 n.12
Zer. 33a18–19 100 n.207
27a4 100 n.209
Kal. 27a5, Zer. 33a20 100 n.211
Kal. 27a8–10, Zer. 33b1–3 100 n.211
III.3.4.2, 28a5–18 50 n.60
28a10–12 45 n.28, 50 n.63
28a15–17 45 n.28, **51 n.66**
28a17–30a24 12 n.12
28a18–b26 50 n.60
28a24–b6 51 n.72
28b26–29b26 50 n.60
30a1–6 50 n.60
30a6–24 50 n.60
III.3.5, 31a22–5, b4–10 **153 n.76**
31b4–32a6 161 n.118
31b17–19 160 n.116
III.3.7, Kal. 32b12–14, Zer. 40a13–16 **158 n.107**
IV.1.1–2, 12 n.12
IV .1.1, 34a26–b1 24 n.18
IV.1.2, 35b16–19 45 n.27

[1] In the Arabic edition each page is divided: the upper part is version B, the lower version A. In the Hebrew edition version B appears first and then version A.

IV.1.3, 35b19–36a1 12 n.12
IV.1.6, 36b 12 n.12
IV.1.8, 37a24–6 45 n.27 and 30; 47 n.44
IV.1.9, 26 n.37
39b14–25 **168 n.172**
40a1 23 n.14
40a14 23 n.14, 24 n.16
40a22 23 n.14
IV.2.3, 41b12–16 12 n.12
IV.2.5, 26 n.37
IV.2.5, 43a–46a 12 n.12
44b19–20 23 n.14
45a17 23 n.14
IV.3.3, 48a13–19 23 n. 12, 45 n.27 and 29; 170 n.179
VI, 66a18–19 **161 n.121**
VI.1, 66a19 **161 n.122**
67b16–26 45 n.27–8, n.30
67b18 **161 n.123**
67b20 47 n.44
67b26–68a7, Zer. 83a19–b2 24 n. 18, **67 n.30**
68a7 24 n.18
VI.2, 68b12 48 n.46
VI.3, 69a 12 n.12
VI.4, 100
VI.7, 4 n.16; 5 n.18; 26 n.37; 134; 137; 139
72a5–19 **121 n.62**; 134 n.126
72a19–b9 134 n.127
72a20–22 24 n. 20, 116 n.36
72a23–5 24 n. 21, 116 n.38, 139 n.154
72a25–b4 116 n.37
72b4–9 23 n.14, 117 n.43
72b9–73a2 134 n.128
72b11 24 n.20
72b14–17 **4 n.14; 60 n.**7; **136 n.146**
72b15, 17, 20 23 n.14
72b23–73a2 45 n.27 and 30
73a2–4 **5 n.17**; **60 n.12**; 134 n.129
73a4–20 24 n. 20, 134 n.130
73a4–8 **117 n.46**
Kal. 73a13–14, Zer. 89a1–13 **117 n.45**
73a20–74a23 134 n.131
Kal. 73a20–b10, Zer. 89a18–b12 112 n.15, **118 n.49**
Kal. 73b8–10, Zer. 89b10–12 **118 n.48**
Kal. 73b10–14, Zer. 89b13–16 **119 n.52**
Kal. 73b14–23, Zer. 89b16–90a1 **119 n.53**
73b15 24 n.20
Kal. 74a1–5, Zer. 90a5–7 **118 n.50**
74a3–6 118 n.50
74a5–9 **119 n.51**
74a14 24 n.20
Kal 74a23–b4, Zer. 90b2–10 **140 n.161**
74a23–b7 134 n.132
74a25 24 n.21
74b2 24 n.21
74b7–11 **4 n.16**; 23 n. 14, 24 n.20, **60 n.10**, 134 n.133, 140 n.162
74b11–23 134 n.134
Kal. 74b11–17, Zer. 90b13–19 **5 n.18; 61 n.14**
74b14–15, 17 140 n.162
Kal. 74b 21–2, Zer. 90b23–91a1 **5 n.18; 61 n.14**
75a10, 17, 23 88 n.153
75a23–b1 162 n.128
VI.8, 75b7–8 137 n.148
VI.9 77a26 24 n.20
VI.11 81b1–2 23 n.15
VI.12, 81b 12 n.12
VII.1–2, 26 n.37
VII.1, 100; 163; 165; 167
82b14–83a15 164 n.141
Kal. 83a2–13, Zer. 99b21–100a9 **152 n.73**
83a13–15 **154 n.80**
83a15–b12 164 n.142
83a26–b4 **154 n.81**
83b8–12 **154 n.82**
83b12–16 164 n.143

Averroes (*cont.*)
83b12–13 **165 n.154**
83b13–16 **166 n.157**
83b16–20 **157 n.99**
Kal. 83b16–25, Zer. 100b11–19 164 n.144
Zer. 100b19–21 **164 n.145**
Zer. 100b21–2 **164 n.146**
Zer. 100b22–101a3 **164 n.147**
83b25–6 **164 n.148**
83b25–84a1 **4 n.14; 60 n.8**
83b26–84a8 **165 n.149**
84a2–4 24 n.19, **4 n.11; 59 n.3, 154 n.79**
84a3–8 23 n.14, **4 n.12; 60 n.5**
84a8–11 24 nn. 20–1, **165 n.150**
84a11–13 **165 n.152**
VII.2 85a9 23 n.14
VII.4, 88a24–5 224 nn.21–2
VIII.2, 97
VIII.2.1–2, 30
VIII.2.1, ver. A, anon. 65b12–22 74 n.64
ver. A, anon. 65b20–26; Zer. 110a10–111.5 **90 n.159**
ver. A, anon. 65b20–22; Zer. 110a16–18 **87 n.140**
ver. A anon. 65b22–66b5 74 n.65
ver. A, anon. 65b25–6, Zer. 110b1–3 **91 n.166**
ver. A, anon. 66a1–3, Zer. 110b3–9 **91 n.164**
ver. A, anon. 66a3–6, Zer. 110b9–12 **91 n.167**
ver. A anon. 66a21 23 n.11
ver. A anon 24 n.16
ver. B, 92b5–15 75 n.69
ver. B 92b9–11 **87 n.143**
ver. B, 92b17–20 **99 n.198**
VIII.2.2, 98 n.197; 99; 105 n.229; 138
ver. A, anon. 66b5–30 74 n.66
ver. A, anon. 66b29–30 **87 n.141**
ver. A, anon. 66b30–67a6; Oxford MS 96a16–22; Zer. 112a5–13 **76 n.80**
ver. A, anon. 66b30–67a15 74 n.67
ver. A, anon. 67a5–6 **105 n.228**
ver. A, anon. 67a6–14, Oxford MS 96a21–b2; Zer. 112a12–23 77 **n.91**
ver. A, anon. 67a8 **4 n.15; 60 n.9**
ver. A, anon. 67a13–22, Oxford MS 96b1–15; Zer. 112a20–b7 **84 n.125; 99 n.198**
ver. A, anon. 67a15–28 74 n.68
ver. A, anon. 67a20–21 **88 n.147**
ver. A anon. 67a26–7 **5 n.20; 60 n.16**
ver. B, 92b16–94a5 75 n.70, 87 n.144
ver. B, 92b25–93a11 **87 n.145**
ver. B 93a17–b1 88 n.146
ver. B, 94a6–19 24 n.18, 75 n.71, **79 n.101**
ver. B, 94a19–26 75 n.72, **82 n.120**
ver. B, 94a21–3 **88 n.148**
ver. B, 94a24–6 23 n.11, 24 n.16, **4 n.13; 60 n.6; 85 n.133**
VIII.2.4, 78; 98 n.197; 99
95b4–6 **78 n.96**
VIII.4.4 100a26 23 n.11
VIII.5.3, 107b2–4 **120–1 n.58**
108a20–22 **121 n.58**
VIII.6.5, Kal. 115a5–17, Zer. 137b20–138a10 **19 n.6**
Colophon 115a9–10 24 n.17, n.20
Long Commentary on Aristotle's Physics
Introduction:
Heb. 1a1–5 **53 n.81**
Heb. 1a2 20 n.9
Heb. 1a3 53 n.79
Heb. 1a3, 25 24 n.23
Heb. 1a25–6 **54 n.89**
Heb. 1b20, 3 24 n.23
Heb. 2a14–17 43 n.14
Book I:
I.4, Heb. 5a28–30 33 n.31; 37 n.53, **43 n.13**

I.5, Lat. 8H2–5 **43 n.11**
Heb. 6a24–5 33 n.31; 37 n.53, 43 n.11, **43 n.12**
I.10, Heb. 8b15–16, 22–23 44 n.23
I.11, Lat. 11K2–6 33 n.32; 37 n.53
I.15, Heb. 11a17–18 33 n.31; 37 n.53; 48 n.49
I.18, Lat. 14B5–8, Heb. 12a18–19 37 n.53
I.21, Heb. 13b10–11 33 n.31; 37 n.53
I.22, Heb. 13b25 37 n.53
Lat. 15G14, Heb. 13b25 48 n.49
I.23, Heb. 14a23 37 n.53
Heb. 14a25–9 37 n.53
Heb. 14a30 37 n.53
Heb. 14b2–3, 6 37 n.53
I.25, Heb. 15a30 37 n.53
Heb. 15b8–11 37 n.53
Heb. 15b16–18 37 n.53
Lat. 17K7, Heb. 16a30 25 n.27
I.27, 34 n.37–8; 37; 40
I.28, Heb. 18b6–7 33 n.31
I.30–31, 34 n.37; 40; 54–5
I.30, Heb. 19b28 24 n.23; 54 n.92
Heb. 19b29–20a4 25 n.25, 55 n.93
Heb. 20a10 26 n.38
Heb. 20a14 24 n.23; 25 n.24; 54 n.92
Heb. 20a 23 24 n.23; 54 n.92
I.31, Heb. 20b27 24 n.23; 25 n.24; 54 n.92
I.35, 48
Lat. 23C13, Heb. 23a13–14 **49 n.54**
Lat. 23D1–2, Heb. 23a14–15 49 n.54
Lat. 23D6–E1, Heb. 23a16–20 **49 n.55**
Lat. 23F1–12, Heb. 23a25–9 **49 n.56**
Lat. 23G10–H1, Heb. 23b1–5 **49 n.57**
Lat. 23H1–4, Heb. 23b5–6 50 n.58
Lat. 23I5–13, Heb. 23b15–18 **46 n.33**
Lat. 23I7, Heb. 23b16 46 n.32
Heb. 23b18–21 33 n.31, **46 n.34**
I.37, Lat. 24M13–25A4, Heb. 25a3–4 **146 n.25**
I.40, Heb. 26b17–18 33 n.31
I.41, Lat. 27F6–9, Heb. 27b18–19 33 n.30
I.47, Heb. 30a14–17 33 n.31
I.52, 34 n.37; 40; 54–5
Lat. 32E15, F1 24 n.23
I.54, Lat. 33A2–6 33 n.32
I.57, 35 n.40; 39
Lat. 34K9–11, Heb. 35b11–16 **20.7**; 33 n.31
I.60, 34 n.37
Lat. 36D4, Heb. 37b5 26 n.38
Lat. 36E2, Heb. 37b13 26 n.38
Lat. 36E4, Heb. 37b14 27 n.40
Heb. 37b15 26 n.35
Lat. 36F6, Heb. 37b22 26 n.38
Lat. 36I7, Heb. 38a8 26 n.33, n.36
I.61, Heb. 38b1–6 33 n.31, 33 n.33, 25 n.27
I.63, Lat. 37M1–38F14, Heb. 13 n.24
I.67, Heb. 41a7–9 33 n.31
I.68, Heb. 41a14–5 48 n.49
I.71, Lat. 42C1, Heb. 43b3 26 n.38
I.83, Lat. 47G10, Heb. 49a20 26 n.35
Lat. 47K5, Heb. 49b11 26 n.35
Lat. 47K13–L2 33 n.32
Book II:
II.1, Heb. 50a27–30 33 n.31
II.3, Lat. 49B14, Heb. 51a5–6 26 n.35
Heb. 51b2–4 47 n.40
II.9, Lat. 51H10,Heb. 54a11 24 n.23; 25 n.25
II.18, Lat. 54M, Heb. 57b17–19 160 n.117
II.19, Lat. 55C, Heb. 57b28–58a2 **160 n.115**
II.22, Lat. 56M, Heb. 59b19 26 n.35
Lat. 57B3, Heb. 60a7 26 n.35
Lat. 57B6, Heb. 60a11 26 n.30
Lat. 57B7, Heb. 60a11 26 n.38
II.26, Lat. 59C2, Heb. 62b7 26 n.35

Averroes (*cont.*)
II.30, Lat. 60L1, Heb. 64a18 24 n.23
II.35, Lat. 62I11, Heb. 66b4 24 n.23; 25 n.24
II.36, Heb. 66b30–67a1 33 n.31
II.37, Lat. 63E2, Heb. 67a11 24 n.23; 25 n.24
II.42, Heb. 68b4–10 33 n.31
II.48, Lat. 66G11, Heb. 70b10 26 n.30 and 35
Lat. 66G15, Heb. 70b12 25 n.27; 26 n.35
Lat. 66H9, Heb. 70b15 26 n.35
Lat. 66M3, Heb. 71a7 26 n.35
II.50, Lat. 68A12, Heb. 72a19 25 n.29
II.55, Lat. 70A14, Heb. 74b6 25 n.27
II.66–7, 34 n.37–8
II.75, Heb. 82a10–14 33 n.31
II.77, Lat. 77I9, Heb. 83b27 24 n.23
II.88, Lat. 82M9, Heb. 90a12 24 n.23; 25 n.24
II.90, Lat. 84H7, Heb. 92a17 24 n.23
II.91, Heb. 92b18–19 33 n.31
II.92, Heb. 93a3–14 34 n.37
Lat. 85C13–D5 34 n.37
Book III:
III.3, Lat. 86L2–3 33 n.32
III.4, Lat. 87C11–D4, Heb. 95a11–15 **113 n.25**
Lat. 87D13–E2, Heb. 95a19–22 114 n.28
Heb. 95a22–6 33 n.31
III.6, 34 n.37
Lat. 88A14–B4, Heb. 96a16–17 **113 n.24**
Lat. 88C5–8, Heb. 96a28–b1 **129–30 n.105**
Heb. 96a30–b1 129 n.101
Lat. 88C8–D13, Heb. 96b1–10 **130 n.105**
Lat. 88D15–E 33 n.32
III.7, 34 n.37
III.9, Lat. 89D1–15 Heb. 97b16–21 34 n.37
III.12, 47 n.45
Heb. 98b19–21, 25–7, 30–99a1 34 n.37; 47 n.45
Heb. 99a3–6, 11–14, 17–20 34 n.37; 47 n.45
Lat. 90G4–10 Heb. 99a21–30 34 n.37
Heb. 99a 23–30 **47 n.45**
III.19, Lat. 94A13–B4, Heb. 103b29–104a4 33 n.30
III.21, Heb. 105a5–7 33 n.31
III.26, Heb. 107b3 33 n.31
III.34, Lat. 100F4–I5, Heb. 111b3–29 100 n.208
III.36, Heb. 113a22–4 33 n.31; 48 n.49
III.40, Lat. 103B5–C6, Heb. 114b20–22 50 n.63
Lat. 103C6–D4, Heb. 114b28–115a4 50 n.64
III.41, Lat. 103E14–F5, Heb. 115a12–15 **51 n.67**
Lat. 103F5–11, Heb. 115a15–17 **51 n.68**
Heb. 115a18–19 33 n.31; 47 n.40
Heb. Paris MS 884, 115a19–20; Paris MS 883, 88a18 51 n.70
III.42, Heb. 115b2–3 47 n.40
Lat. 103M1–10, Heb. 115b17–22 **52 n.75**
Heb. 116a20–21 33 n.31
Lat. 104B16–C6, Heb. 116a15–21 **52 n.76**
III.45, Lat., Heb. 117a10–12 13 n.24
Lat., Heb. 117a17–20 13 n.24
III.48, Heb. 118a22 48 n.46
Lat. 106B10 48 n.47
Lat. 106C4–5, Heb. 118a26 46 n.32
Heb. 118a28 47 n.40
III.49, Heb. 120a23 46 n.32
Heb. 120a25–9 47 n.40
III.52, Heb. 122a28–9 47 n.40
Heb. 122a29 46 n.32
III.53, Lat. 110A13, Heb. 123a17 25 n.27 and 29
III.54, Heb. 123b7–8 33 n.31
III.55, Heb. 124a13–14 33 n.31
III.60, Lat. 114D–E, Heb. 128a21–3 **161 n.118**
Lat. 114E, Heb. 128a23–25 **161 n.118**
Lat. 114G1–6 33 n.32

III.63, Heb. 130a7–9 33 n.31
III.66, Arab. 260.15–16, Lat. 116K7–90 32 n.29
III.72, Heb. 134a17 33 n.31
Book IV:
IV.3, Heb. 137a19–22 48 n.49
IV.6, Lat. 124A5, Heb. 138b29 27 n.38
IV.9, Heb. 139b22–3, 25–6, 28, 47 n.40
Heb. 140a1, 2, 8 47 n.40
Lat. 125B1–2, Heb. 140a10 46 n.32
Heb. 140a15–17 33 n.31; 48 n.49
IV.10, Heb. 140b4–5 33 n.31
IV.11, 170 n.181
Heb. 140b19 24 n.23; 170 n.181
IV.20, Lat. 129E11, Heb. 144b8 24 n.23
Lat. 129F10, (Lat. and the Heb. MS Oxford 1388 fo. 122b) 24 n.23
Lat. 129F10–14 33 n.32
IV.23, Heb. 145b4–5 27 n.39; 33 n.31
IV.24, Heb. 145b25 27 n.38
IV.26, Heb. 147a27 33 n.31
IV.27, 32 n.29; 34 n.37; 55
Heb. 147b21–5 48 n.49; 55 **n.98**
IV.28, 32 n.29
Lat. 132L14–M5 33 n.32
IV.30, Lat. 133H1, Heb. 148b30 24 n.23; 170 n.180
Lat. 133H7, Heb. 149a3 24 n.23; 170 n.180
IV.32, Lat. 134F10, Heb. 149b17 26 n.35
IV.37, Lat. 137L15–138E2, Heb. 153a2–b1 25 n.26
Lat. 137M1, Heb. 153a2 24 n.23
Heb. 153a30–b1 33 n.31
IV.39, Heb. 154a24 48 n.49
IV.43, Lat. 141F9, Heb. 157b3 25 n.28
Lat. 141F12, Heb. 157b 25 n.27
Lat. 141H14–15, Heb. 157b17 25 n.27
Lat. 141I3, Heb. 157b23 25 n.27
Lat. 141L5, Heb. 158a3 25 n.27
Lat. 141L7, Heb. 158a6 25 n.27
Lat. 141M2 25 n.27
Lat. 141M11, Heb. 158a10 26 n.37
Lat. 142B14, Heb. 158a21 26 n.37
Lat. 142B14, 15, Heb. 158a22 26 n.34
Lat. 142C1, Heb. 158a22 25 n.28
Lat. 142C4, Heb. 158a24 26 n.37
Lat. 142G4, Heb. 158b14 26 n.37
Heb. 158b16 26 n.37
Heb. 158b23 25 n.29
Lat. 142K1 24 n.23
Lat. 142K6, Heb. 158b24 25–6 n.29
Lat. 142K8, Heb. 158b25 26 n.37
Lat. 143A5, Heb. 159a11 24 n.23
Heb. 159a25 33 n.31
IV.45, Lat. 144G7, Heb. 160b15 26 n.35
Lat. 144H9, Heb. 160b21 26 n.35
Lat. 144H13, Heb. 160b22 26 n.35
Lat. 144H16, Heb. 160b22 24 n.23
IV.50, Lat. 147E10, Heb. 163a27 24 n.23; 25 n.24
Heb. 163b16 33 n.31; 46 n.32
IV.53, Heb. 165b2–4 33 n.31
IV.57, Heb. 167a11 33 n.31
IV.58, Lat. 151C2, Heb. 167a16 14 n.25
Lat. 151E5, Heb. 167b3 24 n.23; 25 n.25

Averroes (*cont.*)
IV.64, Lat. 154B15, Heb. 170a30 24 n.23
IV.65, Lat. 154I1, Heb. 170b23 46 n.32
Lat. 154K6, Heb. 170b30 24 n.23
Lat. 154M8, 26 n.37
Lat. 155C9, Heb. 171b2 24 n.23
IV.67, Lat. 156B10, Heb. 172a19 26 n.35
IV.70, Lat. 157I14, Heb. 174a17 24 n.23; 25 n.24
Lat. 157K13–L9 33 n.32
Lat. 157L6 24 n.23
IV.71, 26, n.37; 125 n.77
Heb. 177a14 26 n.29, n.30
Heb. 177a16 26 n.29
Lat. 161G13–I3, Heb. 178a22–5 **125 n.79**
Lat. 161K15–L11, Heb. 178b11–14 **125 n.80**
Heb. 178b16–23 33 n.31
Heb. 178b21 26 n.30
IV.72, Lat. 163 Heb. **153 n.76**
IV.73–4, 32 n.29
IV.74, Heb. 181a28 26 n.37
IV.77, 55
Heb. 183a25 24 n.23; 25 n.24; **55 n.95**
Heb. 183a25–6 33 n.31
IV.86, Lat. 173F11–14, Heb. 189b21–7 33 n.30
IV.88, Heb. 190b6 33 n.31
IV.89, Lat. 174D8, Heb. 190b11 48 n.49
IV.90, 170 n.181
Heb. 191a29–30 170 n.181
Heb. 191a30 24 n.23; 25 n.24
IV.94, 170 n.179
IV.95–6, 170 n.179
IV.95, Heb. 193a29–b4 44 n.23
Heb. 193a30–b4 33 n.31
IV 97–8, 32 n.29
IV.97, Lat. 177M2 26 n.31
Lat. 177M8 26 n.31
IV.98, Lat. 179E6, Heb. 195b6 26 n.31
Lat. 179E15, Heb. 196b8 26 n.31
Lat. 179G7–8 26 n.29
IV.101–2, 170 n.181; 171 n.184
IV.101, Arab. 420.2–3, Lat. 181B12–14 32 n.29
Lat. 181E7, Heb. 197a29 26 n.34
Lat. 181G6, Heb. 197b10, 11 24 n.23; 25 n.25; 170 n.181
Lat. 181G13, Heb. 197b10, 11 24 n.23; 170 n.181
IV.102, Heb. 197b20–30 44 n.23; 170 n.181
Heb. 197b23, 26 46 n.32
Heb. 197b29 24 n.23; 170 n.181
Lat. 182A5, Heb. 198a9 24 n.23; 170 n.181
Lat. 182C2, Heb. 198a19 25 n.27
Lat. 182E5 24 n.23; 170 n.181
IV.106, Lat. 185H5, Heb. 201b5 25 n.27
IV.108, Heb. 202b21 33 n.31
IV.115, Heb. 206a24–8 33 n.31
Heb. 206a26–7 27 n.39
IV.119, Heb. 209b7 27 n.39
Heb. 209b6–9 33 n.31
IV.126, Heb. 214a4–6 33 n.31
IV.127, 14 n.24
Heb. 214a15 25 n.27
IV.128, Arab. 466.11, Lat. 199D3–4 32 n.29
Lat. 199H6- 200A4, Heb. 214b10 33 n.31
IV.129, Heb. 215a3 26 n.29
Lat. 201B4, 6, Heb. 215b11 24 n.23
IV.132, Lat. 203E4–203M14, Heb. 217a14 34 n.37
Lat. 203L10 25 n.27
Book V:
V.4–5, 32 n.29
V.5, Lat. 209 I4–17, Heb. 8b21–2 33 n.30

V.8, 39
Lat. 212G3–H2; Heb. 11a1–5 **39 n.64**
Lat. 213I1–9, Heb. 12a11–19 44 n.23
V.9, Heb. 12b3, 13 47 n.40
Lat. 214K7–8, Heb. 13a16 26 n.29
Lat. 215A1–8, Heb. 13a28–31 **114 n.26**
Lat. 215B1–7, Heb. 13b2–3 **114 n.28**
V.10, Lat. 215F11, Heb. 13b20 24 n.23
Lat. 215I6, Heb. 14a2 24 n.23
Lat. 215K9, Heb. 14a8 25 n.27
Lat. 215L10, Heb. 14a12 24 n.23; 25 n.27
Lat. 215L10–216A14, Heb. 14a12–22 34 n.37
Lat. 215M6, Heb. 14a15 24 n.23
Lat. 216A8 24 n.23; 25 n.27
Heb. 14a20 24 n.23; 25 n.27
V.11, Heb. 14b30 33 n.31
V.12, Lat. 217B16–C8, Heb. 15a19–22 **132 n.119**
Lat. 217C13–D4, Heb. 15a24–6 **78 n.95, 132 n.119**
Lat. 217E13, Heb. 15b2 34 n.37
V.13, Heb. 16b13–14 78 n.95; 132 n.119
Lat. 218I11, Heb. 16b18 27 n.38
V.15, 34 n.37
V.16, Lat., Heb. 17a20–8 14 n.24
Lat., Heb. 17a28–b23 14 n.24
V.17, Lat. 220C5–9, Heb. 17b15–17 46 n.32 **78 n.94**
V.19–20, 32 n.29
V.20, Lat. 222B10, Heb. 19b15 24 n.23
Heb. 19b23 24 n.23
V.22, Lat. 223C–D, Heb. 20b19–25 161 n.118
Heb. 20b30 24 n.23
V.24, Heb. 21b14 26 n.32; 33 n.34
V.28, Lat. 226A3, Heb. 23a31 25 n.27
V.29, Heb. 23b17–18 33 n.33
V.33, Lat. 227K14–L4, Heb. 25a17–20 33 n.30
Heb. 25a17–20 33 n.31
V.34, Lat. 228D5–7 33 n.32
V.36, Lat. 229G10–12, Heb. 27a7–8 **126 n.84**
Lat. 229G12–H1, Heb. 27a8–12 **126 n.85**
Lat. 229H15–K3, Heb. 27a14–22 **126 n.87**
Heb. 27b5 33 n.31
V.38, 55
Lat. 231C1–4, Heb. 28b17–18 **55 n.99**
Lat. 231C2, Heb. 28b18 24 n.23
Heb. 29a3 27 n.38
V.50, Lat. 238B4, Heb. 35b0 24 n.23
Heb. 36a7–9 33 n.31
V.51, Lat. 238H8–9, Heb. 36b2–3 118 n.49
V.52, Lat. 239D10–11 33 n.32
V.56, Heb. 40a10–11 33 n.31
V.59, Lat. 243H4, Heb. 41b11 24 n.23; 25 n.24
Lat. 243H6, Heb. 41b12 24 n.23
Heb. 41b23 33 n.31
Book VI:
VI.1–3, 47
VI.1, Lat. 246M2, Heb. 45a6 24 n.23
Heb. 45a8 47 n.41–2
Lat. 247A6, Heb. 45a16 47 n.41
Lat. 247B10, Heb. 45a25–6 47 n.41
VI.2, Heb. 45b7–8 47 n.41–2
Heb. 45b12–13 47 n.41–2
Lat. 247K11, Heb. 46a14–15 47 n.41
VI.3, Lat. 248D5–6, Heb. 46b2 121 n.60
Lat. 248F12–G6, Heb. 46b16–19 47 n.40–2
VI.9, Lat. 251G6–15, Heb. 49b21–4 47 n.40
Lat. 251G14, Heb. 49b23 47 n.40
VI.10, Lat. 252A10, Heb. 50a20 24 n.23; 25 n.24

Averroes (*cont.*)
VI.15, Lat. 255K3–8, Heb. 53a12–14 **111 n.10**
Lat. 255K11–13, Heb. 53a15–16 111 n.13
Lat. 255L7, Heb. 53a20 24 n.23
Lat. 255L7–M7, Heb. 53a20–27 25 n.26
VI.23, Lat. 261K1, Heb. 57b27 34 n.37
VI.26, Lat. 263A15–B1 33 n.32
VI.27, Lat. 263E7–10; Heb. 60a7–11 33 n.30
VI.28, Heb. 60a27–8 33 n.31
VI.30, Heb. 61a11–13 33 n.31
VI.32–9, 39 n.63
VI.32, 134; 137
61b24 121 n.61
Lat. 265I12–K14, Heb. 61b26–62a2 **138 n.153**
Lat. 265I12–L12, Heb. 61b26–62a7 135 n.135
Lat. 265L12, Heb. 62a7 26 n.29
Lat. 265L13–266C4; Heb. 62a7–30 135 n.136
Lat. 265L14, Heb. 62a7 24 n.23
Lat. 265M9, Heb. 62a11 24 n.23
Lat. 265M9–13, Heb. 62a 11–12 **139 n.156**
Lat. 266A1, Heb. 62a14 25 n.27
Heb. 62a22–4 137 n.152
Lat. 266B7, Heb. 62a25 26 n.37
Heb. 62a25–9 117 n.43
Lat. 266C2, Heb. 62a29 25 n.27; 26 n.29
Lat. 266C3–6, Heb. 62a29–31 **136 n.146**
Lat. 266C4–C8; Heb. 62a30–b2 135 n.137
Lat. 266C7–9, Heb. 62b1–2 **137 n.150**
Heb. 62b2–5 **5 n.17; 60 n.13;** 135 n.138
Lat. 266C8–D5, Heb. 62b5–10 **118 n.47**
Lat. 266C8–F11, Heb. 62b5–22 135 n.139
Lat. 266C12, Heb. 62b6 117 n.45
Lat. 266D7–14, Heb. 62b11–13 **118 n.50**
Lat. 266F11–12, Heb. 62b22–3 **4 n.11; 60 n.4;** 135 n.140
Heb. 62b23–5 **5 n.19; 60 n.15**
Heb. 62b23–31 135 n.141
Heb. 63a1–2 117 n.45
Lat. 266F12–G6, Heb. 63a1–4 **122 n.66**
Lat. 266F12–K11, Heb. 63a1–26 135 n.142
Lat. 266F14–G4, Heb. 63a1–4 132 n.119
Lat. 266I2, K4, Heb. 63a16, 22–3 122 n.65
Lat. 267D **153 n.76**
Lat. 267D6–12, Heb. 64a1–4 **158 n.108**
VI.33, 34 n.37; 166 n.158
Lat. 267M5–14 33 n.32
Heb. 64a23–7 **162 n.135**
VI.34, 34 n.37
Heb. 65a27 24 n.23
VI.36, Lat. 269K4–5 33 n.32
VI.37, 34 n.37; 39
Heb. 67a11 24 n.23
Lat. 270F11G4, Heb. 67a16–22 162 n.128
VI 38, 34 n.37; 166 n.158
Heb. 68a23–5 **156 n.96**
VI.39, Heb. 68b27–31 33 n.31
VI.40, 122 n.65; 137 n.148
Lat. 272B11–C10, Heb. 69a10–14 **122 n.65**
Lat. 272D8–13, Heb. 69a25–7 **122 n.65**
Lat. 272D13–15, Heb. 69a27–30 33 n.30
VI.41, Lat. 272K2–7, Heb. 69b31–70a1 33 n.30
VI.45, Heb. 72a16–18 33 n.31; 44 n.23
VI.46, Lat. 275I5, Heb. 72b15 24 n.23
Lat. 275K3, Heb. 72b21 26 n.29
Heb. 73b22–3 33 n.31
VI.51, Heb. 77a29–30 33 n.31
VI.54, Lat. 281M8–13 33 n.32

VI.56, Heb. 80a4–7 33 n.31
Lat. 283C2, C9, Heb. 80a20 24 n.23
Lat. 283C9, Heb. 80a21 25 n.24
VI.59, Lat. 284H10–I2, Heb. 81b24–5 **119 n.52**
Lat. 284L3–7, Heb. 82a31–b6 119 n.52
VI.61, Lat. 288A2, Heb. 85b24 25 n.28
VI.62, Lat. 289C14–D2 33 n.32
VI.68, Heb. 90a15–17 44 n.23
Heb. 90a23–6 33 n.31
Heb. 90a23–7 47 n.40
VI.74, Heb. 94a21–2 33 n.31
VI.87, Heb. 101a1–11, 15–18, 25–7, 29–30 14 n.24
Book VII:
VII.1, 104
Lat. 306A5, Heb. 105b3 147 n.30
Lat. 306C1, Heb. 105b12 26 n.31
Lat. 306C2–3, Heb. 105b13 26 n.29
Lat. 306F1–12 **167 n.164**
Lat. 306F12–G5, Heb. 106a3–8 167 n.164
Lat. 306G1–5, Heb. 106a6–8 **167 n.165**
Lat. 306G6, Heb. 106a8 26 n.31
VII.2 Lat. 307G3–9, Heb. 107a14–16 **154 n.79**
Lat. 307G15-H1, Heb. 107a19–20 26 n.31, 4 **n.12; 60 n.5**
Lat. 307I3–9; Heb. 107a25–7 **154 n.**77
Lat. 308A10–C14 34 n.37
VII.3, Heb. 108a6–7 33 n.34
Heb. 108a11–16 33 n.31; 48 n.49
VII.4, 33 n.32
Lat. 309B14, Heb. 109a2 26 n.31
VII.7, Heb. 110b13–14 33 n.31; 44 n.23
VII.9, 34 n.37; 38
Heb. 111b2–112b14 **38 n.58**–9
Heb. 111b27 25 n.27, 26 n.29
Heb. 112a5–11 44 n.23
Heb. 112b9–12 33 n.31
Lat. 311L2–13 38 n.61
Lat. 311L15–M11 38 n.61, 44 n.23
Lat. 311M12–312 B5 38 n.61
Lat. 312B5–C7 **104 n.224**
Lat. 312B10–F11 38 n.61
VII.10, 33 n.32
Lat. 314D9, Heb. 113a19 46 n.32
Heb. 113b29 26 n.31
VII.13, Lat. 317L6–M4, Heb. 116b29–117a2 34 n.37
VII.15, Heb. 118a27 26 n.29
Heb. 118b10 26 n.31
VII.16–17, 32 n.29
VII.18, Lat. 320K8–10, Heb. 120a27–8 118 n.49
VII.20, Lat. 323I11, Heb. 123b21 46 n.32
Lat. 323I13, Heb. 123b23 24 n.23; 54 n.88
Lat. 323I13–15, Heb. 123b23–4 56 n.100
Lat. 323K4–9 33 n.32
VII.24, Heb. 126a26–7 33 n.31
VII.31, Heb. 130b21–3 33 n.31
VII.34, Lat. 334B12–14 33 n.32
VII.35, Lat. 334F5–6 32 n.29
Lat. 335E1–6 33 n.32
VII.37, Lat., Heb. 133b27–134a23 13 n.24
Lat., Heb. 134a23–6 13 n.24
Lat., Heb. 134a26–b4 13 n.24
Lat., Heb. 134b4–8 13 n.24
BookVIII:
VIII.1–5, 92
VIII.1–9, 97
VIII.1, 38; 86 n.135; 93–7; 101–3; 105 n.229
Lat. 338F6–10, Heb. 136a20–22 94 n.172
Lat. 338F6–H9, Heb. 136a20–b4 **95 n.178**
Heb. 136a28–b1 **68 n.33**
Lat. 339A3–5, Heb. 137a9–10 **101 n.214**
Lat. 339A5–F7 34 n.37; **102 n.215**

Averroes (*cont.*)
Lat. 339B5–6 26 n.34
Lat. 339B5–13 **105 n.230**
Lat. 339D9–E1 **103 n.220**
VIII.2, 101 n.214
Lat. 339L4, Heb. 137a28 46 n.32
VIII.3, Lat. 340E10–11, Heb. 138a8 26 n.35
Lat. 340E14, Heb. 138a10 26 n.36
Lat. 340F6, Heb. 138a12 26 n.36
VIII.4, 86 n.135; 95; 101, 102 n.216; 103; 105 n.229; 106 n.237
Lat. 340K3–8, Heb. 138a25–7 95 n.180
Lat. 340L3–8, Heb. 138b1–2 **95 n.180**
Lat. 340L8–M3, Heb. 138b3–6 90 n.159
Lat. 341A2–7, Heb. 138b10–12 91 n.167
Lat. 341A2–11, Heb. 138b10–14 90 n.159
Lat. 341A7–11, Heb. 138b12–14 **91 n.165**
Lat. 341A10–11, Heb. 138b13–14 **90 n.162**
Lat. 341A12, Heb. 138b14 25 n.28
Lat. 341E3, Heb. 139a2 27 n.38
Lat. 341G1–2, Heb. 139a15 **95 n.181**
Lat. 341I1–2, Heb. 139a28–9 27 n.38
Lat. 341I10 26 n.34
Lat. 341K3–6 **103 n.221**
Lat. 341K11 24 n.23; 53 n.87
Lat. 341I9–K13 **103 n.219**
Lat. 341I9–L7 34 n.37
VIII. 5, 38; 95 n.179; 101; 104
Lat. 341M1–13, Heb. 139b2–7 95 n.179
Lat. 341M12–13 **101 n.214**
Lat. 341M13–342B5 34 n.37
Lat. 341M14–15 **104 n.222**
Lat. 342A6–B2 **166 n.159**
VIII.6, 98 n.196; 101 n.214; 104
Lat. 342D14–E7, Heb. 139b18–21 **78 n.93**
Lat. 342E7–F4, Heb. 139b21–6 98 n.196
Lat. 342G3–13, Heb. 139b29–140a3 98 n.196
VIII.7, 34 n.37; 101; 104
Lat. 342L9–M10 **104 n.223**
VIII.8, Lat. 344I1, Heb. 142a5 27 n.38
Heb. 142a13–14 33 n.31
VIII.9, 86 n.135; 92; 96–7; 98 n.196; 101; 105 n.229; 106 n.237
Lat. 345A6, Heb. 142b20 26 n.34
Lat. 345C6–11, Heb. 142b9–10 **96 n.183**
Lat. 345C11–D1, Heb. 142b10–12 **94 n.171**; **96 n.185**
Lat. 345C11–E6, Heb. 142b10–20 **96 n.186**
Lat. 345D14–E6, Heb. 142b17–20 **105 n.230**
Lat. 345F7–9, Heb. 142b25–6 **98 n.196**
Lat. 345F7–I4, Heb. 142b25–143a8 98 n.196
Lat. 345F15–G11, Heb. 142b28–143a1 **80 n.103**
Lat. 345I4–7, Heb. 143a8–9 **96 n.188**
Lat. 345L3–M2, Heb. 143a17–21 **97 n.189**
VIII.12–14, 34 n.37
VIII.15, Lat. 349I10, Heb. 146b22 27 n.38
Lat. 349M15, Heb. 147a8 27 n.38
Lat. 350A10, Heb. 147a11 27 n.38
Lat. 350D4, Heb. 147a22 27 n.38
Lat. 350D12–M1; Heb. 147a25–b15 34 n.37
Lat. 350E7 27 n.38
Lat. 350 I11 27 n.38
Heb. 147b 9,12 27 n.38

Heb. 149b10–17 33 n.31; 44 n.23
Heb. 149b17 25 n.28
VIII.17, Arab. 819.3, Lat. 353A5–7 32 n.29
Lat. 353I1–14, Heb. 151a10–15 33 n.30
VIII.20, Lat. 355B10, Heb. 152b4 27 n.38
VIII.21, Lat. 356H10–I7, Heb. 154a1–5 **97 n.190**
VIII.23, 130 n.105
Lat. 358H, Heb. 155b19–20 **130 n.105**
Lat. 359K3, Heb. 156b28 25 n.28; 26 n.29
Lat. 360E5 26, n.34
Lat. 360F5, Heb. 157b6 26 n.34
VIII.28, Heb. 164a10–11 33 n.31
VIII.29, 34 n.37
Heb. 164b2–3, 6–7 47 n.40
Heb. 164b14–30 47 n.40
Heb. 164b16 46 n.32
VIII.32, Heb. 168b22–3 91 n.167
Heb. 169b5–6 33 n.31
VIII.33, Lat. 372B4, Heb. 169b20 25 n.27
VIII.37, Lat. 377B13, 25 n.27
VIII.38, 34 n.37
VIII.40–2, 34 n.37
VIII.42, 53 n.87
Lat. 381I4, 25 n.27; 26 n.29
Lat. 381I5, 24 n.23; 53 n.87
Lat. 382C2 26 n.29; 53 n.87
VIII.44, Lat. 384K **153 n.76**
Heb. 184a30–b6 33 n.31; 34 n.35
VIII.47, Lat. 388K10, Heb. 188b18, 27 n.38
VIII.49–50, 34 n.37
VIII.49, Heb. 189b20–25 **97 n.191**
VIII.51, Lat. 392A13, Heb. 192b19 46 n.32
VIII.52, Arab. 872.15–873.2, Heb. 193a4–5 32 n.29
Lat. 393C6–E8 34 n.37
VIII.53, Lat. 394K9–L1 33 n.32
Lat. 394K16–L1 27 n.38
VIII.54, Heb. 195b1–3 33 n.31
VIII.55, Heb. 197a11–16 33 n.31
VIII.56, Lat. 397G2–4, Heb. 197b27–8 **82 n.116**
VIII.62, Lat. D7–E6 123 n.68
Heb. 202b24–8 **123 n.70**
Heb. 202b28–203a3 **123 n.70**
Heb. 203b26–8 33 n.31; 44 n.23
VIII.65, Lat. 407C10–D3, Heb. 208a13–17 33 n.30
VIII.66, 34 n.37
VIII.68, Lat. 411B9–10, Heb. 212a6 27 n.40
VIII.74, Lat. 418I14, 27 n.38
Lat. 418K4–5, Heb. 219a4 27 n.38
VIII.76, Lat. 421F4, Heb. 221B11 25 n.27
VIII.78, 34 n.37
Lat. 424L1, 27 n.38
Lat. 424L2, 26 n.35
Lat. 424L10, 26 n.35
Lat. 424L14, 26 n.31
Lat. 424M1, 26 n.34
VIII.79, 54 n.87
Lat. 426K2, Heb. 226a14 24 n.23; 54 n.87
Lat. 426K14, Heb. 226a18 25 n.28; 26 n.30
Lat. 426L10, Heb. 226a22 26 n.35
Lat. 426L11, Heb. 226a22 24 n.23; 54 n.87
VIII.82, Lat. 431B11, Heb. 229B30 25 n.27
VIII.83, Lat. 432D1, Heb. 231a12–13 26 n.35
VIII.85, Lat. 432M1–3, Heb. 231b15–17 **125 n.81**
Lat. 433C6–D6, Heb. 232a6–11 **125 n.76**
Questions in Physics
Quest. I, 18
Quest. VI, 17
Quest. VII, 17–18
18, # 13 88 n.152
18–19, # 15 **82 n.117, 86 n.134**
19, # 17 **105 n.230**
19, # 18 **89 n.155**
Question VIII 18

Averroes (*cont.*)
De caelo:
Long Commentary on Aristotle's De caelo 44–5
Middle Commentary on Aristotle's De caelo
III.3.1, Arab. 285.10–13, Heb. 60b20–22 168 n.169
III.3.2.1 Arab. 289.3–6; Heb. 61b22–4 153 n.76
Arab. 291.17–21, Heb. 62b5–8 **168 n.170**
De generatione et corruptione:
Short Commentary on Aristotle's De generatione et corruptione
Heb. 121.67–122.78, English 133 **79 n.99**
Middle Commentary on Aristotle's De generatione et corruptione
Heb. 31.87–32.96, English 38 **159 n.109**
Heb. 91.75–92.81, English 104 **107 n.245**
De anima:
Middle Commentary on Aristotle's De anima 22.61 64 n.15
Arab. and English 22.61 **85 n.130**
English 32–3, ## 87–8 **169 n.176**
121 # 312 160 n.115
Metaphysics:
Short Commentary on Aristotle's Metaphysics
German, 107 106 n.233
Arab. 60–61, Heb. 128a col. b19–128b col. a5 160 n.117
Middle Commentary on Aristotle's Metaphysics
136b26–7 **160 n.116**
137a4 **160 n.116**
137a15–16 **160 n.116**
137a15–23 161 n.118
137a22–3 160 n.116
138a1–6 **162 n.131**
138a9–11 **162 n.132**
Long Commentary on Aristotle's Metaphysics
A.16, Heb. 4b20–1 36 n.49
A.15, Heb. 5a24–5 36 n.49
A.9, Heb. 8a20 36 n.49
A.14, Heb. 9a40 36 n.49
A.16, Heb. 10a28–9 36 n.49
A.17, Heb. 10b11 36 n.49
A.19, Heb. 11a23–4 36 n.49
A.23, Heb. 11b38–19 36 n.49
A.24, Heb. 12a6–10 36 n.49
B.1, Heb. 18a37–8 36 n.49
B.3, Heb. 20b11–12 36 n.49
Arab. vol. II 192.4–5, Heb. 20b11–12 36 n.49
B.4, 36 n.49
Arab. 193.11–194.4 36 n.47
Heb. 20b24 35 n.47
B.5, Heb. 6b12 35 n.47
B.8, Heb. 7b8 35 n.47
Lat. 9E11 36 n.48
B.9, Heb. 7b39 35 n.47
Heb. 23a22 36 n.49
B.10, Heb. 24a12 36 n.49
B.12, 36 n.49
B.17, Heb. 29a18 35 n.47
Γ 12, Heb. 37b25 35 n.47
Γ.29, Heb. 47a39 35 n.47
Γ.29, Heb. 47b27–8 35 n.46
Δ.13, 36 n.49
Δ.15, Heb. 56b1–2 36 n.49
Δ.24, Heb. 62b39–40 36 n.49
Δ.32, Heb. 66a41–42 36 n.49
E.1, Heb. 69a1–2 35 n.46
Lat. 145C3–5 36 n.48
E.5, Heb. 70b15 35 n.47
E.7, Heb. 71b32 36 n.49
E.8, Heb. 72a2 35 n.47
Z.1, Heb. 72b22, 36 n.49
Z.17, Heb. 79b27–8 36 n.49
Z.18, Lat. 167K4–6 36 n.49
Z.23, Heb. 82b26, 32, 35 n.47
Heb. 82b43 36 n.49
Z.24, Heb. 83b19 35 n.47
Z.25, Heb. 84a22 36 n.49
Z.28, Heb. 85b26 36 n.49
Z.37, Heb. 91b21 36 n.49
Z.42, Heb. 93b40 35 n.47
Z.43, Heb. 94b7 35 n.47
Heb. 95a12–14 36 n.49
Z.44, Heb. 96a15–16 36 n.49
Z.45, Heb. 96a24 36 n.47
Z.46, Heb. 96b1 36 n.49
Z.48, Heb. 96b32 36 n.47
Heb. 96b39 35 n.46
Z.50, Heb. 97b18 36 n.49
Z.51, Heb. 98a1 36 n.49
Z.54, 36 n.49
Lat. 202D10–11 36 n.48
Z.60, Heb. 101b36 36 n.49

Z epilogue Arab., 1020.13–1021.6; Heb., 102b19–24 **52 n.77**
H.1, Heb. 103a12 36 n.49
H.8, Heb. 106b38 36 n.49
H.12, Heb. 109a17–18 36 n.49
Θ.21, Heb. 122b19, 20–1, 23, 35 n.46
I.2, 36 n.49
I.4, Lat. 254D9 36 n.49
I.6, Heb. 127a27 35 n.46
I.13, Heb. 130b2 36 n.49
I.17, Heb. 132a39–40 36 n.49
Λ prologue, Arab. 1393.4–1394.2; Heb., 139a9–13 20 n. 9, **53 n.78**
Λ.1, Heb. 140b15–16 36 n.49
Λ.9, Heb. 144b23–4 36 n.49
Λ.17, Heb. 149a1–2 36 n.49
Λ.18, Lat. 305I6–7 36 n.49
Λ.26, Heb. 153b8, 153b15–16 35 n.46
Λ, 26, Arab. 1537.12–14; Heb. 153b15–16: 25 n.24
Λ.28, Heb. 155a16–18 36 n.49
Λ.29, Heb. 155b31–2 36 n.49
Λ.34, Heb. 157b10 35 n.46
Λ.41, Heb. 163a33–4 36 n.49
Λ.48,Lat. 333C8–9 36 n.49
Λ.71,Heb. 171b7–9 36 n.49

De substantia orbis
IV.20, Heb. 48, English 115 **125 n.82**

Al-Kashf ᶜan Manāhij al-Adilla fi ᶜAqā'id al-Milla 82 **107 n.243**
138–9, English 22 174 n.1

Tahāfut al-Tahāfut 44 n.18
162 **107 n.241**
172 **107 n.244**
188–9 **81 n.114**
229, English 136–7 **65 n.20**
283 **82 n.115**
421 106 n.239
479, English 291–2 **65 n.20**
480.11–13, English 292 **163 n.138**
487.5–8 **81 n.113**
495 106 n.239

Hebrew Authors

Shem-Tov ben Yosef Ibn Falaquera
De ᶜot ha-Filosofim
256b18–19 **158 n.103**

Yedaᶜaya ha-Penini
A commentary on Ibn Rushd's short commentary on the Physics
V.1, 91a5 29 n.9
V.2, 100a5 29 n.9
VI.4, 141b24–6 29 n.9, 136 n.144
VII.1, 156a11–16, 156b16–20,157a15–24 29 n.9
VII.4, 188a2–16 29 n.9

Levi ben Gershom (Gersonides),
Commentary on the Short Commentary on the Physics
Berlin MS 31b col. b 10–13, 24–7 **136 n.144**
Commentary on the Middle Commentary on the Physics
111b1 121 n.61
112a14–15 **139 n.155**
118a18–b4 **158 n.105**

Medieval Lat. Authors

Thomas Aquinas
On Physics: Commentary on Aristotle's Physics
book I, lecture 9, 34 **145 n.21**